Praise for Evan Hughes's

PAIN HUSTLERS

"A richly reported, mesmerizing tale, and a devastating indictment of our broken pharmaceutical industry. Everyone should read this book."   —Sheelah Kolhatkar,
New York Times bestselling author of *Black Edge*

"Filled with odd and scintillating details, [*Pain Hustlers*] plots the winding way one drug company and its associated doctors helped to beget the latest wave in our ongoing opioid crisis."
—Errol Morris, Academy Award–winning filmmaker

"A fast-paced and maddening account. . . . What's most surprising and powerful about [this book] is not one company's criminality—we've grown inured to corporations behaving badly—as much as how institutionalized these practices were across the modern drug industry."   —*The New York Times Book Review*

"A pacey crime caper set against the backdrop of the opioid crisis. . . . When I tell you that reading [this book] is like watching a Scorsese film, you will assume I am exaggerating. Pick it up and tell me I'm wrong."   —Patrick Radden Keefe,
"By the Book," *The New York Times Book Review*

"Fascinating in the fashion of a slow-moving train wreck. . . . A study of corruption in which we see how the actions of key executives make a kind of awful sense, given the ecosystem in which they operate."
—Ted Conover, National Book Critics Circle Award–winning author of *Newjack* and *The Routes of Man*

"A revelatory deep dive into the ignominious history of the pharmaceutical manufacturer Insys Therapeutics. . . . Hughes does an excellent job of illuminating the inner workings of Big Pharma's malicious practices. . . . A powerful indictment of abhorrent industry practices."   —*Publishers Weekly* (starred review)

"As compelling as a true crime documentary. . . . Hughes perfectly captures the human impact of pharmaceutical sales and corporate greed. . . . Anyone who picks up this title will be left reflecting on how the U.S. medical system and drug companies have recklessly destroyed countless lives. A book readers will not soon forget."
—*Library Journal* (starred review)

"A journalist pulls back the curtain on the scandals that sent the first pharmaceutical executives to prison for their role in the opioid crisis. . . . A brisk and engaging account."   —*Kirkus Reviews*

"Unfolds like a blockbuster film. Fans of *Bad Blood* by John Carreyrou will be captivated by this story of unbelievable greed and hubris. A must-read."   —*Booklist* (starred review)

WINNER OF THE 2023
EXCELLENCE IN FINANCIAL JOURNALISM AWARD FROM THE NYSSCPA

Evan Hughes

PAIN HUSTLERS

Evan Hughes has written feature-length articles for *The New York Times Magazine*, *The Atlantic*, *GQ*, *New York*, *Wired*, and *The New York Review of Books*. He was a finalist for the National Magazine Award in Reporting in 2015. He is the author of *Literary Brooklyn*.

Also by Evan Hughes

Literary Brooklyn

PAIN HUSTLERS

Crime and Punishment at an Opioid Startup

EVAN HUGHES

Originally published as *The Hard Sell*

ANCHOR BOOKS
A DIVISION OF PENGUIN RANDOM HOUSE LLC
NEW YORK

The Library of Congress has cataloged the Doubleday edition as follows:
Name: Hughes, Evan, [date] author.
Title: The hard sell : crime and punishment at an opioid startup / Evan Hughes.
Description: First edition. | New York : Doubleday, 2022.
Identifiers: LCCN 2021018682 (print) | LCCN 2021018683 (ebook).
Subjects: LCSH: Insys Therapeutics, Inc. | Opioids—Marketing. |
    Pharmaceutical industry—Corrupt practices.
Classification: LCC HD9675.O644 I5748 2022 (print) |
    LCC HD9675.O644 (ebook) | DDC 338.4/76153—dc23
LC record available at https://lccn.loc.gov/2021018682
LC ebook record available at https://lccn.loc.gov/2021018683

Anchor Books Trade Paperback ISBN: 978-0-525-56632-8
eBook ISBN: 978-0-385-54491-7

Author photograph © Mike Lawrie
Book design by Maria Carella

anchorbooks.com

Printed in the United States of America
1st Printing

For Adelle and Isabel

CONTENTS

PAIN HUSTLERS

Gavin Awerbuch had a long commute, but often he arrived at work before dawn. After an hour and a half's drive, his headlights would swing into the parking lot, illuminating a one-story beige brick building that resembled a shopping plaza, divided into storefronts.

It was Saginaw, Michigan. In the winters it was frigid. Awerbuch would get out of his Chevrolet HHR, and when he was the first one there, he would unlock the door. He worked in the unit farthest to the right, where his name was stenciled in white letters on the glass door.

Awerbuch was too busy to pay much attention to his appearance. His graying hair sprouted in every direction, and he was often unshaven. At the office, he wore casual clothes—a sweatshirt and jeans, perhaps. He was disheveled enough that people wondered if he had slept in his outfit. His lab coat looked as if it could use a wash. He would shrug it on over his street clothes after he arrived at the office. Then the people would come, in a constant flow.

Awerbuch was a doctor. He was educated at Michigan State, the University of Arizona, and Wayne State University in Detroit. In 1989, he completed the specialized training to become a neurologist, treating conditions of the nervous system. In the early years, his practice evolved from focusing on disorders such as stroke and multiple sclerosis into managing pain in a broader set of patients. People came to him suffering from migraines, neck pain, back pain.

By 2012, Awerbuch's clinic was a major medical destination in the area, about ninety miles northwest of Detroit, not far from Flint. Awerbuch had around five thousand active patients, pouring into the small office suite at a rate of perhaps fifty a day. Some of them drove for hours to see him, from as far away as Michigan's Upper Peninsula. The wait was long once they got there.

Awerbuch had opened his clinic in the area in order to cater to an underserved population. The city core of Saginaw is predominantly black, but Awerbuch's clinic was located on the outskirts, where the city gives way quickly to farmland with a majority-white, blue-collar population. In the wake of the global financial collapse, jobs were in short supply. With the near collapse of the Big Three carmakers, a top local employer, an auto-parts manufacturer, had become a shell of its former self, shedding workers and entering bankruptcy before being purchased by Chinese interests.

A lot of Awerbuch's patients wore work jackets or camouflage. Many were retired or on disability. More than half were on Medicaid or Medicare. Walkers, braces, and wheelchairs were a common sight at the clinic.

To patients, Dr. Awerbuch appeared to be a man of great decency, ministering one at a time to their deeply personal needs, with the unpretentious air of a social worker. He was a small man and never intimidating or confrontational. He wasn't one of those doctors who let you know that he had power over you. He cared for his patients, many of them said. He took their pain seriously.

By this time the medical community was grappling with the fact that the prolonged boom in opioid prescribing that had begun in the late 1990s had helped to create a nationwide health crisis. Now, heightened scrutiny and changing medical opinion were altering the landscape of pain management. Many physicians were beginning to turn away from prescribing opioids over the long term or at high doses. Instead, doctors were referring patients struggling with chronic pain to specialists such as Awerbuch. This was not simply a matter of deferring to the experts; it was also a way of dumping a difficult problem on someone else. Treating pain is demanding and sensitive, and liability comes with the territory. Awerbuch became, for many patients, a port of last resort, a man who would give them the potent medications they depended on when other doctors would not.

In January 2013, a regular patient made the trip to the clinic in Saginaw. He told Dr. Awerbuch that his back pain was manageable, ranging from a 3 to a 4 on a scale of 1 to 10. He had been riding motorcycles lately, he added, making conversation. The patient said the Vicodin that Awerbuch had put him on seemed okay, but he asked for a prescription of the painkiller OxyContin. Awerbuch told him that he ought to try a new medication instead, and showed it to him.

The doctor held in his hand a small plastic bottle with a spout that extended from the top like a periscope. The medication was a liquid spray, and Awerbuch explained that you shoot it under your tongue. The drug had only just been approved the previous year. It was called Subsys. It is an opioid many times more powerful than OxyContin.

What Awerbuch didn't know was that the patient at this appointment was an undercover agent. The whole encounter was covertly recorded on video. At least three agents had been seeing Awerbuch for many months, posing as patients and concocting fake medical complaints.

At the outset of their investigation, the authorities were looking into the doctor's prolific billing for certain diagnostic tests, which measure electrical activity in nerves and muscles. Their suspicions turned out to be well founded. Over and over in their undercover visits, Awerbuch used needles and probes that may have looked right to patients, but the exams were bogus—a brief pantomime performed for show. Sometimes the needles and probes weren't even connected to a machine.

Agents at the U.S. Department of Health and Human Services Office of Inspector General, or HHS-OIG, see a lot of insurance fraud like this. It's a major drain on federal programs. Some doctors look at the checks that come back from Medicare or Medicaid when they invoice for testing and they get ideas: Who would know if the tests they administered were even real? They might rationalize their cheating with the thought that the patients aren't getting hurt.

But prescribing Subsys for moderate back pain—that was something different. Awerbuch's permissiveness with opioids had already raised flags, but the HHS–OIG special agent on the case, Marc Heggemeyer, straightened up and took notice when Subsys appeared unprompted in that undercover visit. "That was where we first started really drilling into it, the amount he was prescribing," he recalled. "Because once you did the research on that drug, it was like, 'Whoa, this is serious stuff.'"

The liquid in the Subsys spray bottle that Awerbuch held in his hand was fentanyl. For decades after it was first synthesized in 1960, fentanyl had been approved only for patients under medical supervision, in hospital settings. Subsys doses are measured in micrograms—one-millionth of a gram—because fentanyl is up to a hundred times as powerful as morphine, and roughly fifty times as potent as heroin. At the time of the investigation, illicitly manufactured fentanyl, often pressed into counterfeit pills or spiked into heroin, was starting to become the leading culprit in the opioid crisis, the deadliest drug epidemic in American history. By 2017, fentanyl and its analogs would be implicated in more than half of all opioid fatalities.

Subsys had been approved by the Food and Drug Administration solely to treat a relatively small group of people in dire circumstances: cancer patients who are already taking an around-the-clock regimen of opioids but still suffering from so-called breakthrough cancer pain. The term refers to spikes of pain that pierce through the protection of a longer-acting painkiller such as OxyContin. Drugs in Subsys's class are valuable for this use because they're fast. They can combat pain so severe that the patient might otherwise go to the emergency room. They can give comfort to a person near the end of life.

The narrow profile of this powerful drug was not stopping Dr. Awerbuch from handing out an extraordinary number of Subsys prescriptions.

———

Heggemeyer and a special agent at the Federal Bureau of Investigation, Travis Lloyd, set out together to interview some of Awerbuch's Subsys patients. They were disturbed by what they found.

They visited a young mother named Kendra. She was a tall woman in her early twenties, with a narrow face, light-colored hair, and a wispy voice. It took her some time to answer the door. She seemed worried that she was in trouble. In the family room of her small house, the two agents sat on one wing of an L-shaped couch while she sat on the other. Little natural light penetrated the room.

Awerbuch had treated Kendra's mother, who was glad to find him after she had been passed around by other providers. Kendra had gone to the doctor complaining of back and neck problems stemming from a car crash, among other chronic conditions. She had never had cancer, nor did she know that Subsys was only approved to treat cancer pain, she said. She gazed at the agents with glassy eyes, they recalled. It was as if she were looking through them. They asked for her driver's license. "The young woman in the photo was not the person we saw sitting before us," Lloyd recalled. "It looked like the life had been drawn from her face." Across the room, a young girl played at a toy kitchen. They worried for the child.

Heggemeyer sensed that Kendra was initially hesitant to implicate Awerbuch. They wondered if she didn't want the prescriptions to stop coming. This became a recurring issue in their interviews; patients were protective of Awerbuch, for a range of reasons. They seemed loyal to the doctor they thought they knew.

When the agents went to see another woman Awerbuch had put on Subsys, however, her husband had no problem condemning the doctor. He was furious. Awerbuch had kept feeding his wife opioids, he said, until finally she had to go into an inpatient facility in Pontiac for eight days and then into rehab. She had only just come back. She was around fifty and had been seeing Awerbuch for years, complaining of a litany of medical issues and a pain that never seemed to improve. It wasn't clear what the core problem was; she didn't have cancer. The Subsys was too much for her, her husband said. It made her incoherent, unable to function. The woman herself didn't say much at all, though she later acknowledged that she had passed out twice in the linen closet, facedown. It was the dog who found her there.

When authorities see suspicious prescribing of opioids, it typically involves high volumes of widely known drugs, usually containing oxycodone (branded as OxyContin, Roxicodone, Percocet) or hydrocodone (Vicodin, Lortab). These products are household names, and patients ask for them. Awerbuch often prescribed the drugs that patients requested, which can be a way of keeping people coming back for more appointments and lucrative procedures. But no one was asking for Subsys. Almost no one had even heard of it at the time.

Subsys is not only more powerful than most painkillers; it is also far rarer, and much more expensive. A typical prescription in 2013 ranged from approximately $3,000 to $17,000 a month, depending on the dosage. Medicare paid over $70,000 for one Awerbuch patient's Subsys supply over a ten-month period.

Persuading insurance companies to cover Subsys was an elaborate process. With such a potent and costly drug, most insurers required prior authorization before they would pay for it. For staff at a clinic, the paperwork could be a time-consuming hassle. Yet Awerbuch was opting to go through with it time and again.

Authorities were gathering that Awerbuch was working a number of different financial angles, that the fraudulent tests were only a piece of the puzzle. But the Subsys bit was hard to figure out at first. Why run this kind of risk?

But Awerbuch's motives weren't the most urgent matter. Investigators were worried about "how deadly that drug can be," Heggemeyer said, and who was getting it from him. "We had to do something."

On May 6, 2014, not long after the clinic in Saginaw opened in the morning, law-enforcement vehicles swarmed the parking lot. More than a dozen agents came through the doors. They began clearing people out of the waiting room and boxing up medical charts for removal.

Heggemeyer and Lloyd confronted Awerbuch to tell him they had a search warrant and that he was under arrest. He was accused of health-care fraud and of prescribing Subsys without a legitimate medical purpose.

Awerbuch was quiet and defeated, apparently not shocked by this development. "As soon as he saw us, he knew," Heggemeyer said.

By this point, Awerbuch was well aware that he was being watched. The two agents and their colleagues had already executed a search warrant on Awerbuch's house and clinic early in their probe, before Subsys was even on the market. During that search, the investigators found that the man who came to the office in rumpled clothes led a different life at home. He lived in a six-thousand-square-foot lakefront house on a cul-de-sac in West Bloomfield, a prosperous Detroit suburb a world away from Saginaw. The doctor drove his modest Chevy to work, but stored in his garage was a 2005 Lotus Elise, a rare British sports car so low to the road that it looks like a go-kart. Awerbuch also owned an extensive collection of rare coins, stamps, and sports cards, stashed all around the house and in safe-deposit boxes. When agents were searching his clinic, they signed for a FedEx package of collectible coins and medals sent from overseas that happened to arrive for the doctor.

When the two lead agents arrested him that day in 2014, they led him away from his patients, into his personal office, so as not to embarrass him. They didn't want to alienate him; they wanted to bring him around. They asked Awerbuch if he would be willing to talk to another set of investigators who were waiting for him down in Detroit. For the Department of Justice, there was an endgame here that was bigger than just one doctor.

After Awerbuch had his initial appearance in court that afternoon, in downtown Detroit, he crossed the street to the offices of the U.S. Attorney. Waiting for him in a conference room were three people who had flown in from Boston, including an FBI special agent named Paul Baumrind. The timing of the arrest had been coordinated so that they could be there to try to talk to Awerbuch. The

Boston group had nothing to do with prosecuting the doctor, but his arrest represented a big moment for them. He was a potential asset to their own investigation, which had national implications. They were pursuing an entire drug company.

The agents wanted to know what Awerbuch had to say about a pharmaceutical manufacturer called Insys Therapeutics. Insys was a small but highly successful startup, led by an Indian-born visionary founder named John Kapoor. The Arizona-based firm had grown at an enormous rate in the preceding two years. After going public the previous May, Insys had become the best-performing initial public offering of 2013, on a gain of over 400 percent. Investors were thrilled with the skyrocketing sales numbers, which came almost entirely from one source: Subsys. It was the only branded product the company marketed. The CEO, Michael Babich, had held up that little plastic fentanyl spray bottle on CNBC a few months before, in an interview about the incredible run of Insys's stock. Boston investigators knew that Awerbuch had a close relationship with the company, but they were looking for details. In secret, he began to provide them.

A few days later, Awerbuch called Baumrind and told him that something unexpected had happened. With the media reporting that the doctor had been criminally charged with overprescribing Insys's flagship drug, the company was distancing itself from him in the public eye. But a top executive at Insys had just privately contacted him, Awerbuch told the FBI agent. The executive had said that he was going to be in the Detroit area, and he and some other Insys employees wanted to come see him and go out for a meal.

The executive was a man called Alec Burlakoff. Baumrind already knew the name well. It was coming up again and again in the Boston team's investigation. There was John Kapoor, the founder; Mike Babich, the CEO; and Alec Burlakoff, the leader of the Subsys sales effort. This was the trio of men at the top of Insys.

Kapoor was a relentless boss but at heart a scientist, a tinkerer delighted by innovation; Babich was his protégé and like Kapoor the first in his family to come so far; Burlakoff was a salesman with the gift of gab, unmanageable but a genius of persuasion. Together they and their growing company were a model of American entrepreneurship, overcoming obstacles with nimble decision making and unmatched hustle—just what the system is designed to reward in a country that generates more new drugs than any other.

The investigative pursuit of these men and their company would lay bare how that system really works, revealing in extraordinary detail the inner workings of the prescription-opioid machine. The story of Insys would span the nation, unfolding inside pain clinics and high-end restaurants, boardrooms and call centers, gentlemen's clubs and Wall Street office towers, before culminating in Boston's federal courthouse. The investigation would become a landmark event in the government's efforts to hold the pharmaceutical industry accountable for its role in the spread of potent and addictive painkillers.

While a flood of prescription opioids has driven a national health crisis, the drug companies responsible, showered in riches, have been able to operate largely in secrecy, paying to settle cases that might otherwise crack open their ways of doing business. This time the story would be different. The Insys saga would afford an unprecedented view into the marketing of painkillers in the midst of a deadly epidemic.

All of this would take years to unfold. When Awerbuch was arrested, it was still the early days. Burlakoff's impending visit held out the prospect of a major break.

The FBI agent was amazed to hear that Insys's sales chief was headed to see a doctor who had just been arrested. He told Awerbuch to accept the invitation. When the doctor showed up at the meal, Baumrind told him, he was going to be wearing a wire.

It was a quiet day in the office, a holiday weekend in 2001, when the head of Mike Babich's division asked him out to breakfast. Babich had been working at Northern Trust, a storied Chicago banking institution, for a few years by then, since graduating from college. He had started out in a two-year program, similar to a med-school rotation, cycling through various departments. But he was plucked out of the pool early and promoted.

Babich joined an elite team within the bank's wealth management division. Serving so-called high-net-worth individuals, this unit had carved out an excellent reputation, competing with global players such as Merrill Lynch and Morgan Stanley. If you wanted them to manage your money, you had to maintain a balance of at least $10 million.

Babich was a Chicago native, but he had already come a considerable distance. He was born in 1976 to a large, close-knit Catholic family on the South Side. His father was an electrician who worked for the city, his mother a receptionist. All his grandparents lived within walking distance. After graduating from Catholic school, Babich became the first in his family to get a four-year degree, earning his bachelor's at the University of Illinois in 1998.

Babich was very tall, with brown hair and a broad build and face. He had the look of a former All-American athlete who has put on a few pounds since his playing days. You could picture him as the president of a fraternity, the one who leads the rowdy rituals but also knows how to conduct himself when he meets with university administrators. Out of the office, he kept a messy apartment and liked talking about football and pro wrestling (the staged kind). At work, he spoke crisply and could find his way quickly to the heart of the matter in a business discussion. He showed a talent for picking apart investment opportunities. He was regarded as a young man on the rise.

So it was a surprise, at their breakfast, when the head of Babich's division told him about a potential job that would mean leaving the bank. Northern Trust was a large bureaucracy, full of lifers. Babich would have a hard time leapfrogging those ahead of him in line for promotions, the boss said. There was another opportunity he might want to consider. An enormously wealthy man, a longtime client of Northern Trust's, was drawing attention in the pharmaceutical business, and he was looking for help managing his finances. He was based in the biotech hotbed of Lake Forest, Illinois, an affluent suburb north of Chicago. The man's name was John Kapoor.

Babich decided to venture an hour north for an interview with Kapoor. The job represented an uncertain prospect. Based in the distant suburbs, Kapoor's company, EJ Financial, had just eight or nine employees. It wasn't a pharmaceutical firm per se. It was a "family office," managing Kapoor's substantial investments in an array of ventures, along with his personal wealth. The company was dominated by a single person, from an older generation—Babich was twenty-four years old, while Kapoor was fifty-seven—and Babich didn't know a lot about him.

As Babich would come to learn, Kapoor in many respects fit the American archetype of the immigrant striver. He was born to a respected family in the Indian subcontinent. His grandfather was a highly placed judge in Lahore under British colonial rule. But when Kapoor was a young child, his Hindu family lived right along the fault line created when India was separated from Pakistan by partition in 1947, producing an enormous eruption of sectarian violence that he would remember all his life. Kapoor's parents found themselves on the wrong side of the new border, and they lost their home and business amid the rioting.

As his family sought to build a new future in India, Kapoor excelled in school. He was identified as a great talent, a boy with the promise to lift the family's fortunes single-handedly. He graduated from high school at thirteen. When his parents resettled in Bombay (now Mumbai), he lived with them in a two-bedroom household of eight or nine people while he attended the University of Bombay, eventually earning a pharmacy degree. He and a brother slept on the small, uncovered balcony. When it rained, they covered themselves with plastic or a spare mattress.

Looking to forge a career in pharmaceuticals, Kapoor felt constrained by what his home country could offer him. In India, he said, when you were training to be in the drug business, they taught you how to work in a factory. Onward to America then. Kapoor came to the United States with $5 in his pocket, he later said, to earn his graduate degree, on a fellowship, at the pharmacy school at the State University of New York at Buffalo, the biggest public university in the state.

By the time Babich met him, Kapoor was the largest shareholder in at least five companies. He had made a fortune as a biotech entrepreneur. For most of us, the words "pharmaceutical industry" call to mind giants such as Pfizer, AstraZeneca, and Eli Lilly, but the vast majority of drug ventures are obscure. It was in the lesser-known pockets of the industry that Kapoor had made his name.

Several of Kapoor's companies were in the unglamorous business of generic medications. When a new branded drug comes to market—those products with familiar names such as Humira, Zoloft, and Viagra—the government grants years of patent protection and market exclusivity to the novel product, out of a recognition that no one would undertake the immensely difficult and expensive research-and-development process if competitors could immediately copy the results. It is only after that period of exclusivity lapses that generic versions are permitted to enter the fray, driving down prices. Patients pay no attention to the name of the manufacturer of a generic, printed in tiny letters on the prescription bottle, but there's plenty of money to be made in the niche.

Kapoor's first big break, the coup that had earned him the capital to seed everything that followed, provoked lasting controversy.

In his mid-thirties, after earning his PhD and working in operations at a small drug company near Buffalo, Kapoor saw potential at Lypho-Med in Chicago, a neglected generic-drug subsidiary of a manufacturer better known for making cardboard boxes. After he approached the parent company, Stone Container, the bosses there agreed to hire him as Lypho-Med general manager, but they warned him they planned to sell the money-losing drug unit. Kapoor asked for right of first refusal, and in 1981 he took Lypho-Med off their hands. Not yet wealthy, Kapoor borrowed from Northern Trust and recruited a group of investors for the leveraged buyout, limiting his own personal investment to around $50,000, a small fraction of the total price.

Kapoor took the reins and quickly turned the company (rebranded as Lyphomed) into a powerhouse in the generic drug business, selling hundreds of injectable medications for use in hospitals. The 1980s were a go-go decade in generics, with government incentives favoring cheaper alternatives to branded medications. The name of the game in generics is to be first out of the gate with a competitor once a branded product loses exclusivity. If you don't win that race, or at least come in second, you're just "hoping to get your pennies back," as Babich later said. At Lyphomed, Kapoor was a consistent winner, bursting into the market at the earliest moment. "At midnight," his Lyphomed business partner Brian Tambi later said, "we would start trucking."

During the AIDS epidemic, Lyphomed had a de facto monopoly on an antibiotic that became a go-to treatment for a deadly pneumonia common to AIDS patients. The company attracted outrage from activists when it quadrupled the price. Protesters lay down en masse in front of its Chicago headquarters for a "die-in."

Still, under Kapoor's ownership, Lyphomed grew in less than a decade from fewer than twenty employees to about eight hundred, as total sales increased more than twenty-five-fold. Beginning in 1987, however, Lyphomed ran into major trouble with government regulators. The Food and Drug Administration flagged a host of "serious violations" related to patient health at Lyphomed facilities. Investigators in 1988 seized drugs from a Lyphomed plant. Shareholders sued the company for failing to promptly disclose the FDA troubles, resulting in a settlement. Later, the FDA found that the company had submitted false or misleading information for years in applications for new-product approvals, during Kapoor's tenure.

The precise sequence of events is a matter of dispute, but it was during the time that this wrongdoing was being uncovered—but before the revelations could seriously damage the company—that Kapoor cashed out: in 1989, he agreed to sell Lyphomed to the Japanese firm Fujisawa at a valuation of nearly $1 billion. He personally reaped more than $130 million in the sale, nine years after investing no more than $50,000 of his own money.

Fujisawa's big acquisition signaled a confidence that Lyphomed had overcome its regulatory troubles and was on a promising path. Within a couple of years of Kapoor's big deal, however, Lyphomed's value and reputation were in pieces. In 1992, Fujisawa sued Kapoor, alleging that he had concealed devastating FDA problems during the sale. The buyer was accusing Kapoor of, essentially, selling a lemon. Kapoor countersued, and the fight persisted for years. In pretrial litigation, Kapoor scored some victories, but the argument that carried the day in his favor was not that his company was innocent. It was the opposite. Fujisawa had been a major shareholder for years while Kapoor was still in charge. Lyphomed was so rife with misconduct during that time, judges found, that if Fujisawa officials didn't know about it or did not suspect Kapoor of deceit, they should have.

Kapoor has consistently described the suit as face-saving nonsense on the part of Fujisawa's owners. He said the questionable data submissions to the FDA were merely a matter of "somebody not keeping good records." When a congressional panel took up corruption in the generic-drug business and lambasted Lyphomed in a hearing, citing its "legendary" manufacturing problems, Kapoor invoked his Fifth Amendment right to remain silent.

He settled the Fujisawa matter out of court, for much less than Fujisawa was seeking. Fujisawa was left to recall Lyphomed drugs and withdraw new-product applications to the FDA. Ultimately, Fujisawa retired the name Lyphomed altogether.

Meanwhile, Kapoor moved on. On the strength of his Lyphomed profits, the boy who slept on a balcony had become an American business mogul.

With his newfound wealth, Kapoor immediately set about giving extensively to charitable causes, in both India and the United States, and he lent support to a vast network of relatives, not only with money, but with time and attention. He and his wife, Editha, adopted four children. Several of them had significant challenges or special needs. Three came from orphanages in India. Whenever Kapoor visited his native country, family would gather to greet and celebrate him.

Meanwhile, drawing on his Lyphomed proceeds, Kapoor continued to be a fierce and relentless businessman. He spread his bets widely, seeding dozens of startups as well as taking major positions in several larger ventures. When companies he played a central role in were dogged by dire financial troubles and litigation, which happened repeatedly, he tended to plunge in only deeper, taking on bigger roles, refusing to concede defeat. "If something happens," he once said, "I just don't run away."

Now, in 2001, Kapoor was looking for a low-level employee to join the team of EJ Financial, managing his complex tangle of investments. Mike Babich would be interviewing for the position of portfolio analyst. Arriving in Lake Forest, he found that he towered over his would-be boss; Babich was well over six feet and Kapoor well under that. In his large glasses, Kapoor looked more like a distinguished professor than a business titan. His signature physical trait was a wavy mop of graying hair. Still, Kapoor was intimidating, with an air of intensity. While relatives and friends knew him for his generosity and heart, colleagues spoke of the need to "survive" him.

The meeting was not an instant match. Weeks passed afterward with no word, and Babich began to feel he had been quietly passed over for the job. A second interview was followed by another lengthy unexplained silence. When Babich finally got a job offer, it came in the form of a letter in the mail. He accepted.

For the first couple of years at EJ Financial, Babich barely got to know Kapoor any better than he had in those interviews. The office in Lake Forest was U-shaped, and the two worked at opposite ends. Babich was the young new guy, rarely in direct contact with the man in charge.

Kapoor was busy in this period, his business interests often under siege. As the largest shareholder in the generic drugmaker Akorn, he was steering it through dire regulatory and financial trouble, stepping in for a time as chief executive. Akorn was in lien default and the lender was foreclosing. Kapoor was also a director and the largest stakeholder in First Horizon, another drug company (later called Sciele Pharma); after its stock dropped 81 percent in one day in 2002, shareholders sued the firm and members of the board, including Kapoor, for manipulating and misrepresenting its true financial condition before the bottom fell out. (The suit later settled.) Another company Kapoor co-founded, Neopharm, was faltering, prompting him to later instigate a fierce battle for control. He publicly called for the ouster of the majority of his fellow board members, citing their "'DO NOTHING' style."

Meanwhile, down the hall, in a room with three other cubicles, Babich read balance sheets, created spreadsheets, and prepared buy-and-sell recommendations. When Babich did communicate with his boss, it was from an arm's length, almost comically so for such a small company. Typically Babich would send his investing ideas to Kapoor by email. But email didn't come naturally to Kapoor, being of an older generation; his assistant Nellie Oquendo tried to teach him several times, but he lacked the patience to learn. So Oquendo would print out Babich's memos, Kapoor would scribble his agreement or disagreement in the margin, and Oquendo would interpret his handwriting and leave a note for Babich in his cubicle with Kapoor's reply. That was Kapoor and Babich's version of a dialogue for some time.

Even from a remove, Babich could glean certain things about his boss and his manner. Kapoor was serious and sometimes severe. His affable demeanor could vanish in an instant, some colleagues said. A number of people owed their careers to him, and they tended to stick by his side, while he in turn brought them from project to project. But he could turn cold on a partner or employee, especially for the mistake of being overly cautious and missing a business opportunity. When the coldness set in, that was the beginning of the end. Recovering Kapoor's good opinion was almost impossible.

In his primary role, Babich managed a $100 million personal portfolio. Assessing it in those early years, he grew skeptical of Kapoor's large investment in the giant health-care firm Health-South, which composed around a quarter of the portfolio. Studying its regulatory filings and management's conference calls with investors, Babich detected some discrepancies in what HealthSouth was saying about its finances. This came on the heels of revelations of earlier misconduct at the company. Babich detected an odor. He recommended that Kapoor shed 80 percent of his stake—an enormous move—and Kapoor agreed.

"That turned out to be a great idea," Babich said later. Health-South was committing fraud, which resulted in criminal charges. When the scheme was revealed, the company stock tanked. Babich had saved Kapoor millions of dollars. That was a language he understood.

Not long after the HealthSouth trade, according to Babich, Nellie Oquendo left an envelope with his name on it at his cubicle. It was a check for $5,000 from Kapoor's personal checking account. Babich called his parents: "You're not going to believe what just happened."

Soon, Kapoor started dropping by Babich's desk more often and soliciting his opinions. There was still little in the way of personal chatter, but a relationship of substance was taking hold, a give-and-take. Babich wanted to earn an MBA, and he broached the topic with Kapoor, who asked him what other firms did for their employees in this situation. Babich looked into it and presented a few possible scenarios. Kapoor elected to pay nearly the entire tuition for Babich's degree. Babich didn't leave EJ Financial to pursue the MBA; he earned it in an evening program at Northwestern's prestigious Kellogg School of Management and stayed under Kapoor's wing.

Babich was learning how to please his boss, and he was learning that it could bring rewards.

In 2002, not long after Babich arrived, John Kapoor summoned a young Indian-born man he knew in the industry, George Kottayil, to discuss some business ideas. Together they soon founded Insys Therapeutics. Kapoor would provide the funding for the fledgling drugmaker, beginning with a $1 million loan, and hold a 75 percent stake. Kottayil, as president, would be tasked with overseeing the day-to-day science of developing potential new drugs. The company was only one of the numerous Kapoor projects operated out of EJ Financial, and initially Babich was only peripherally involved in it. The entity that would eventually launch Subsys existed more on paper than in actuality. Its assets, early on, consisted of some equipment in a rented lab space in Mundelein, Illinois, not far from Kapoor's home base in Lake Forest.

For any pharmaceutical startup, a central challenge is how to sustain the company financially for the years required to push drugs through the pipeline to regulatory approval. Until a prized letter from the FDA arrives, a drug doesn't bring in the first dollar. With Insys, the initial plan was to win the race to market the first generic version of Marinol, a branded treatment for nausea and vomiting induced by chemotherapy, and for wasting caused by AIDS. The active ingredient is dronabinol, or synthetic THC (the compound found in marijuana that stimulates the appetite). Kapoor thought that his dronabinol medication would take perhaps two or three years and $5 million to develop—small numbers in the business. At that point, according to the plan, the drug would start bringing in substantial revenue, which could be used to fund the lengthy and more expensive development of other products that he and Kottayil were exploring.

One of those products was a fentanyl spray.

In the origin story that Kapoor has often told, it was the travails of his wife that drove him to develop Subsys. Kapoor had met Editha Hillock back when he was living in the Buffalo area, shortly after earning his PhD. Eight years younger than Kapoor, she had been raised and educated in Grand Island, New York, and had been a cheerleader at Niagara County Community College. They married in 1974, holding two traditional ceremonies, one Hindu and one Catholic. Editha took his last name. Kapoor was deeply devoted to her. The initials in EJ Financial stand for Editha and John.

Editha Kapoor battled breast cancer in the 1990s, prior to the founding of Insys, and then suffered a recurrence in 2004, when she was in her early fifties. Her health declined, and Kapoor spent a lot of time at her bedside. He consulted doctors nationwide. He tried everything. "I've never seen a husband fight the way he fought to save her life," a relative of Editha's said. Kapoor's wife lost a lot of weight. She suffered terribly.

"I can tell you," Kapoor later told *Forbes,* "pain is such a misunderstood thing for cancer patients. Nobody understands pain. They think pain is just pain. My wife went through it." In her final days, family gathered in the Kapoor house could hear her wailing from the other room.

Editha Kapoor died at home in 2005, at fifty-four years old. Kapoor called out his nickname for Editha as he wept, saying the word "Bunny" over and over, like an incantation.

For many months, Kapoor withdrew almost completely from social and professional life. Nothing could hold his interest. Family wondered if he would ever recover.

His absence and sudden indifference to work created difficulties at EJ Financial; Kapoor was a central figure in a number of companies, private and public. In this period, Mike Babich often stepped up in Kapoor's stead. Increasingly, he was at his boss's right hand.

After his wife's death, Kapoor invested more and more into pushing Subsys forward. The aim of the product, Kapoor said, was to help people like his wife—seriously ill people battling severe pain.

Unlike the generics that had largely been Kapoor's stock-in-trade, Subsys was to be a branded drug. When applying for FDA approval, a drugmaker must specify a so-called indication, meaning a diagnosis the medication is meant to treat. For Subsys, the indication would be breakthrough cancer pain—sudden flares of pain that exceed the threshold of a long-acting painkiller the cancer patient would be taking simultaneously.

Subsys had the potential to ease the suffering of people in devastating pain, improving their lives immeasurably. It was also a great business idea.

Developing a brand-name drug that is truly novel can bring a pharmaceutical company a huge windfall, but it's an inherently risky endeavor. After years of sunk costs, failure is far more common than success. Drugs that look promising in the early stages of testing frequently fail in late-stage clinical trials, dealing a massive financial blow to the companies behind them. Creating a generic product is a much safer play, but it comes with smaller rewards.

Subsys had the potential to occupy a sweet spot somewhere in between: a large payoff without the enormous commercial risk. It would cost tens of millions to bring to market, but many branded products cost far more than that to develop and need to traverse more pitfalls, because they're based on a new chemical entity; in simple terms, they're made from scratch. Subsys, by contrast, was a "reformulation" of a drug that already existed, a molecule with known effects on the body.

Fentanyl, the active ingredient in Subsys, dates back to 1960. In the decades after it was first synthesized, it came into widespread use in hospitals, as an intravenous anesthetic during surgery and in epidural injections for women in labor. By the time Subsys entered the picture, despite rising concerns about addiction and abuse, a few take-home fentanyl prescription drugs were also available or in the pipeline. The most widely used was a slow-release patch worn on the skin, branded as Duragesic, but other products on the landscape were even more similar to Subsys.

Kapoor's intention with Subsys was not to forge a new market but to enter this small class of existing medications in the hopes of convincing doctors that his was the best in class. These products—Subsys's future competitors—are sometimes called rapid-onset opioids. The more technical term is TIRF medications (pronounced "turf"), for transmucosal immediate-release fentanyl. Rather than being swallowed in pill form, the fentanyl in these products passes through the highly permeable mucous membrane lining the mouth or nose, providing fast and efficient absorption of the drug into the bloodstream. "Rapid onset" is meant to indicate that they are quicker than long-acting and short-acting opioids. Only intravenous injection is faster.

All the TIRFs on the market were FDA approved solely for breakthrough cancer pain. The first TIRF for out-of-hospital use, called Actiq, was approved in 1998. Actiq was acquired two years later by a drugmaker called Cephalon. In 2003, Cephalon bought out a potential future competitor too; it announced that it would acquire through a merger another TIRF that was in the pipeline. That product came to be called Fentora, and Cephalon launched it in 2006, just after Actiq lost U.S. patent protection (ensuring that the company kept a branded drug on the market, rather than ceding territory to generics). By that time, several other competitors, including Subsys, were on the way.

The only distinction among the TIRF products was how exactly the fentanyl was delivered into the body. Actiq is a lozenge on a stick—a lollipop, essentially—to be rubbed against the inside of the cheek. Fentora is an effervescent tablet that dissolves between the gum and the cheek.

Subsys was conceived as a spray that a patient would shoot under the tongue. This distinction in delivery method would be enough to make it a branded drug, not a generic. Assuming it cleared the bar of FDA approval, Kapoor could secure the brass ring of the pharma business: a period of patent protection and market exclusivity. No one else could sell a fentanyl spray for years. If Kapoor could show that delivering fentanyl in a spray was superior to the other formulations, he could potentially dominate a market that his competitors had already built, by applying a twist to their idea.

What's more, this was a lucrative market. On the one hand, TIRFs were not widely used, in relative terms. In total prescriptions, they were dwarfed by household-name opioids such as OxyContin and Vicodin, which were indicated for a broader set of patients. However, TIRFs still produced tremendous revenue because they commanded a high price. A one-month prescription typically cost thousands of dollars, an order of magnitude more than the price of OxyContin, not to mention generic opioid pills available for less than $20. And TIRF prices were rising rapidly. In 2006, Actiq generated over half a billion dollars in sales for Cephalon, a number not far from the OxyContin stratosphere. That was the year that Insys first filed a patent application for a sublingual fentanyl spray.

Babich's version of the Subsys origin story has a less altruistic cast to it than Kapoor's. In Babich's narrative, the clear business potential of the product figures more heavily than Editha Kapoor's health history. Everything stemmed from Kapoor's observation that spray delivery was not only scientifically promising but remunerative. When Kapoor was a director of First Horizon, that company had marketed a successful oral spray to treat angina attacks. According to Babich, Kapoor observed that sublingual sprays could be priced much higher than pills and compete with generics. He couldn't see why more sprays weren't being developed. As Kapoor has said himself, he was very familiar with Cephalon's Actiq and thought fentanyl might work in a spray and compete with it. He tasked his scientists with simultaneously exploring spray delivery formulations of fentanyl and other molecules, intended to treat different conditions. Fentanyl won out.

Part of what made TIRF products so financially promising was that despite the FDA's intentions the drugs were not, in actuality, restricted solely to patients with breakthrough cancer pain—not even

close. More often than not, in fact, they were prescribed "off label"—
for uses other than the FDA-approved indication. Pain management
doctors, rather than oncologists, were the major players, and they
were using TIRFs to treat all kinds of pain. A Cephalon internal
study of 2004 data showed that Actiq was used most commonly to
treat back pain. Only around one out of five patients taking Fentora
actually suffered from breakthrough cancer pain, a 2008 FDA analysis found.

These doctors weren't doing anything illegal. Health-care providers are permitted to prescribe off label, and they commonly do.
Medications developed to treat seizures are used by psychiatrists
to treat bipolar disorder. Drugs indicated for psychiatric disorders
are prescribed for insomnia, for premature ejaculation, and to help
patients quit smoking.

But regulators draw an important distinction between what is
permitted for doctors and what is permitted for drug companies.
While clinicians can *prescribe* off label, using their own judgment,
it is generally forbidden for a pharmaceutical company to *promote* a
product for off-label uses. The rationale is that in determining what
is safe and appropriate for a patient, a highly trained doctor should be
given leeway to depart from FDA guidance, but a drugmaker should
be given no leeway at all, in view of its obvious bias. (Recent legal
challenges have carved out exceptions and eroded enforcement, but
the prohibition against off-label marketing remains in place.)

Even as drug manufacturers are barred from encouraging it, off-
label prescribing nevertheless represents a major boon to the industry.
The fact that a doctor can prescribe a drug for any reason naturally
grows the potential market for it. With TIRF drugs in particular,
off-label uses constituted the lion's share of the business.

Was Kapoor in fact developing a drug for cancer patients, then?
Yes and no.

On the years-long path to FDA approval that lay ahead, Insys
would sponsor a lengthy series of clinical trials for Subsys. In the
critical late-stage trials, the fentanyl spray would be tested only on
cancer patients, because the sole indication Insys was applying for

was breakthrough cancer pain. In the end, fully a quarter of the patients died during the period of the final trial—a jarring figure, but not a major setback for Subsys. The trial subjects were extremely ill to begin with. That was the kind of patient Subsys was ostensibly meant to reach: a person in dire health, a person for whom dependence and addiction are not the foremost concerns. Describing the use of TIRF products, Dr. Lewis Nelson, then of the New York University School of Medicine, told *The New York Times*, "If you're waiting to die, you should die in comfort and dignity. . . . It's very different than if you're attempting to have a functional life, because these drugs are relatively incompatible with having a functional life."

With Subsys, as with any drug candidate, the FDA's job would be to study the trial results and conduct a careful risk-benefit analysis tailored to the indication. The agency was tasked with determining if the drug was safe and effective. But the FDA doesn't use the word "safe" in quite the way the rest of us do, as its officials sometimes try to publicly explain. The agency determines whether a product is safe *enough* relative to the benefits, under a particular set of circumstances—if the risks, in other words, are worth it.

What is appropriate in medicine depends greatly, of course, on a patient's condition. Prying open a person's chest to grab and palpate the heart by hand may be the best course of action in a cardiac emergency; it is obviously not a wise thing to do in other cases. Likewise, a highly addictive opioid may be the right choice for a terminally ill person in terrible suffering but totally inappropriate as a treatment for, say, moderate lower back pain.

With FDA approval, however, Insys would have a "crowbar" to pry open a wider market, as a former Insys sales trainer put it. The track record of other TIRFs had already shown that doctors would prescribe Subsys to people who were nothing like the patients in the clinical trial, and the FDA would be unable to stop them. For Insys, that was a business opportunity too big to ignore. If the company marketed its drug only to cancer specialists, it could never compete with Cephalon.

———

When Kapoor dove headlong into developing Subsys, he was already in his sixties and wealthy enough to retire in luxury. He spent time at a second home in Phoenix, a large, desert-hillside property with an amoeba-shaped pool in a gated community on the southern edge of the Piestewa Peak hiking area, to the north of downtown. The city skyline looms in the distance, and helicopters can be heard overhead. The neighborhood overlooks the Arizona Biltmore, a mammoth resort hotel that opened in 1929 and has since drawn presidents and celebrities. Kapoor was deeply involved in charities, many of them related to cancer; donated to Republican political candidates; and was setting out to open a series of restaurants. The plentiful golf courses of metro Phoenix are full of entrepreneurs of Kapoor's generation who no longer work and instead spend time perfecting their swings and renovating their kitchens.

But here was Kapoor, launching a major new startup. Despite his extensive tangle of investments and board seats and the demands on his time, he was obsessed with pushing Subsys toward approval and getting Insys off the ground. He leaned hard on his protégé Babich to help him fulfill his vision.

In banking on Subsys, Kapoor was stepping into risky territory. The danger was not just that the venture might fail. If Subsys were approved, Kapoor would be stepping straight into the middle of a public health emergency.

What separates the opioid crisis from all previous drug epidemics is that it has its roots in drugs that are perfectly legal to use— FDA-approved and highly regulated painkillers much like Subsys. In the 1990s and early in the following decade, new voices in the medical community advanced the idea that pain needed to be treated more forcefully, that fear of opioids was excessive and had to be overcome so that patients wouldn't needlessly suffer. Medical students and doctors were widely taught that legitimate pain patients would not become addicted.

This idea never rested on a solid scientific foundation, and it simply wasn't true. Pharmaceutical companies played a central role in fostering this misimpression, downplaying the risks as they aggressively marketed their painkillers. Drugmakers handed megaphones to physicians who celebrated the benefits of opioids and embraced more liberal prescribing of narcotics, anointing the doctors "key opinion leaders." These physicians presented themselves in the manner of evangelists, giving talks designed to break down resistance to opioid therapy. In 1997, a North Carolina pain specialist named Alan Spanos said, "These drugs, which are—I repeat—our best, strongest pain medicines, should be used much more often than they are" and "do not have serious medical side effects." The doctor made these remarks in a promotional video for OxyContin.

Local doctors, many of them in primary care and not pain specialists, fell under the sway of these voices. They looked at patients they had known all their lives and saw people who needed pain relief; they didn't see potential addicts. Their intentions were usually good. The national outcome was catastrophic.

It would be wrong to suggest that everyone who was prescribed painkillers became addicted; most of them did not, and many of them were, and are, profoundly grateful for opioids. But even prominent early advocates of liberal practices now acknowledge that far too little care was taken in prescribing these drugs. People experience pain all over the globe, of course, but no foreign country consumes as many opioids as the United States.

As the years went on, and as liberal prescribing created a widespread dependence on opioids, illicit drugs stepped in to meet the excess demand. Heroin, also an opioid, targets the same receptor in the brain that prescription painkillers do. Heroin had been in decline since the 1970s and suddenly returned in full force. Regions that had been "tenderized," in the journalist Sam Quinones's description, by pharmaceutical sales reps selling painkillers fell prey to traffickers in heroin and, later, synthetic opioids such as fentanyl.

Fentanyl—the same substance found in Subsys—has become a prolific killer. Fentanyl and its analogs were implicated in about two-thirds of all opioid overdose deaths in 2018. In the vast majority of cases, the fentanyl that is causing overdose deaths is illicitly manufactured, not made by pharmaceutical companies. Fentanyl is a synthetic opioid, meaning it is not derived from the poppy flower, which for centuries has been harvested to create opium, morphine, and heroin. Fentanyl needs no fields and can be made in a clandestine lab. It is easily trafficked, often from China or Mexico; its potency means a small package can deliver a large payload.

Even as street drugs have overtaken prescription products as the leading culprits in the crisis, it has become only clearer that the opioid disaster began with government-regulated painkillers. As many as four out of five heroin users have reported that they started out by misusing prescription drugs. An enormous public health crisis began not with hand-to-hand transactions on darkened street corners or covert shipments over the border but under the sanitized fluorescent glare of neighborhood pharmacies and Walgreens. The drugs at issue were packaged and trafficked by men in suits who worked at companies celebrated on Wall Street and in the pages of business magazines.

The dramatic deepening of the opioid crisis brought heightened attention and heavy litigation focused on the pharmaceutical industry. Most notably, Purdue Pharma and its founding family, the Sacklers, came under intense scrutiny over the marketing of OxyContin. Purdue Pharma had launched OxyContin in early 1996, and by 1999 at the latest, according to a secret Department of Justice report later obtained by *The New York Times*, the company's top executives had learned from their sales force that the product was being misused, abused, and sold on the street. Already in 2001, the world was learning of the scourge of OxyContin in West Virginia and throughout Appalachia, where it earned the nickname hillbilly heroin. A Kentucky prosecutor, Michael Pratt, told *The Guardian* that year, "The bodies are stacking up like cordwood." The opioid crisis, in other words, was already in full swing when John Kapoor and his new drug came along.

So too was the government's battle with opioid makers. Throughout the first decade of this century, pharmaceutical manufacturers clashed with public officials over their role in the spread of powerful painkillers. Authorities were trying to confine opioids to a select population of pain patients who desperately needed them, but manufacturers were pushing legal boundaries—sometimes to the breaking point—to get their products out to a wider market. Regulators were slow, tentative, and overmatched.

Still, drugmakers were beginning to face consequences. Purdue Pharma pled guilty in 2007 to the euphemistic felony of "misbranding" OxyContin and agreed to pay $600 million to resolve the charges. Three top executives also pled guilty to misdemeanors, escaping prison sentences. Purdue acknowledged that "with the intent to defraud or mislead," it falsely promoted OxyContin to prescribers as a drug that was less addictive and prone to abuse than other narcotic painkillers.

Meanwhile, even closer to home for Kapoor, government authorities were investigating the marketing of TIRF products. Cephalon disclosed federal and state probes into its sales and promotion practices for Actiq in 2004, when Subsys was still on the drawing board. Cephalon told investors that year that it was in "ongoing discussions" with two states regarding reports of abuse and diversion of Actiq. The company ultimately pled guilty in federal court in 2008 and paid a $425 million settlement in connection with its unlawful marketing tactics for Actiq and two other drugs.

The Cephalon litigation revealed that it was not an unintended quirk that TIRFs had come to be prescribed so commonly for noncancer pain. When Actiq was first awaiting regulatory approval, before Cephalon acquired it, an executive of the company that was poised to market the drug, Abbott Laboratories, told an FDA advisory committee, "We are only going to focus our promotional efforts on the Hem/Oncs [hematologists and oncologists] or the cancer pain specialists. These are the only clinicians that we will be approaching to give them information on this drug. As a company we do not tolerate off-label use of our products." Cephalon didn't abide by that pledge. The drugmaker's sales force illegally promoted Actiq for off-label uses, including for migraines. Cephalon targeted physicians who had almost no cancer patients, and employees touted the drug's benefits for anyone suffering from pain, as the company acknowledged in court. (Similar allegations would later be leveled at the promotional efforts for Fentora.) Sales reps and managers at Cephalon made the case to doctors that Actiq was useful to a wide range of patients, and this message was passed on to other practitioners through purported educational programs. Trainers and reps used the mantra "pain is pain."

What's more, there were signs that TIRF drugs were leading to serious harm, especially in off-label use. This was not the widespread damage associated with, say, oxycodone or hydrocodone, because TIRF products were not as plentiful, but no one doubted that they were dangerous.

"We all know [Actiq] is being misused and abused," a health insurance manager told *The Wall Street Journal* in 2006. The paper reported that the drug had appeared on the streets in Philadelphia, where it bore the nickname perc-a-pop, a bit of wordplay combining "Percocet" and "lollipop." In 2007, the FDA issued a public health advisory about the proper prescribing of Fentora, after several patient deaths.

And yet, in late 2007, Cephalon applied to the FDA for approval to expand the indication for Fentora so that its sales force could lawfully market it more broadly, for non-cancer pain. At a 2008 FDA joint meeting of advisory committees to address the issue, panelists expressed alarm at the prospect of TIRF drugs being prescribed any more widely than they already were. A risk-management program designed to ensure proper patient selection plainly wasn't working, the data showed. One scientist noted that in Fentora's clinical study, some of the product was stolen, and study participants showed "aberrant drug use behavior," which is "uncommon in controlled clinical trials." Her presentation concluded, "The risks of unintentional potentially fatal overdose, misuse, abuse or diversion of fentanyl and of Fentora in particular are extremely high." The FDA denied Cephalon's bid for a broader indication. The government was making a conscious effort, if a feeble one, to restrict the use of TIRFs.

The legal allegations that continued to dog Cephalon were different from the charges against Purdue, but the underlying concept was the same. The companies had enabled and encouraged doctors to prescribe their potent products to far more patients than they should have, with costly and sometimes fatal results. The Department of

Justice, by prosecuting these companies, was trying to put two horses back in the barn. Kapoor, meanwhile, was just mounting a third horse to gallop out the door.

In early 2007, Kapoor told Babich he was interested in moving Insys to Arizona, near his second home, and he saw Babich becoming a key player in the company. Babich, a lifelong Chicagoan, was not particularly excited about relocating, but the opportunity to be a major figure at Insys was hard to ignore. Still, it wasn't at all certain what the company would become. The generic Marinol project was dragging on, beset by technical problems. Kapoor was unhappy with the delays, and Kottayil, the co-founder and scientific lead, was seeing his role reduced. Subsys had fared well in an early trial but was still years away. There was no revenue and no guarantee that any of the products would pan out.

At Kapoor's direction, Babich broached the idea of a move with Kottayil and the other couple of scientists who were working for Insys out of its Illinois lab. Along with Kapoor and Babich, they constituted, in practical terms, virtually the entirety of the company. Babich was surprised to find that they were all willing to uproot their lives and go to Arizona. If the science people were on board, Babich thought, maybe Insys was for real.

Babich moved to Arizona in 2007 and got to work finding office and lab space. He was soon named chief operating officer of the company. For the first half year or so, while still commuting to Chicago to finish his MBA, Babich lived in Kapoor's Arizona "guesthouse," as Kapoor called it (though it was about a mile from his residence). Kapoor was entrusting him not only with his business interests but with his home.

The two men had grown closer over the years. Babich had shown ambition at EJ Financial, which Kapoor always liked to see. He had taken on more work on his own initiative and proven his value during Kapoor's long absence following his wife's death. Given how small Kapoor's home office was, there was a certain intimacy to the relationship, an inevitable father-son dimension to it. Kapoor was serving as Babich's entire financial support, paying his salary out of his own pocket and funding his tuition for business school.

For the next several years, the two men worked together to bring Insys to life, with a small rotating cast of other players in Kapoor's orbit. It was a difficult period, to say the least.

In 2007, the long-delayed generic Marinol still had the potential to be the first to market and generate needed funds. It would buy them time for Subsys, which was going to require at least a few more years and an additional investment of tens of millions of dollars.

One option to raise cash during all this waiting would have been to court private equity, but Kapoor ruled that out, according to Babich: "John's theory was, as soon as you take a dollar from someone, you gotta listen to them."

Another option would be to take the company public. In 2007, the market was hot for IPOs, and a phase I trial for Subsys had shown strong results. Kapoor decided to try for a public offering, with Babich's help. They beefed up the management team and brought on new directors to meet the requirements. But by the time they were ready, a twofold disaster had struck. For one, they lost the race to get a generic Marinol approved. (Their own version, which Kapoor had spent more than $15 million developing, had to be retooled and wound up coming in a distant third. It would never bring in much revenue.) Meanwhile, the economy was cratering worldwide, and investor money was drying up. Bankers told Kapoor there was no use in trying to go public. He soon fired much of the senior management team, leaving Insys with a skeleton crew. But Babich stayed on.

The company was in "a desperate position," Kapoor said later. "It had no money." Attempts to form partnerships with other pharma companies had failed. In mid-2009, Insys had $21,000 in a checking account and carried over $25 million in debt, owed mostly to Kapoor. If he decided to stop pouring money into this sinkhole, it was over. Given the historic financial crisis and the mounting scrutiny and litigation surrounding opioids, no one would have blamed him.

But Kapoor believed in Subsys and pushed onward. Much of his funding for Insys had come in the form of loans, but partly to signal confidence in hopes of attracting other potential investors, he later said, he converted around $20 million of the debt to equity. As a consequence of this transaction, George Kottayil's stake in Insys was virtually wiped out. (He would later sue Kapoor and the company, alleging that Subsys was his invention, not Kapoor's, and the litigation would last for years.)

For Insys, everything was riding on Subsys now. It was a precarious position to be in. Babich said, "We had one product, one shot on goal." Meanwhile, the overall number of TIRF prescriptions had entered a decline starting in 2006. Insurers were placing tighter restrictions on the drug class, and some doctors were opting to prescribe the cheaper generics. The controversies surrounding the marketing and abuse potential of Actiq and Fentora were not helping Subsys's cause, as Kapoor was well aware.

On the other hand, TIRFs commanded an ever-higher price, which considerably softened the blow of the loss of prescriptions. The market was still worth upwards of $400 million. But the fact remained that through no fault of his own, Kapoor was going to be fighting for a slice of a shrinking pie.

Still, Subsys continued to show potential. Anecdotal evidence from the ongoing pivotal phase III trial was encouraging. When investor interest in the health-care sector returned in 2010, he and Babich tried to take Insys public again. When the two met with bankers in preparation, one of them asked Kapoor who was going to head up the company as chief executive. Kapoor said, "Mike's going to do it." It was the first Babich heard that he was being hired as the CEO of Insys Therapeutics.

In private, Babich later asked Kapoor why he didn't become CEO himself, with so much invested. Kapoor said that he had done it before; it was Babich's turn. But he also made clear that Babich's primary role would be to serve as the face of Insys, traveling and handling Wall Street investors. Babich was clean-cut, American-born, fluent in the language and folkways of finance. But in terms of the particulars of pharmaceuticals, he was a beginner. Kapoor was still going to run the company, as executive chairman of the board.

Kapoor and Babich were trying to go public from a position of need, rather than a position of strength; they were looking to raise cash because Kapoor was losing patience with carrying the whole bag. Their second attempt at a public offering also came to nothing. Despite Kapoor and Babich's great efforts, again the bankers determined an IPO would be a waste of time. But Kapoor owed his career to not giving up, and he wasn't going to do it now either, not with Subsys getting close.

At last, the phase III results came in. For Kapoor and Babich, it was a make-or-break moment. They had contracted an outside firm to oversee the trial, and the company arranged a conference call in early 2011 to deliver the news.

The scientists got right to the point: Subsys really worked. The "primary endpoint" of the study, meaning the measure of success, would be to demonstrate a significant fentanyl blood level at thirty minutes after the dose. When the team learned they had hit that target, "we were ecstatic," Babich said.

The news got better. Subsys had hit each and every secondary endpoint they had elected to study. Not only was the drug working at thirty minutes; it was working at fifteen minutes, at ten minutes after the dose. It was working even at five. No TIRF product had ever been shown to relieve pain so rapidly. This was close to the speed of IV drugs administered in a hospital. For a patient in terrible pain, a TIRF with a faster onset could be a godsend. For Kapoor and Babich, it could bring a fortune.

3   THE PLAYBOOK

The fact that regulatory approval of Subsys now finally seemed near, in the fall of 2011, was a huge milestone for Kapoor and Babich, but it also placed them in a vulnerable new position. The pharmaceutical business can be understood as encompassing two functions that are quite distinct: first, drug development, and second, "commercialization." *Science,* then *selling.* Small entrepreneurial outfits like Insys predominate in the first step. The second is often the domain of massive corporations; once a drug succeeds in clinical trials, its developer frequently sells it to a Big Pharma name, a company with the regulatory experience and sales and marketing firepower to fully exploit its financial potential.

Kapoor's plan, however, called for controlling Subsys end to end. He wanted Insys to bring Subsys to the market on its own. That meant Kapoor and Babich would have to build out a marketing and sales infrastructure that was capable of competing with larger, entrenched competitors and could capture the attention of doctors who had never heard of them or of Insys Therapeutics. To do that, they needed a far better understanding of the TIRF marketplace than they had.

Babich in particular, who hadn't worked in the drug business for anyone other than John Kapoor, needed more know-how around him. His public-facing Insys bio looked more impressive than it really was. He had never worked for a company that was out in the world marketing medications. "My opinions were those of those around me telling me," Babich later said. "I've never launched a pharmaceutical

drug in my life at this time." So Kapoor and Babich looked for someone to head up their marketing effort.

Babich learned of an executive named Matt Napoletano who
might be interested. Kapoor agreed right away that they should fly
him out from the East Coast to Arizona for an interview.

Napoletano grew up in Pennsylvania, graduated from Shippens-
burg University, and later pursued an MBA at St. Joseph's University
in Philadelphia. More to the point from Kapoor's perspective, Napoletano worked at Cephalon. He had held senior management positions at the company, based near Philadelphia, for about six years.
Better still, he had been intimately involved in the 2007 launch of
Fentora, which would be Subsys's top branded competitor. Napoletano knew the TIRF world cold.

A person with this kind of experience wasn't easy to come by.
Only five branded TIRF products had ever been launched. Three of
them were new and struggling to get off the ground. Of the two that
had so far succeeded, Cephalon marketed both. It was the pioneer in
the niche and still the dominant player.

Babich and Kapoor could quickly see that Napoletano was gun-
ning for their job opening. The Israeli industry giant Teva Pharmaceuticals had recently bought and swallowed Cephalon, which made
Napoletano a part of a larger bureaucracy. At Insys, Napoletano
sensed an opportunity to get in early and play a bigger role than his
résumé would merit in Big Pharma. With stock options on offer at
Insys, there was real "upside," as he put it. Napoletano saw potential
in their new drug, and he liked the fact that Insys was in the sup-
portive care niche, meaning that its portfolio of drugs was centered
on managing serious illness, particularly cancer. The subject was personal for him; Napoletano's young son suffered from cancer.

For Napoletano, a job at Insys would mean uprooting his wife
and family, moving far from where he was raised, and finding a new
medical team to treat his son. There would be a lot of persuading to
do at home. But he was ready for that.

For his interviews with Kapoor and Babich—he met them
both separately and then together—Napoletano came prepared. He
already had a detailed plan for how to market Subsys, broken down

into component initiatives, and he spoke extensively of the specific audience Insys needed to target. His insight into the competition was impressive. When Kapoor and Babich conferred following the interviews, the decision wasn't difficult. Napoletano was their new vice president of marketing.

Matt Napoletano was forty-three years old, closer to Babich's age than to Kapoor's. He was clean-cut and slender and usually wore glasses. In demeanor, he was not an obvious top executive; he was no swaggering Master of the Universe. In a slightly nasal voice, he spoke without embarrassment in the management-theory lingo of the moment: *stratifying* the data, *pulsing out* a budget, *the learnings* from a day of meetings.

He was a very different animal from Kapoor, who wasn't in touch with the latest thinking out of the top MBA programs. Kapoor had never gone to business school. He wasn't in the habit of getting deep into the math or anticipating trends. He liked to see hard proof of success on the page before giving a green light, but he would get annoyed if his employees' presentations were more than a few pages. Once briefed, he acted on his instincts, which had served him well over a long career. After that he didn't like being questioned.

Napoletano wasn't a lot like Babich either. Napoletano was more analytical, more of a worrier. He was highly intelligent—"a genius," one co-worker said—and also a talented pianist. He didn't have Babich's towering physical presence. Napoletano was said to be a flirt with women, but not always a successful one. ("He was a total goob," one female senior Insys manager said.) Babich spoke more simply, acted faster, presented with more confidence. He attracted more romantic interest, too.

Babich might have felt a twinge of self-doubt or competitiveness as Napoletano entered the picture and won Kapoor's respect. But Babich could be certain that as the face of the company he had no competition.

In meetings with Kapoor, Napoletano, and a chief medical officer Kapoor had hired, Babich let the others handle the fine points of marketing, regulatory matters, and pharmacokinetics. "I am not going to start throwing out things that make me sound like an idiot," Babich said later. "I'm on my Blackberry dealing with how are we going to get this thing public. . . . That was my job. How do we get this company public."

Napoletano, meanwhile, brought his Cephalon experience to bear. When he had arrived at Cephalon in 2005, the company's marketing schemes were already under government investigation. Department of Justice officials were engaged in the years-long process of doing what they usually do in such cases: extracting a settlement and, in this instance, a guilty plea from the company.

As part of the terms of the settlement, finalized in 2008, Cephalon was required to enter into what's known as a corporate integrity agreement. This mandated that the company undergo audits and submit itself to close scrutiny for a period of five years, under the threat of heavy sanctions if it strayed. The company was ostensibly in its getting-clean phase, in other words. For a time, Napoletano led a training program in the appropriate use of opioids.

He therefore became extremely familiar with the raft of rules that govern pharmaceutical marketing and sales, particularly in the arena of controlled substances. The Drug Enforcement Administration classifies all TIRFs as Schedule II products, the most tightly regulated category of legal drugs. These regulations and guidelines are issued and enforced by an alphabet soup of federal and state agencies, including the FDA, HHS–OIG, state medical and pharmacy boards, and, most ominously, the DOJ and its agencies the FBI and the DEA. The rules are complicated and extensive, and violating them brings potentially huge legal and financial penalties.

A studious person by nature, Napoletano knew very well what you couldn't get away with if you were marketing a fentanyl drug. Seen another way, he also knew what you could.

He was taken aback that Kapoor wasn't planning to hire either a general counsel or a compliance officer. Because pharmaceutical regulations are so complex, compliance is an entire field within the industry. At a large firm such as Eli Lilly or Pfizer, there are dozens of employees working in compliance.

But Kapoor insisted he wanted to use a "low-cost model" to build Insys. He took pride in spending the minimum in business, thereby bringing the goalposts of profitability closer. When Napoletano would ask about hiring legal and compliance executives, Kapoor would raise his voice: "Do you have a checkbook? Do you want to pay that salary?" Napoletano was not one to back down easily, and some friction developed between the two. Babich kept explaining to Napoletano—as he would come to explain to people around him over and over—that it wasn't a good idea to push back against Kapoor. "Once he makes up his mind," Babich said, "the decision is done."

Before he was even hired, Napoletano had created a substantial document outlining his business plan for Subsys. "Matt's not very short-winded," Babich said. "He loved to have hundreds and hundreds of pages in front of him." Napoletano called this document the "playbook." After he was hired, everyone else at Insys called it that too. Napoletano wrote it more as a wish list than a final game plan; of course Kapoor would ultimately decide how to spend his own money. But with a few exceptions, Napoletano's playbook became the road map that Kapoor began to follow in marketing their new drug.

A core idea that animated the entire playbook was that in order for Subsys to win market share, they needed to win the loyalty of a relatively small group of doctors. Insys had limited resources, but that could be overcome if the company targeted its efforts just right. It was a simple notion, but the significance of it would prove to be enormous.

To drill down and identify where to direct their sales and marketing campaign, the Insys leadership drew on a wealth of data derived from the commerce in prescription drugs. Drugmakers ship their products to wholesale distributors, principally the "big three" of McKesson, AmerisourceBergen, and Cardinal Health. (These companies are among the largest corporations in the country, each of them bringing in more than $100 billion in annual revenue.) From the distributors, the product goes to pharmacies—CVS and neighborhood independents and mail-order outlets—where the actual retail sales transpire.

But that flowchart leaves out what is, to the drugmaker, the most important transaction, even though no money changes hands: the prescription, or, in the industry shorthand, the script. For manufacturers, there is almost nothing more valuable than knowing who is prescribing, or "writing," your product, and who is prescribing the competition.

Third-party firms have stepped in to supply that knowledge, at a price. The most well known is IQVIA, formed through a merger of industry leader IMS Health and Quintiles. Companies like this acquire sales data for drugs at the pharmacy level. Because each prescription is tied to a prescriber ID number, IQVIA can link up each ring of the cash register to the name of a physician and then sell that data to drugmakers.

Many physicians object to this practice. To have a "private interaction" with a patient be "subsequently sold and repackaged as marketing ammunition to use to influence my prescribing habits is distasteful to me and to many of my colleagues," a Vermont doctor named Norman Ward has said. That state passed a law banning the sale of prescription data for marketing purposes. But IMS and its competitors joined with PhRMA, the major drugmaker consortium and lobbying group, to challenge the measure in court, and they won: the Supreme Court in 2011 overturned the law on First Amendment grounds. So whenever you fill a prescription at your pharmacy, pharma firms nationwide are going to know about it, and they're going to know who gave it to you. This allows drug companies to target physicians with great precision.

In many industries, the sales function has migrated online and become less personal. People selling insurance or Bibles or hairbrushes rarely ring doorbells anymore. But the pharmaceutical business still typically does things the old-fashioned way: face to face.

Drug manufacturers blanket the country with sales reps, assigning each one to a territory. The sales reps get a "call list" of healthcare practitioners, then make the rounds to visit their offices day after day, putting incredible mileage on their cars. They often come to know "their" doctors well, because they return again and again to reinforce their message and push for more prescriptions.

Back at headquarters, executives figure out where to deploy reps and even what routes they should take in their cars, to maximize efficiency. On their fishing trips for "customers" (a term they use for doctors), drugmakers don't wander around on their boat with a line in the water. They head out with a near-perfect radar image of what's happening below the surface. "You fish where the fish are," a former Insys manager said.

The data that Insys was most interested in showed that the universe of TIRF prescribers was small, in relative terms. These were niche drugs, amassing between 100,000 and 200,000 prescriptions a year, whereas the total number for all opioids by this time was a staggering 250 million. Many doctors hadn't heard of TIRF drugs, even some pain management specialists and oncologists. Approximately 1,100 practitioners accounted for 80 percent of the TIRF prescriptions. Anyone outside that group had prescribed drugs in the class so rarely that they might not merit a sales rep's attention—which was, for a startup, a precious commodity.

And in fact, as Napoletano knew from firsthand experience, the number 1,100 understated how concentrated the market really was. The Insys team divided TIRF prescribers into deciles, according to how many scripts they wrote. This revealed that roughly 30 percent of the TIRF prescriptions in the United States were written by just the top 170 doctors or so.

For Insys, this was great news. Because there were so few big names—the equivalent of three per state—a company with a comparatively small sales force had an opportunity to win them over. Furthermore, the marquee doctors were geographically concentrated, tending to cluster in, for example, Florida, California, and New Jersey, and rarely in low-density states.

If Insys could position its sales reps wisely around the country and persuade a lot of these 170 doctors to switch their TIRF patients to Subsys, Insys stood to win control of the market. Because most TIRF scripts at the time—around 60 percent—were written for the much less expensive generic versions, a 30 percent share would almost certainly make Subsys the revenue leader. Winning even a 20 percent share would likely make the top Insys executives extremely wealthy men.

To get to the core group of 170, it made sense to start with the core of the core. The true all-stars were the top 25 or so. These were the "decile 10" prescribers, accounting for fully 10 percent of the TIRF drugs distributed in the nation, totaling around fifteen thousand prescriptions.

With the beginnings of a plan laid out, Kapoor decided to grant Napoletano one of the first items on his wish list. He authorized his marketing head to create an advisory board, or "ad board," consisting of around a dozen doctors. The physicians invited were not randomly chosen, of course. They were key opinion leaders, or KOLs—"the gurus of fentanyl," Babich called them later. "It just so happened that the majority of those gurus were also decile 9s and 10s." ("KOL is a very loose term," a onetime Insys manager said.)

In late 2011, those on the ad board were compensated and flown out for a weekend in Arizona for a half-day meeting, plus some fine dining. Dinner was held at Roka Akor, an ultraexpensive Scottsdale restaurant that Kapoor owned. Kapoor always wanted business dinners to take place at Roka, a sushi restaurant fused with a steak house, housed in its own large sand-colored building. In the open kitchen, a small army, dressed in black robes, sliced precise cuts of fish and flipped Wagyu steaks over open flame in full view of the diners.

At the ad board meeting, the KOLs gave some advice on Insys's plans for Subsys, which hadn't yet reached the market. But Insys did most of the talking. Kapoor offered some remarks, telling the doctors how his late wife's suffering had led him on this journey. Napoletano zoomed in on the details, delivering an hours-long presentation about their fledgling product.

Though it wasn't billed as a sales effort, the aim was partly to tout the drug. Perhaps more important, it was about getting the top customers in a room, in order to start forming relationships with them—to "touch" them, as an Insys executive called it. Unlike its competitors, Insys had no track record, no corporate name recognition. Here was a chance to gain a foothold with just the right people. Those competitors would not have been pleased to know this event was occurring. They already had ties to these doctors. Insys was trying to woo them away.

The gathering seemed like a success, though it would be hard to know if anything was working until Subsys went on sale. The timing of that was still uncertain. But just a few weeks later, Kapoor and his small team reached a milestone they had been waiting for and counting on. On January 4, 2012, the Food and Drug Administration approved Subsys.

Now Insys leadership would need to hire up a full sales force, to pitch the product out in the field. With a growing payroll, their costs were mounting. The faster they could begin selling, the better their prospects for success.

4   THE ROOKIES

Tracy Krane was living with her in-laws when she got the call. Her family of three was crammed into a house that wasn't theirs, the in-laws occupying the master bedroom. The house was in Venice, Florida, near Sarasota. Krane hated Florida. But she and her then husband were short of money, and their options were limited. He had been let go from jobs several times and was unemployed.

Krane had a confident and warm manner, with a big laugh, but at that moment in her life she was worried and on edge. She felt the pressure of needing to support her young family. But she hadn't held a job since before she had her two-year-old daughter, when she worked in sales at an import-export company.

In late 2011, Krane was trawling online job boards and sending out résumés in bulk. On Monster.com, she came across an ad from Insys Therapeutics. The company was looking for sales reps.

By this point, Insys had hired a vice president of sales, Shawn Simon, who would run the sales force out of the Arizona headquarters, along with five regional managers who would be based around the country and report to Simon. Each of those regional managers would oversee nine reps or so. Out in the field, then, would be five managers and forty-five reps going door to door in all fifty states.

After submitting her résumé, Krane got a call from the manager of the Southeast region, Tony Bryant. She walked out to the humid backyard of her in-laws' house so that her toddler wouldn't be overheard, and she paced nervously with her cell phone pressed to her ear. Of course she would come in for an interview.

Krane drove to Tampa to meet with Bryant in January 2012. He was hiring his team of nine reps in a region that would stretch from Florida to as far west as Texas and as far north as North Carolina. Bryant had summoned people from around the Southeast for interviews at a Tampa hotel suite with him and his boss, Shawn Simon. The fact that the head of sales was meeting with potential reps, who would occupy the lowest level in the hierarchy, seemed telling to Krane. This was a small outfit.

Finding good pharmaceutical sales reps is a challenge. It's a tricky and demanding job. Many physicians find drug reps to be an annoyance, or worse. They don't like being told how to practice medicine, much less by someone with an obvious agenda, and they object to unannounced doorstep visits. Office staff try to fend off reps and dissuade them from coming so often. Reps call them the "gate-keepers." The challenge for reps is to "get back"—both literally and figuratively, to get past the front desk and into the doctor's realm. An unending battle for access is the norm, and a sales rep's day is littered with failures. It isn't unusual to drive fifty or a hundred miles to see a doctor, only to be turned away immediately.

Reps need to at least appear to be sufficiently educated and knowledgeable to be training a doctor about a medication. They also need to turn on the charm, to get creative and stand out from the competition. The good ones are persuasive, even pushy. Some industry insiders believe that if you haven't gotten kicked out of a doctor's office as a rep, you aren't pushing hard enough. The job takes chutzpah. It isn't for everyone.

One by one, at the Tampa hotel, job candidates entered the suite for their interviews, looking their best. The job market was still tough going in the wake of the global financial crisis. Krane was worried, when she walked in, that pharma wasn't in her wheelhouse, that there could easily be questions she didn't know how to answer. Bryant asked her what she thought the job of a drug rep entailed. A little flummoxed, she decided on a straightforward answer. Well, she said, she thought it involved driving around trying to persuade doctors to prescribe a medication. The two men chuckled, not unkindly. Bryant said, "That's basically it!"

It didn't take long for him to decide, mid-interview, that they should hire Krane. It was clear that she had the intelligence to learn what she needed to, and she was vivacious and appealing in person.

Getting an offer from Insys, in a follow-up call from Bryant, was a highlight for Krane at a dismal time. But she was taken aback when she learned the base salary: $40,000. She thought that when it came to sales, pharma was supposed to be the pinnacle. She didn't imagine anyone in drug sales could make so little. A typical company would offer twice that amount, or more.

Bryant had years of industry experience. He knew the number was awfully low, but he wasn't empowered to improve it: with very few exceptions, that was going to be the base pay for Insys reps across the board. He quickly added that there would be stock options and generous commissions on sales. He assured Krane that Insys had an amazing product on its hands. The company was going to succeed, and she would share in that success.

Krane was skeptical. She had googled Insys Therapeutics and come up with almost nothing. It was hard to know what this job was all about. The company was a startup, and its big product wasn't even on the market yet. It sounded a little like one of those Silicon Valley upstarts that touts its compelling "story" but has barely any revenue, never mind profits. Tracy had worked for one of those already, in the first dot-com boom, and her stock options had become worthless when the company folded.

She told Bryant that story on the phone, pressing him a little on what she could expect in pay. But privately, she already knew she was going to accept the offer. *Who am I kidding?* she thought to herself. She needed a job.

It wasn't until a couple months later that Krane got a sense of Insys as a whole. In late March 2012, Insys gathered all its employees in the desert sprawl of greater Phoenix for a company conference. The location was the Saguaro Scottsdale, a colorful and hip boutique hotel close to Kapoor's restaurant and not far from the Insys corporate headquarters in Chandler. It was the launch meeting for Subsys: the product was about to go on sale.

There was an upbeat feeling to the event, a crowd of people getting together to start something new. It was a little like the first day of college. Nearly everyone at the meeting had been hired within the last few months. It was the first time that many of the reps would meet one another; they all lived in different areas, of course, and they would scatter again at the end.

Tracy wound up spending a lot of time with another new rep based in Florida, Mia Guzman. The Southeast region team had gathered briefly in Miami the week before, for a little preliminary training with Bryant, and the two had become fast friends.

Guzman was a fellow pharma rookie. She was petite and energetic, a little bit feisty. She loved delving into various conspiracy theories online and nursed a paranoid streak. Mia had aspired to a career in dance when she was younger. But she had bounced around in various jobs: she worked at Sephora and did hair and makeup on photo shoots during college and later taught dance in Florida schools. She was selling protective wear for workers to corporations when she came across the same Insys ad that Tracy found.

Guzman was a single mother, with a seven-year-old son. She had split with her husband when the boy was a toddler. She was tired of relying on child support, which was always a source of fighting with her ex. Her goal was to make enough to stay afloat whether the child support came or not. She wasn't greedy for money, she said, but she was greedy for independence.

The idea of a pharma job caught her attention. That's where the money is, she thought. She had also heard that so-called specialty drugs like Subsys, which typically cost more, meant higher pay for the reps. (Usually reps don't begin their career in specialty pharma; they start by calling on primary care offices.) Guzman's title at Insys as a rep would be specialty sales professional.

At the Scottsdale hotel, Krane and Guzman talked in private about their new co-workers. They couldn't help noticing that the average rep was younger and even greener than they were. The job listing they had seen said that a bachelor's degree and two years' experience in sales were required. Evidently, those were loose guidelines.

Most of Bryant's reps, for the Southeast region, were in their thirties like Guzman and Krane and had at least some relevant job history. But it turned out that his hires were not the norm. Many of the new reps from elsewhere were ten or even fifteen years younger. Some were straight out of college.

The reps were overwhelmingly female. They were also remarkably attractive, and some of them flaunted it. The same was true of the men. The West region in particular drew a lot of chatter. Krane and Guzman weren't shocked that good-looking people had been hired to work in pharmaceutical sales; it's not an uncommon phenomenon in the industry, where former cheerleaders and athletes abound. Still, Krane and Guzman marveled at the overall picture. They felt as if they had stumbled into an audition for a reality TV show.

There was a flirtatious atmosphere that made them a little wary—people in hot tubs with higher-ups they had just met, rumors of heavy drinking and hookups. One female rep was spotted arm in arm with a senior executive in an upstairs hallway of the hotel around 3:00 a.m. It was the night before the conference even began. At another point, a manager noticed that Kapoor gave his phone number to a rep from New Jersey, an outgoing and brassy woman in her thirties named Sue Beisler.

The gender dynamics of the company were noticeable. Until the reps had been hired in the preceding weeks, Insys was composed of a small group of executives who were almost entirely male (with female assistants). Now, suddenly, there were a lot of women around. For the most part, they had been hand selected by men who would supervise them closely. Their job would be to use their powers of persuasion with doctors, also mostly male.

Mike Babich had been working since his twenties in a somewhat claustrophobic atmosphere alongside Kapoor, with few co-workers. Now he was surrounded by women his age, and he was their CEO. He appeared to be enjoying the attention. The amount of personal space between Babich and one female employee raised some eyebrows. She was not in fact a rep; she was the head of human resources.

Later, Babich had a "one-day relationship" with her, he said. At Insys, he became involved, eventually, with at least five women who worked under him.

Some of what Krane and Guzman were observing was the result of decisions made above them and outside their view. If John Kapoor had a philosophy of drug sales, not his specific area of expertise, it was a simple one. He believed in the "low-cost model," and the company publicly touted it as a strategic choice. In building a sales force, Kapoor had opted to hire on the cheap, with the carrot of high bonuses based on performance. The same model had been used at Sciele Pharma, co-founded by Kapoor as First Horizon in the 1990s, and it worked out well; although the company went through serious troubles, it sold for over $1 billion in 2008.

The green reps at Sciele weren't selling a Schedule II narcotic, however. Not all the managers at Insys were convinced that this approach was a wise idea for a fentanyl product. A beginner rep could easily violate the rules unintentionally, and the consequences could be serious. But Kapoor stayed the course.

Those attracted to the modest salary at Insys were people who yearned to be drug reps, usually for the first time. "We were willing to give them the shot where most companies would not," Babich said. While Insys spoke to investors of its "cost-efficient" sales force, the terms used internally were more frank, more crude. Top executives discussed their intention to hire reps who were PhDs—"poor, hungry, and driven." Or that's how the term first started being used. Later it morphed into "poor, hungry, and dumb."

Kapoor, Babich, and Napoletano also spoke openly of hiring "folks who were, you know, easy on the eyes," Babich said. "No physician wanted a quote-unquote, you know, unattractive person to walk in their door." If a sales rep didn't have what it took—and this was bound to happen sometimes—the answer was simple: you fired her. If, however, she showed she could "drive business," you paid her handsomely. At Insys, sales commissions would be higher than the industry norm, to compensate for the low salary. Bonuses would also be uncapped; there would be no limit to what a rep could make.

Kapoor had a reputation as a stingy owner, and it was well deserved, but for those who produced results, the opposite was true. If you raked in revenue, it didn't matter that you were only a few years out of college; you could earn more money than an upper-level executive. (One rep in his mid-twenties would end up earning close to $2 million in four and a half years.)

"That was John's philosophy," Babich said. "It was an 'eat what you kill' philosophy. If you sell a lot, you make a lot."

In some sense, this idea was only a reflection of Kapoor's overall approach to business: risk as little as possible and back what works. Whenever Kapoor decided to spend capital to launch a new initiative at Insys, he started with a pilot program. *Let's see how this goes* was a common refrain. If the trial run failed, he would put a quick stop to it. If it paid dividends, he would take it off the leash.

When business got going on day one of the launch conference, Kapoor and Babich addressed the company, but it was Matt Napoletano who did most of the talking, leading a detailed presentation of the Subsys FDA label and the "messaging" that the reps were going to use when they called on doctors. He went over his allotted time. There were a lot of scientific facts to memorize, Guzman thought, watching from the audience.

Around dawn the next day, Kapoor awakened Babich with a phone call. The boss was extremely upset, the anger thick in his voice. Babich had experienced his wrath before, many times, but the timing now, days before the launch of their flagship product, made it more unnerving. Kapoor said that he and Napoletano had no idea what they were doing, Babich said, and the messaging was "fucking terrible." Kapoor told Babich that he was coming to the hotel right away, and he ordered him to gather the brass for a meeting in a room there.

Babich scrambled to summon everyone, telling them to "hurry

up and get dressed" as he got ready himself. He gave them some words of warning about the thrashing that was coming. With Napoletano especially, who had put in long hours developing the messaging, Babich wanted to prepare him and talk him off the ledge.

It was a big part of Babich's role at Insys: he absorbed the brunt of the hits from Kapoor, then tried to soften and translate the message down the chain of command, drawing on his longtime relationship with Kapoor to give advice on how to placate the boss. In the reverse direction, he was the one to convey and frame any unpleasant information from below up to Kapoor, without igniting his anger. Kapoor would call him around six times a day, and Babich told people never to email Kapoor without clueing him in because he'd be blindsided when Kapoor would call him about the email. The message from Babich was *I have to deal with this guy, so let me do it.*

At the meeting, Kapoor was fuming. In Napoletano's talk to the sales force, he had been characteristically cautious, anticipating issues that might draw trouble. He told the beginner reps that their opening remarks about Subsys to a doctor should include, right up front, the approved indication of breakthrough cancer pain. They should also highlight that Subsys achieved measurable pain relief at thirty minutes after the dose in the final clinical trial.

Kapoor thought this was all wrong. Instead of mentioning breakthrough cancer pain, he wanted reps to say Subsys had the same indication as the chief competitors, Cephalon's Actiq and Fentora. That approach conveniently omitted the word "cancer" and steered clear of the inconvenient fact that Subsys was only approved for a relatively small group of patients. It also implied, without saying so, that Subsys was appropriate for non-cancer pain, because that was in fact the primary use for those two competing drugs, partly owing to Cephalon's illegal off-label promotion.

Kapoor also wanted the words "five minutes," not "thirty minutes," to come up early and often on sales calls. The rapid onset was the entire key to success for Subsys, as he saw it. He wanted each rep to carry around a five-minute hourglass and flip it over on a doctor's desk to underscore how fast that was. This was risky because the

FDA label did not explicitly back the five-minute claim, but to him that was a technicality.

When Kapoor left the room, "Matt was distraught," Babich recalled. The VP of sales, Shawn Simon, who had many years of pharma experience, "basically said, 'We can't do this.'" Kapoor was telling his lieutenants, they thought, to ignore the FDA's rules. The group was in a bind. They had to take some consideration of Kapoor's view, whatever they thought of it. He was the boss.

Kapoor took matters out of Napoletano's hands at the launch. He had his protégé take the lead instead. With Simon alongside him, Babich emphasized the five-minute onset to the young reps gathered before him. He also told them, toward the end of the conference, that he had been getting a lot of questions about whom this product was for, a natural area of concern. According to Napoletano, Babich told the entire sales force, "Subsys is good for everybody, any pain patient."

It's likely that only a small percentage of the audience found this to be a notable or controversial statement. To Matt Napoletano, however, it was ruinous. The entire basis of the Actiq debacle he had witnessed at Cephalon, resulting in a criminal charge, was that the sales force had made the claim that its fentanyl drug was for everyone, rather than promoting it only for breakthrough cancer pain. One of the smoking-gun quotations cited by Cephalon whistleblowers was the company message that "pain is pain." Now Babich, the CEO, was telling his beginner reps the same thing. Napoletano went home and had a heart-to-heart with his wife, telling her how upset he was.

Meanwhile, at the Saguaro hotel, everyone continued having a great time. One night at a club, Krane and Guzman stayed out until 4:00 a.m. They were among the first to leave. At the end of the week, the sales reps dispersed across the country. The following Monday, they would be going door to door to start moving the product.

The launch of Subsys, in late March 2012, represented a long-awaited landmark for John Kapoor. He had carried the company on his back for a decade and had pushed Subsys all the way through the pipeline, shoveling approximately $80 million into Insys. Another founder might easily have given up, but Kapoor had persevered and emerged as the victor. He had good reason to believe that he was going to market with the best drug in its class. He was ready to reap the rewards, and he expected them to come quickly.

It didn't work out that way. When the Insys sales reps hit the field, they found they had a lot to learn. Each of them was given a call list loaded onto a company-issued iPad. In addition to providing contact details for the clinics they should be visiting in their territories, the lists indicated how often each target had been writing TIRF prescriptions. Reps were to lavish the most attention on the high-decile prescribers, returning to their clinics again and again in hopes of getting face time with the doctors and winning them over to Subsys.

But apart from the decile number, the Insys reps typically knew very little about the people they were trying to persuade. In a relationship business, they had to create relationships from scratch. After summoning the courage to walk into a clinic uninvited on a cold call, they commonly found themselves rejected out of hand. Often their best pitch for Subsys, if they even got past the front desk and had a chance to deliver it, was received to little or no effect. Mia Guzman and Tracy Krane would talk about the frustrating fact that in this industry the "customer"—the doctor—was not in fact a *buyer* of anything. When you left the room after a sales pitch, you couldn't tell if you had closed the deal. A doctor might grant an audience and make noises about being on the lookout for the right patients, but then you were left to wait for scripts that might never materialize.

Clinics would allow reps to schedule a "lunch and learn," which involved bringing in a restaurant lunch for the office and pitching a product to the doctor and staff. But the calendar could be booked up weeks or even months in advance. When the day finally arrived, the doctor might check his phone during the talk and then duck out early with his free sandwich in hand, if he bothered to drop by at all.

Krane saw a glimmer of promise early with a major account in her territory, Dr. Steven Chun, based in Lakewood Ranch, Florida. Chun was a top priority for the company not only in her corner of Florida but nationwide. In week one, Shawn Simon, the head of sales, flew to Florida and joined her for an introductory lunch in Chun's clinic, with the doctor and his nurses. It was a coup for Tracy just to get the meeting. Over lunch, Chun said repeatedly that he would "take care of us with Subsys," Simon later said. Before Krane left, one of Chun's staffers motioned to a patient chart and gave her the thumbs-up. The doctor had come out of the meeting and written a script for Subsys immediately. After years of joblessness, Krane had just earned her first commission. A few days later, Simon gave her a rave performance review, writing in an email, "That Fentora representative better be looking for another job."

But after a relatively strong couple of months, Chun's Subsys numbers began to fall off. He was a mercurial man, and at one point, according to Krane, he kicked her out of his office for a month. This was potentially disastrous for her prospects at her new job, but having scoped out the situation at the clinic for a while, she wasn't sure if there was anything to be done about it. She had been told by then, she said, that Dr. Chun had previously dated a rep for Cephalon. And she suspected that Chun's current girlfriend, a woman in her early twenties named Aqsa Nawaz who was sometimes present in the clinic, had played a role in barring Krane from the office (though Nawaz later disputed it).

The rookies at Insys came to see that many of their targets had long-standing relationships, professional and personal, with competing reps, and that mattered more than they had anticipated. Once they grew acquainted with the clinics on their call lists, they saw that each of them was a social ecosystem, with a cast of staffers surrounding the doctor and a circle of reps jockeying for position. On every call, the Insys reps were stumbling onto someone else's territory. By asking a doctor to start opting for Subsys as his go-to TIRF drug, the Insys rep was asking him to deal a serious blow to a Cephalon rep who might have been visiting his office and seeing him at dinners for years. Particularly at the high-decile end, reps began to detect a subtext coming from the doctors: *What's in it for me?*

It was an uncomfortable dynamic, especially when the doctor's clinic itself provoked an uneasy feeling. Many of the addresses on the Insys call lists seemed like your typical medical office: a tidy waiting room with stacks of magazines and fluorescent lighting, a smattering of patients scrolling on their phones, some staffers wearing scrubs, a doctor who seemed professional and informed running the place. But sometimes, it was different. Mia Guzman tried to call on one office in South Florida for the first time and arrived at a downmarket strip club. The two businesses were in the same shopping center, the clinic tucked behind the club. She later learned that the doctor had acquired a financial stake in the strip club. At the doctor's office, reps were directed to queue up in chairs as they waited to pitch their drugs. Guzman talked to her manager, Tony Bryant, about it. He told her not to go back there.

When a young Insys rep just out of school, Holly Brown, first visited a clinic near Chicago's O'Hare International Airport, to call on an anesthesiologist named Paul Madison, she found it "markedly different" from the others in her territory, and she was troubled. It was located in a "kind of dingy strip mall in a not-so-nice area of town," she said. "I walk in and there's a guy sitting behind the desk counting this big wad of cash out of a safe. The patients that hung around the office were people that looked like they probably had some kind of problem."

Madison was a high-priority target for Insys, but in the first few months Brown didn't succeed in bringing him on board. "He kind of gave me the brush-off," she said. She started fudging her paperwork to make it look as if she called on him more often than she did.

Other reps had better luck finding traction with Subsys in the early days. Clinicians on the call lists were typically experienced with TIRF drugs, which meant that reps only had to make the case that Subsys was the latest and greatest version of something they already used in their practice. Some prescribers responded to the notion of a faster onset of pain relief, and they began making the switch from Fentora and Actiq to Subsys. The shift was generally gradual; some patients were understandably reluctant to break with the treatment they knew.

A few high-decile targets started prescribing Subsys quickly. The ad board that Insys had convened the previous December appeared to pay dividends; several of the top early prescribers had been in attendance.

Insys executives had unusually deep insight into how the sales force was faring, from an ironic source. During the period when Subsys was being developed, the Food and Drug Administration had determined that TIRFs represented so much risk for inappropriate patients that distribution of the products needed to be monitored through a special protocol—a Risk Evaluation and Mitigation Strategy, or REMS, governing the entire supply chain. Consequently, to prescribe Subsys or any of the competitors, prescribers needed to enroll in the TIRF REMS Access Program, which required that they pass a "knowledge assessment"—a quiz—and certify that they understood the risks and the narrow indication for the products. New patients were also required to sign an agreement that warned against improper use.

Curiously, the TIRF REMS program was sponsored and administered not by government regulators but by corporations in the industry, most notably the TIRF manufacturers themselves. In other words, the drugmakers were supposed to police the prescribing of drugs they were promoting. Being part of the program meant that Insys had access to reports listing every single Subsys prescription. Each one appeared as a row on a spreadsheet, indicating the doctor, the pharmacy, the dosage, and more. The purpose of collecting this data was to protect patient safety, but Insys found itself with a marketing gold mine. This granular prescribing information flowed into the Arizona headquarters virtually in real time, whereas even the most expensive data that Insys bought from third parties lagged by a few weeks. When a new doctor produced a Subsys prescription, leadership picked up the signal right away and could send their rep to the office to follow up and reinforce the message. The best time to make a sale, one Insys executive said, is right after you made one. In the TIRF REMS system, patient information was anonymized for privacy, but each patient had a unique ID number, which allowed the Insys brass to track individuals over time, each one of them a potential profit center. Kapoor, Babich, Napoletano, and others personally scoured the reports on a near-daily basis.

The top executives were using a government-mandated safety protocol as a marketing tool. They turned a shield into a sword.

Powerful as the reports were, they could be sobering. There weren't very many Subsys prescriptions coming in early on, only a couple dozen per day. For the lieutenants, this was not what you wanted to be showing Kapoor. The documents also invited his close scrutiny: *What's this doctor's story? Why was he writing two weeks ago and then stopped? Who's the rep?*

A deeply worrying trend was that new patients would appear on a report and then disappear. No refills were allowed on Subsys, as a Schedule II narcotic, so patients needed to return to the doctor every thirty days at most for a new prescription. Some of them evidently weren't coming back—either that or they were asking for a different drug.

In the first few months after launch, an internal debate took hold over the company's performance. Some looked at the sales trajectory and saw a little startup taking on entrenched competitors and making some encouraging inroads. Insys had earned a few percentage points of market share more quickly than the other TIRF upstarts that had taken on Cephalon in the past few years, some of which had fallen flat. But that wasn't good enough for Kapoor. He had the best product. It was obvious. What was so hard about selling it? Managers grumbled about unrealistic expectations, to no effect. When they gently explained the challenges they were up against, he didn't want to hear it.

Kapoor directed Babich to fire Shawn Simon, the head of sales, and take over the role himself for the time being. Babich followed the order and tried to run the sales force, but he had no experience in sales, at any level, and was simultaneously carrying the workload of CEO.

The regional managers in the field came under similar pressure from above, asked to fire underperforming reps. Babich kept telling Tony Bryant—Krane and Guzman's boss in the Southeast—that "the board" was making demands like this. Bryant thought this was obvious code for Kapoor. Bryant resisted firing his people. A couple of months just wasn't enough for beginners to prove themselves, he thought. Some reps had been hired away from other jobs. Now Insys was going to put them out on the street?

That is just what happened. Several of Bryant's reps were let go. In other regions, too, the herd was being aggressively culled. Kapoor was angry about the performance of three reps in the Northeast and asked their manager, "Why are they still here?" Suddenly co-workers were gone, with no explanation from corporate. The high turnover had a psychological impact on the remaining reps. Krane and Guzman had made the cut, but they couldn't be sure how long that would last. A lot of people feared for their jobs.

Babich didn't know what to think of the trajectory. Of the three men at the top, only Napoletano had launched a TIRF drug before; he knew the market much better than Babich and Kapoor did. Napoletano kept pointing to positive trends in the Subsys sales data and telling Babich that he was excited about the early returns.

But Kapoor was saying something else into Babich's other ear.

Kapoor had sunk more money into Insys Therapeutics than he'd ever put into a company, he told Babich over and over. With a sales force to pay, the company was spending faster than ever, without enough revenue to compensate.

According to Babich, Kapoor called it "the worst fucking launch in pharmaceutical history."

It was right at this time of tumult at Insys—with Kapoor maximally dissatisfied and furious—that Alec Burlakoff entered the picture, asking about a job. Burlakoff was thirty-eight years old and applying to be a regional sales manager. But when he traveled from his Florida home to meet Babich and Kapoor in Arizona, he made no secret of the fact that he had much bigger designs.

Burlakoff captured Kapoor's attention right away. Kapoor had a serious problem, as he saw it. In Burlakoff, he saw the glimmer of a solution. Burlakoff's arrival would prove to be the most consequential turning point in the entire Insys saga.

To meet Alec Burlakoff was to know that he was a salesman through and through. For him, it was the family business. His father made a living selling Honda Accords, and his brother sold cars too.

Burlakoff stood just five feet nine inches, but he projected a swagger and charisma that made people turn their heads in his direction, and he relished that attention. He was wiry and kept himself in good shape. His close-cropped brown hair had a hint of a widow's peak. His smile always looked a little like a smirk, as if he knew something that everyone else was missing.

By the time he interviewed at Insys, Burlakoff had a history that might have put off some potential employers. He had begun working in pharma a decade earlier as a twenty-seven-year-old sales rep. The story of his early career traced a steep rise and fall.

Before entering the business, the young Burlakoff had worked as a coach and counselor at a prep school in Boca Raton. He liked work-ing with schoolkids and they liked him, but his salary there made him feel like a loser. On a tip from a school parent who was a doctor, he decided to mount a charm offensive in a quest for a job at Eli Lilly, the pharmaceutical giant. Burlakoff put a picture of himself on his résumé—figuring that it's harder to reject a person with a face—and he kept driving to a local Lilly office to bring coffee and snacks while his application was being considered.

He was passed over for one position, but Lilly tapped him for another soon after. He was hired to call on primary care doctors, the entry-level rung on the drug-rep ladder. Lilly assigned him to a divi-sion devoted to selling two products: the antipsychotic Zyprexa and a new slow-release version of Prozac, the antidepressant, called Prozac Weekly. The company provided four weeks of intensive training for new reps, including two at company headquarters in Indianapolis. There, reps were paired up as roommates in corporate apartments and got to know one another.

Among his training class of about forty, all destined to sell the same products, Burlakoff immediately stood out. In training, he sat near the instructor and was often the first to jump in with the answer to a question, the first to volunteer for role-playing exercises. He absorbed the necessary science, but he really homed in on the lessons about identifying the personality type of the doctor you were dealing with and using that to your advantage.

Burlakoff was named MVP of the training class, and when the trainees hit the field to work, he was an instant star. He "blew it out of the water," a co-worker said, quickly climbing to the top of the sales charts, which were visible to all his fellow reps. He was pre-sented with the Rookie of the Year Award at a national meeting.

Burlakoff had a knack for ingratiating himself with a doctor enough to get past the front desk, or, better yet, get the target out of the office for a more personal conversation. The "money hours," he said, were the ones outside the 9:00-to-5:00 workday. Meet with a doctor then and you could find some "hot button," some desire or need that you could fulfill. He developed a close rapport with one prescriber in particular, an internist, and made tens of thousands in bonuses off his scripts. "Since the day I started working for Eli Lilly, I could do nothing wrong," he once stated, with typical brazenness.

Burlakoff came from a Jewish family that had transplanted from Long Island to South Florida when he was in high school. He wasn't especially religious, but in an attempt to feign common ground, he would sometimes put on a yarmulke to call on a doctor who was an observant Jew. He would tell reps about this tactic years later, from the stage at a conference, presenting it as a model of how to sell.

A rep he was coaching once called him on the fact that he would pull a little disingenuous act when talking to a doctor: pretending a lightbulb had gone off and he'd just thought of a great idea that in fact he had planned to pitch all along. Burlakoff wasn't sheepish about his ploy. He was pleased his young charge had noticed.

The fact that everyone on the Lilly sales force knew how well everyone else was doing—as is typical in pharma—fostered a competitive atmosphere. There was resentment and suspicion of Burlakoff's success. But even some people who mistrusted him found themselves liking him, almost against their will. Or at least they enjoyed spending time with him and taking in The Alec Show. That way they could all talk about him later, grinning and shaking their heads.

Burlakoff punched above his weight when it came to attracting women. They would roll their eyes at him and then order another drink, getting a little contact high from his confidence and outsize presence. On an early date on a dinner cruise with the woman who would become his wife, he ducked out for a minute, saying he needed to go to the bathroom, and played a hand of blackjack. Burlakoff could do outrageous things and be easily forgiven.

Still, his oily aggressiveness didn't go unnoticed at Lilly. Word spread that he had sold cars with his dad for a brief spell during college. His fellow reps started giving him a hard time about being—literally—a used-car salesman.

Burlakoff didn't like the snobbish insinuation. He often credited his father with teaching him everything he knew about how to sell. Burlakoff was drawn to people who made their way without having the education or family background that Big Pharma favored. He thought the idea that you need a college degree to be a sales rep was "bullshit." He was proud of his unglamorous origins and sometimes made his story sound more rags to riches than it really was. But people enjoyed his anecdotes anyway. He was a gifted raconteur and had plenty of material to draw from.

When he was a kid in Long Island, his father ran midsize printing businesses before heading to Florida and turning to selling cars. The Burlakoffs' Long Island community, Kings Park, wasn't affluent, but the family had one of the nicer houses around. Young Alec attended a Jewish summer sports camp in Connecticut that he adored, returning year after year. The family had a succession of late-model Cadillacs in the driveway. His father had his initials stenciled in silver on the back of the Caddys.

Burlakoff would sometimes talk obliquely to co-workers about his family's ties to organized crime, which sparked rumors and created a certain aura. His grandfather was a criminal defense attorney and labor lawyer. According to Alec, he represented members of a well-known crime family. Alec's father held tight to the legacy and nursed an affinity for Mob culture. He used the Mafia lingo and was said to carry a gun beneath his leather jacket.

Alec's older brother was physically strong and volatile, constantly getting into trouble. Kings Park was a sports-obsessed town, everyone wearing letter jackets and piling into the gym for high school basketball games, and Alec's father pushed him and his brother to win at all costs. He would jaw with other fathers in the crowd and once got into a fistfight. If Alec didn't play rough when the moment called for it, didn't deliver a hard foul to spoil a layup, he wouldn't get a ride home from his dad. When Alec and his brother shoplifted souvenirs from Disney World, their father smiled and chuckled, proud of them for getting one over.

Burlakoff was a strong student in high school, then earned a bachelor's degree at Florida State. He went on to get a master's in clinical social work at Florida International University in Miami. After an upbringing in a troubled home, full of strife and yelling, he wanted to understand psychology better. When he started thinking about pursuing pharmaceutical sales, his father was adamantly

against it. He wanted better for his son than to be in sales like him.
But then some younger colleagues at the car dealership told his father
that pharma sales is different. It's working with doctors. It's respect-
able, a white-collar career. Alec's father warmed to the idea.

When Burlakoff arrived at Eli Lilly in 2001, the company was
making a strong push to switch Prozac patients over to Prozac
Weekly, for reasons that were obvious to anyone in the industry: the
original Prozac, a blockbuster that had created a huge stir, was set
to lose patent protection that August, at which point revenue would
nose-dive in the face of generic competition. As part of this "conver-
sion" campaign, Burlakoff participated in a promotional scheme that
outraged patients and regulators.

Along with other reps, Burlakoff persuaded high-prescribing
doctors to generate a list of their patients who were taking Prozac
or its competitors and then write a mass prescription for them for
Prozac Weekly. As a result, these patients received, with no warning, a "Dear Patient" form letter, signed by their doctors but sent
from a pharmacy along with a month's supply of the new drug in the
mail. "Congratulations on being one step to full recovery," one letter
said. Burlakoff collected a windfall of bonus money when one doctor's mailing went out to more than a hundred people. For Burlakoff's
paycheck, all those scripts counted, whether or not the recipient ever
took the unsolicited pills. Patients meanwhile felt that their medical
records—sensitive psychiatric information—had been exposed and
exploited. Eli Lilly and Walgreens weren't supposed to be playing
doctor, and a psychoactive drug wasn't supposed to show up in the
junk mail.

The scheme drew widespread publicity and major litigation.
"This is appalling in every possible way," a Georgetown professor
of medicine, David L. Pearle, told The New York Times. Eli Lilly
terminated or disciplined eight members of its sales force for their
involvement. Burlakoff was one of three who were fired. Two security
officers escorted him through the office and reclaimed his company-
issued property while his wife waited in the car.

Burlakoff and the other fired employees soon sued Eli Lilly, claiming the mailing program had the blessing of management. He said in the suit that he had briefed new reps about the program at a training seminar at Lilly headquarters and that he'd been given an award. With a furor already swirling around Eli Lilly, the lawsuit had a newsworthy angle: the core allegation was that the giant corporation itself, not eight rogue employees, was behind the misconduct. The suit settled years later. Burlakoff took home $100,000 after taxes.

Burlakoff's legal claim was defamation, but ironically it was the lawsuit itself that first put his name in the national news. Ever after, anyone interested in googling Burlakoff could read about his role in the scheme at Eli Lilly.

A co-worker told him later that his firing was a raw deal, that his only mistake was going so big: a dozen scripts at once might have flown under the radar, but a hundred-plus? "Well, you know me," Burlakoff replied.

In a 2003 court filing, Burlakoff said that his reputation in the pharmaceutical industry was permanently scarred by the firing. Years later, however, he said that what happened at Lilly didn't damage his ability to get a new job in pharma; it "only enhanced" it. He was hired elsewhere within two or three days of the firing—for a better job. Burlakoff took a step up to the position of specialty sales representative, selling Risperdal at Janssen, the pharmaceutical subsidiary of Johnson & Johnson, another industry powerhouse. A manager there had had his eye on Burlakoff's performance at Lilly—they were competing for the same doctors—and he saw promise in the young salesman. Managers earn bonuses on the strength of their reps' sales, so they are personally and financially invested in their recruits. Some Janssen managers resisted the hire, knowing Burlakoff's history. But the rep with the dubious past prevailed.

From Kapoor's perspective, the more salient part of Burlakoff's résumé came later. After a year at Janssen, he worked at none other than Cephalon from 2003 to 2007. For the majority of his time there, Burlakoff sold Subsys's two biggest competitors: Actiq, before it went generic, and then Fentora. Again he was a top performer on the sales force, first as a rep and then as a manager. "I killed it," he said later. "I was number one every frigging time." He also garnered a reputation inside the company for pushing the rules.

In 2012, Burlakoff heard from a former Cephalon colleague, Karen Hill, that there might be an opportunity for him at the startup she was about to join, Insys Therapeutics. By then, he was working in sales at a company that did sleep studies, and he was doing well, he said, but he was intrigued. Insys was like another Cephalon, but crucially it was smaller and newer. Maybe it would work out or maybe it wouldn't, but if it did, he could play a bigger role and cash in on the public offering the company was shooting for. Burlakoff had collected major bonus money in the past, but the chance to own a chunk of the company—that was new.

When Burlakoff's résumé arrived at Insys and he was discussed internally as a candidate, a regional manager named Mike Hemenway was asked for his views, having worked with Burlakoff at Cephalon. Hemenway warned Babich and Napoletano against making the hire, describing Burlakoff as a compliance problem.

Kapoor and Babich nevertheless flew Burlakoff into Phoenix in the late spring of 2012 for a round of interviews, a couple of months after the launch of Subsys. They already had a manager for the Southeast, Tony Bryant, but Kapoor was ready and eager to make changes. Burlakoff charged into his first meetings with Babich and Kapoor as if he had sprinted from the airport.

"Alec was a very sales-y individual, meaning very aggressive," Babich said of his first impressions. He had invited Burlakoff to join him and a friend for dinner at Roka Akor. Burlakoff knew it was a top-shelf restaurant and wore a designer suit, with Ferragamo shoes and belt. He took off his glasses and tie to match their informality once he saw Babich and his friend ordering shots, but he didn't exactly relax. He seized on opportunities to show he was the guy to hire.

At the corporate office in Chandler the next day, his interview with Babich was a curtain-raiser for the main event, when Burlakoff spoke to Kapoor one on one. Then all three came together in a conference room. Hearing that Kapoor was dissatisfied with sales so far, Burlakoff boasted without compunction of his success at Cephalon. He had brought along his "brag book," a binder showcasing his achievements and awards. He posed himself as just the turnaround artist that Kapoor needed.

Insys already had Matt Napoletano's knowledge of the TIRF marketplace, but Burlakoff offered something else. He had been out in the field at Cephalon making things happen. His pitch was that he knew how to sell fentanyl at the ground level. "Alec made it very clear," Babich later said, "that he was willing to start off as our Southeast manager but that he was already looking for homes in Arizona" because he expected to rise to the top sales job, at Insys headquarters.

At the end of the interview, Kapoor looked at Babich, banged on the table with the palm of his hand, and said, "I think we just found our vice president of sales."

With the arrival of Alec Burlakoff, the quartet of men who would determine the fate of Insys was complete. Kapoor, Babich, Napoletano, and Burlakoff—an intimidating mogul in the twilight of his career and a trio of ambitious men beneath him. The three lieutenants were all in their thirties or early forties. They were young and inexperienced for positions of such power and responsibility. "We were kids," Burlakoff said. They used first names with one another—Mike, Matt, and Alec—but Dr. Kapoor was called Dr. Kapoor. Babich alone would sometimes call him John, one on one. In Burlakoff's view, Babich was like the eldest brother who protects the others from an abusive father. Entering the group last, Burlakoff added a combustible element to the chemistry.

The plan called for Burlakoff to start as the regional manager in the Southeast, as a kind of audition. He had never been close to the VP level before and would have to prove himself if he wanted the top job. His predecessor in the Southeast, Tony Bryant, quit of his own volition, but Babich announced Burlakoff's hiring immediately thereafter. The timing led everyone to conclude that Bryant had been on the verge of being ousted so that Burlakoff could take his place.

The reps in the region quickly got a sense of how their new manager planned to turn things around for Insys. One week after Burlakoff arrived, Tracy Krane met him in person for the first time. He was meeting and coaching each of his new reps in turn, starting with Mia Guzman, who lived near him, and then crossing the state of Florida to join Krane for a day of sales calls. On a "ride-along" like this, a manager accompanies a rep to observe, give guidance, and connect with customers as the two make the rounds of medical offices together.

Krane came into the day feeling wary of her new boss. She liked Bryant, who had hired her, and she and her fellow reps in the Southeast had little connection to anyone else in management, which was headquartered thousands of miles away. They felt cut adrift. It was an uneasy situation.

For the ride-along, Krane met up with Burlakoff at a diner near the offices of Dr. Steven Chun, on a hot Florida morning in late June. Chun worked out of the third floor of a two-tone stucco building flanked by palm trees, in prosperous Lakewood Ranch, a master-planned community not far from Sarasota. Adjacent to the medical complex that housed his clinic was a tidy retail and entertainment area called Main Street at Lakewood Ranch that featured a Star-bucks and a made-to-order salad restaurant.

Burlakoff had made it clear that seeing Dr. Chun was his top pri-ority. Since being shut out of his office for a time, Krane had patched things up enough with Chun that she was able to arrange a meeting with him for that morning, but he still wasn't generating a lot of scripts. The Insys leadership badly wanted to land him. Chun would be a prize for any opioid maker, but he was a particularly important target in the TIRF world, where he amounted to a celebrity. Nothing about his clinic's appearance suggested he was running a pill mill, but he wrote so many prescriptions for drugs in Subsys's class that Insys's top executives would refer to him as the $6 Million Man; the com-pany's data analyst had calculated that he could bring in that much business single-handedly in a year. In the lingo often used at Insys, Dr. Chun was a "whale."

Krane brought Burlakoff up to speed on her recent struggles with Chun, telling him her theory that the doctor's girlfriend was part of the problem. Burlakoff already knew Chun from his Cephalon years, and he projected confidence that he could change the trajectory. But Krane detected some bravado. Winning over Chun was a big deal for his job, not just hers, and she sensed he was more anxious about it than he wanted to show.

When they arrived at Chun's office, Krane had trouble reading the situation. Burlakoff behaved as if he and the doctor were great friends, though they hadn't been in contact for years. Chun meanwhile gave off the impression that he didn't even recognize Burlakoff—either that or he wanted to make a point that they weren't buddies. Impervious to embarrassment, Burlakoff plowed ahead. When he got into a doctor's private office, he would scan the room for photographs, diplomas—any hint of intel, any promising topics to raise. He avoided pitching the product to Chun, instead seeking out conversational common ground.

Once Chun grew less guarded, Burlakoff invited the doctor to have dinner with him and Krane the next time he came to town. He made sure to extend the invitation to include the doctor's girlfriend, Aqsa Nawaz. Chun made encouraging noises in response.

When Krane and her new boss left, Burlakoff seemed pleased. He acted unfazed that after he had boasted of his relationship with Chun, the doctor had initially treated him as if he were an irritating stranger. After Krane and Burlakoff climbed back into her white Cadillac CTS and got the air-conditioning running, Alec talked about the importance of bringing Dr. Chun on board as a speaker for Insys Therapeutics.

From the moment Burlakoff had started work a week before, he had been harping on the topic of the speaker program Insys was preparing to launch. But Krane didn't really understand what a speaker program was, much less why it was so important. She had rarely heard it mentioned at Insys before Burlakoff arrived.

A speaker program is a widely used promotional tool in the pharmaceutical industry. Drug companies pay doctors to give talks about the benefits of their product to other potential prescribers. The sales rep assigned to the doctor helps set up the event and attends it. These are not generally speeches with a lectern and microphone in a hotel banquet room. Usually they are relatively small gatherings, with perhaps four to twelve attendees in addition to the speaker and the sales rep. The talks take place at a clinic or, more often, over dinner in a private room at a restaurant. The speaker is trained in advance and uses a slide deck created by the drug company to make the presentations, usually on an ongoing basis; the doctor signs a contract and joins the drugmaker's "speaker bureau."

Anytime a drug company is paying a doctor, it arouses the suspicions of regulators. The industry defends the practice of speaker programs on the grounds that it's peer-to-peer marketing and education. Doctors who already prescribe the medication can help spread the word about its benefits to other clinicians, and their explanations and endorsement are likely to carry more weight than a pitch from a sales rep with no medical training. The practice can be especially useful for a drug that is new to market and lacks widespread name recognition.

That is not exactly what Burlakoff laid out to Krane, however. As the two of them sat in her idling car outside Chun's office, she behind the wheel, he spelled it out for her.

The real target of the speaker program, Burlakoff said, was not the audience of the talks but the speaker himself. The presentations really didn't matter at all. The idea was to funnel cash to the speaker so that he would prescribe Subsys in return. If he didn't live up to his end of the deal, he wouldn't get paid to speak anymore. It was a quid pro quo.

He "boiled it right down," Krane recalled: We pay doctors to write scripts. That's what the speaker program is.

Krane didn't know all the rules, but this wasn't sounding right. She turned to Burlakoff and asked, "Isn't that illegal?"

He brushed off the question, Krane said, with a tone she likened to patting a child on the head and telling her not to worry; the worst that could happen was the company would have to pay some kind of fine. That's basically built into the budget at a drug company, he said.

A speaker program had already been in the planning stages before Alec Burlakoff arrived at Insys. Paying speakers had been part of the strategy that Matt Napoletano had mapped out for Kapoor from the start; Napoletano had helped develop a speaker program for Fentora. But this was one aspect of his game plan where Napoletano met with resistance from Kapoor. Running a program like this is expensive. At Insys, it would cost seven figures per year at a minimum.

With that kind of expenditure, Kapoor wanted to know for sure that this initiative was going to pay off. He didn't have experience with speaker programs from his prior companies. Napoletano tried repeatedly to explain the benefits to him. According to Babich, when Napoletano was having trouble making headway, "Matt would whisper, 'And let's remember, it's a way to put money in the doctors' pockets.'"

While Kapoor weighed the issue, Napoletano continued laying the groundwork and recruiting doctors. Kapoor kept putting off a decision.

Then Burlakoff arrived and things changed. According to him, in his job interview with Kapoor, Burlakoff boasted of his prowess at using a speaker program to drive sales at Cephalon. What exactly was said in this interview is in dispute. But soon after hiring Burlakoff, Kapoor finally unlocked the money for speaker events, and virtually all of it was entrusted to Burlakoff, one of five regional managers, to get a "pilot program" up and running in the Southeast.

The pilot didn't begin until around six weeks after Burlakoff was hired, but in the interim Mike Babich and Matt Napoletano stepped up their preparations for a nationwide rollout. Babich told all his managers in an email to make sure that reps "understand the important nature of having one of their top targets as a speaker. It can pay big dividends for them."

In that email, Babich was pressing a recruitment drive to bring "key opinion leaders" to a speaker-training event that Napoletano had already begun putting together for the following month in Chicago. Some seventy-five doctors eventually attended this gathering, which took place at JW Marriott Chicago during a sweltering weekend in mid-July 2012. Kapoor told them the story of Subsys and invited them into the fold. They were trained to be Insys speakers and taken out for dinner in a reserved section at the Chicago location of Roka Akor, Kapoor's restaurant. The attendees included some of the nation's top prescribers of drugs in Subsys's class. These were names that just about everyone in the TIRF game knew.

Matt Napoletano, in fact, knew many of these doctors personally, from similar events held at Cephalon. A lot of them had been Cephalon speakers—or still were. He was now making an attempt to woo them to his new employer.

Those relationships and introductions were one of Napoletano's great contributions to Insys's success. "He brought us those whales, quite frankly," Burlakoff later said. A substantial number of the Chicago invitees would become, in the ensuing years, deeply entwined in the Insys saga.

On the ground in the Southeast, the speaker events soon got under way, and Burlakoff showed his reps what the new sales strategy was all about. When Burlakoff traveled again to Krane's territory, in August, the two went out for that dinner with Dr. Chun and his girlfriend. The four met up at a seafood restaurant in Sarasota with linen tablecloths and large windows giving out on the bay. On a summer evening, the sun was still high in the sky, and gleaming powerboats lined the docks outside. Krane had handled the logistics and ensured that Chun showed up. Now, at dinner, the men did most of the talking, while the women sat across from each other, making little eye contact.

Burlakoff knew a great deal about Chun from third parties, but it wasn't a close relationship, as Krane had noticed. "He wasn't one of my *guys*," Burlakoff said later. The stout forty-nine-year-old doctor had the bearing of someone accustomed to being afforded respect and flattery, particularly by drug companies. People didn't question him or tell him what to do. This wasn't an easy target.

Burlakoff had gathered that Dr. Chun liked to visit the Hard Rock Casino up in Tampa, so he made a point of discussing his own gambling, which he said he used to love a little too much. He had a Gamblers Anonymous chip, a medallion earned through recovery, and gave the doctor a glimpse of it. Krane wasn't sure when Burlakoff was telling the truth at this point. She wondered if the chip was even legit.

In this case, it was. Burlakoff had previously struggled with gambling problems for many years. When he was little, his grandfather would sneak him out to the dog tracks and horse tracks of Long Island instead of taking him to school.

Krane had scheduled a couple of dinners where Chun would be the speaker, but they hadn't taken place yet. Burlakoff made it clear that he viewed Chun as a valued business partner who would be an asset to the speaker bureau. To Krane, it was as if they were speaking in code, with oblique references to the good old days when Burlakoff was with Cephalon and everyone made out well. Chun had said he was ambivalent about speaking for drug companies; he had found it a little embarrassing when he had done it in the past. But it seemed to Krane that Chun was getting more comfortable with the idea and more generally with Insys, the new player on the scene.

Chun began speaking for Insys soon after, but he didn't immediately come through with big Subsys numbers. This was a disappointment. But Burlakoff still believed it was a significant victory that a guy like Chun would *let* Insys put money in his pocket. All the competitors were trying to form that kind of relationship with him. Paying the doctor was a way of conferring a sense of obligation. Give a man a Christmas gift and he's more likely to give one to you.

Burlakoff was unsatisfied with the performance of the reps he had inherited in the Southeast. He couldn't believe how bad the sales stats were when he walked in the door (though to be fair they were bad nationwide, by his standards). He was wary of getting rid of anyone on his team, though. "You don't fire people in this industry," Burlakoff said, because they'll run to corporate. "They're just going to turn the gun on you, and you're going down, as a manager."

Still, Alec needed to make his mark and get that promotion. He had a clever idea. He would add without subtracting. Burlakoff reached out to an old friend.

Alec had met Joe Rowan back when they were in high school together in Coral Springs, near Boca Raton, when Joe was a strong athlete, particularly in soccer. Joe hadn't had it easy as a kid. When he was eleven, his father was killed when he stepped in and tried to stop a shooting.

Rowan was rail thin in high school and a well-liked jokester, always ribbing someone in the halls and clowning around. His personality reminded Alec and their friends of the actor Will Smith. Burlakoff and Rowan went on to college together at Florida State, in Tallahassee, where they became roommates and fraternity brothers. They both met their future wives on campus, and the four of them spent time together.

After Burlakoff became a pharma rookie at Eli Lilly, he managed to get Joe an interview there. Rowan was never as strong academically as Burlakoff, but he got the Lilly job. The two went line dancing in Nashville with a few female colleagues during a company conference there. Later, Burlakoff recruited Rowan to Cephalon to work for him as a sales rep. He considered Joe a great friend.

Burlakoff approached Rowan about a job at Insys in the summer of 2012. By then, Rowan lived in the Florida Panhandle and had three children with his wife, Denise, an attorney. They were Methodists and regular churchgoers. They would later take in a fourth child, a boy whose family was troubled and could no longer take care of him. Rowan was working full-time at another pharma company, Sunovion. He wasn't eager to leave for an unproven startup, and Burlakoff understood that.

Burlakoff proposed to Mike Babich instead that they bring on Rowan as a part-time rep at Insys, on top of his other job. It was such an unusual notion, Babich said later, that he consulted Kapoor before giving approval. Rowan would be paid a paltry wage in his new role—$7.65 an hour—and receive no benefits as a freelance employee. But he would make a 10 percent commission on his Subsys sales. The key to the whole arrangement, for both parties, was that Rowan's assignment was to call on a single doctor: Xiulu Ruan, in Mobile, Alabama.

Burlakoff was aware that it was uncommon—maybe unprecedented—for someone to hire a rep with a "territory" consisting of a single physician. But this was a special circumstance. Burlakoff knew that Rowan had a unique bond with the doctor, and Ruan was a decile 10.

Rowan lived in Panama City, Florida, a three-hour drive along the Gulf Coast to Mobile, but in pharma sales three-hour drives aren't so unusual. The Panhandle is closer to the Deep South than it is to South Florida, both literally and culturally. Rowan spoke with a southern lilt that fit in in Mobile, and he showed a warmth that bridged divides. Everyone at Ruan's clinic in Mobile talked about how good-looking Rowan was—blond and tall, with a strong jaw. He had bulked up since high school. Staffers would refer to him as Fine Joe. When he was eating lunch once at a restaurant with Tracy Krane and ducked out to take a call, the waitress approached Krane and said, "That's the most beautiful man I've ever seen." Rowan was gentlemanly with new acquaintances, always holding doors for people and asking after their families, remembering their kids' names.

Back at Cephalon, Rowan had spent a lot of time with Dr. Ruan, a first-generation immigrant with a thick accent. Ruan was a studious man on the one hand and a merciless businessman on the other. He seemed lonely in Alabama. Rowan offered to accompany him on a road trip all the way to New Jersey, where Ruan was planning to drop off a car for his daughter. The doctor enthusiastically accepted, and the two set out together, an unlikely duo. Along the way, Rowan even shared a hotel room with his customer. He flew back home, at his own expense, when the epic drive was over.

This road trip became the stuff of legend at Insys, thanks to Burlakoff. He would often point to it as a model of superb salesmanship. That was part of the reason he hired Joe, beyond the Ruan connection—to show the rest of the team how Rowan operated. Any hungry rep would see the new guy on the leaderboard and get the message, and his approach would rapidly spread.

Dr. Ruan and his partner at the clinic, Dr. John Patrick Couch, were nationally known physicians in the pain world. Their clinic was extraordinarily busy, one of the biggest players in a region that did brisk business in prescription opioids. But Ruan was writing Subsys only a few times a week when Rowan was hired. That wasn't bad in

Insys terms; the company was selling only around a hundred prescriptions a week nationwide. But Ruan's Subsys numbers paled in comparison to how much he was writing the TIRF competitors, not to mention other pain drugs. No matter the opioid product, Ruan was a whale.

Burlakoff's new hire made an immediate impact. Within three months of Rowan's arrival, Dr. Ruan had become an Insys speaker, at $2,400 per dinner event, and he had become far and away the most prolific Subsys prescriber nationwide. He averaged roughly triple the total of anyone else. Later, when Rowan pulled in over $300,000 in gross sales in one quarter, Burlakoff congratulated him in an email, making sure to copy the rest of the Southeast on the message: "I am pretty sure your formula worked, you may want to pass it along."

The weekly graph of sales for the entire Southeast showed a pronounced spike once Dr. Ruan came aboard. With the pilot speaker program now under way, Burlakoff had the top-performing region in the country. Dr. Kapoor and Mike Babich took notice.

In August 2012, just two months after Burlakoff was hired, Babich asked him to put together a memo about how he would approach the job if he were brought to Arizona to run the whole sales force as vice president of sales. Burlakoff could sense he was close to a long-time dream. In just a couple of days, he produced a lengthy document headlined "Plan of Attack."

In the memo, Burlakoff announced his intention to meet personally with the top ten doctors in the nation. He proclaimed he would have zero tolerance for managers who interfered with his access to their reps and prescribers. His lieutenants needed to let him run the show his way. He also proposed reallocating speaker-program funds "based on where we have seen the most significant ROI," or return on investment. "WE MUST OWN AND SOLIDIFY OUR SUBSYS LOYALISTS," he wrote. With its feverish vigor, it was a typical Burlakoff document.

Burlakoff also conveyed to the bosses that he understood Kapoor's "grave concern" that patients were dropping off the REMS reports—that they weren't staying on the medication. He would implement Kapoor's plan to address that: the "effective dose" message. Data analysis had revealed that the patients on the lowest strengths of Subsys were the most likely to stop taking it. Clearly, Kapoor concluded, doctors needed to titrate up—move patients up to higher-strength prescriptions. He pointed to a study in which only 4 percent of participants found the lowest dose of Subsys, 100 micrograms, to be effective. A doctor had remarked to Kapoor that all the participants in that trial were cancer patients, so the results might be misleading, but Kapoor was undeterred. "We need to move patients to higher doses from 100 mcg," he wrote in an email. "I am writing this memo, so that we have no misunderstanding." Kapoor wanted sales reps to "force conversations, force the titration," Babich said, because "he just thought the 100 micrograms was the kiss of death" for business.

This was a dicey proposition. Getting into the particulars of a patient's care and questioning a doctor's judgment were the kind of meddling that could get a rep kicked out of a clinic—not to mention that this was an especially potent Schedule II narcotic. "While all opioids carry serious risks," the former FDA commissioner Scott Gottlieb once said of TIRF drugs, "these are not your typical opioids and should be prescribed by providers with extra care and attention." The FDA label for Insys's medication reads, "Overestimating the SUBSYS dosage can result in a fatal overdose with the first dose."

Napoletano told Kapoor that Purdue Pharma had gotten in trouble for "pushing dose" with OxyContin, he said. But Burlakoff indicated he would get on board with Kapoor's initiative and roll out the direction to the field. The higher strengths of Subsys were more expensive, so reps naturally earned more on those scripts because their commissions were tied to the dollar amount. On top of that, Kapoor authorized an incentive structure where the bonus percentage was higher on the top two strengths, 12.5 percent instead of 10, an extra carrot for the sales force. In late 2012, if a doctor put pen to paper for one Subsys script at the highest strength, the rep would collect $1,830.

With Burlakoff's plan of attack articulated, the bosses flew him to Arizona for an interview to be VP, but by then it was a formality. "John had made up his mind," Babich said. He was going to put Burlakoff in charge. Burlakoff's approach with any new job was "promote me or fire me." After less than three months, Kapoor had made his choice.

Although the outcome wasn't in doubt, the meeting covered a lot of ground, according to Burlakoff. He knew that Kapoor was a fierce boss with incredibly high expectations. The first VP of sales,

Shawn Simon, had been fired after only a few months. If Burlakoff was going to move his wife and two daughters to Arizona so he could work out of corporate, he wanted to ensure that everyone had the same understanding. "You can't leave anything for subjectivity," he said later. "I didn't fluff anything. I was very candid and asked very specific probing questions." Burlakoff made sure, according to Babich, that everyone was on board with awarding speaker money to the doctors who were getting Subsys into their patients' hands.

Burlakoff also told the bosses he planned to fire two of his fellow regional managers on day one. "He just said the majority of them sucked and he doesn't want to work with people who don't understand how quickly he wants to do business," Babich said. Burlakoff got the green light. The fact that one of the fired managers, Mike Hemenway, had warned against hiring Burlakoff didn't help his cause; Babich had since told the new head of sales about it. Burlakoff couldn't tolerate that.

In mid-September, on the eve of a national sales meeting, Babich announced Burlakoff's promotion. "Alec has brought a fire to [his] region that was much-needed and his knowledge of the marketplace is unmatched," he wrote in an email to the company. "I personally believe he can AND WILL bring this same fire across the nation."

With Alec Burlakoff's rise, Matt Napoletano found himself with a new rival. He was accustomed to being the lone Insys executive who had real familiarity with the pain market. Now there was another player in the room. To add to the awkwardness, running the Insys speaker program, or ISP, fell partly under Napoletano's purview, in marketing, but meanwhile Burlakoff felt it was his "greatest strength," he told Babich, and he needed "as much Free reign [*sic*] as possible" to manage it. He didn't want anyone interfering, including even Kapoor. Burlakoff wrote to Babich, "I need your guidance on how to present to Dr Kapoor ISP's in a way—where he won't get involved."

With all this jockeying for control, in the fall of 2012 the speaker program remained a matter of ongoing argument at Insys headquarters, even as Burlakoff was putting it into action. The debate played out over a series of meetings involving the quartet at the top: Kapoor, Babich, Napoletano, and Burlakoff. It would escalate into a dramatic standoff.

Just before Burlakoff became VP, Kapoor had ordered a hold on the speaker program, to allow for more internal discussion. Even in its nascent stage, the program was costing him a good deal of money, and he wanted to know what he was getting for it in return. Kapoor was disturbed that not every Insys speaker was actually prescribing Subsys in any significant volume; even in Burlakoff's region, there were freeloaders, which Burlakoff found embarrassing.

Kapoor said in a meeting that he wanted every doctor the company was paying to write his product, Napoletano recalled. The boss told his marketing chief to run the numbers on how much Subsys they were prescribing.

"You don't do that," Napoletano said, exasperated. A speaker program was supposed to be about influencing the attendees, not the speakers. He knew the government kept an eye on things like this. Babich always warned that it was dangerous to talk back to Kapoor, but Napoletano had a temper, and he needed to get across that they were wading into perilous waters.

Napoletano was also seeing that Burlakoff was gaining traction with Kapoor while he was losing it. In the beginning, Napoletano had been the "favored child," Babich said, because he brought Kapoor his Rolodex of top doctors, as Napoletano called it. But now Burlakoff was starting to get in Kapoor's good graces with his aggressive style and his early results. It wounded Napoletano's ego, according to Babich. But it also seemed to worry him on a deeper level. To him, Burlakoff was not only a rival but a danger to everyone.

Napoletano knew the rules. Burlakoff had never gotten any blowback for what he did at Cephalon, he said, but Napoletano was in the home office during the fallout and still working there when the company was forced to plead guilty and face sanctions. In a text message to Mike Babich, Matt wrote, "Last thing we want is the walls to come crumbling down."

In one meeting, Burlakoff proposed that Insys hold speaker

events that were as small as possible. They could be breakfasts or calls on a pharmacy, rather than dinners. That way you could still get money into the doctor's pocket without having to buy steak and wine for four people, let alone ten or twenty. He didn't want to waste his limited budget on anything that didn't juice sales. "I don't care if any attendees show up," Burlakoff said. "It's about paying the doctor." Napoletano saw Kapoor nodding along and despaired. "I knew I had lost," Matt said later.

Napoletano pushed back nonetheless, saying that Insys really needed to have at least a couple of licensed prescribers attending each event. There were sign-in sheets at speaker programs, and part of the purpose was to document that there was a legitimate audience in case there was scrutiny. Napoletano was a smart guy, and at times he took on the demeanor of someone who could hardly believe he had to say something *so goddamn basic:* if you just paid a doctor who wasn't actually spreading the word about Subsys, it would look like a bribe.

But Burlakoff wouldn't back down or let it rest. The two were "out of control," according to Babich, who always hated to see discord aired out in front of the boss.

Kapoor kept pressing Napoletano. At another meeting of the top brass, Kapoor asked him to put together a report that would calculate the return on investment for each speaker—how much money their scripts were bringing in for every dollar Insys was paying them. In other words, Kapoor wanted a written analysis of whether the bribes were working.

It was at that point that Napoletano completely lost it. He stood up and screamed at Kapoor, "No! I told you before, you don't do that!"

Everything came to a stop in the room. No one ever yelled at Dr. Kapoor.

After a silence, Kapoor shouted back that he wrote the checks at this company and he wanted it done, according to Babich. But Napoletano was already on his way out of the room.

Napoletano went back to his office utterly distraught. He prepared himself to be fired. He thought about how he would negotiate a severance, how he needed his health insurance to be covered as long as possible. He'd moved to Arizona to take this job only a year before.

His family was just getting comfortable with a new treatment team for his son with cancer.

Babich gave Napoletano some time to calm down and then came to see him. "Matt was almost in tears," Babich said, "talking about he's not going to run the effing report, he can't do it, he won't do it."

Napoletano wanted Insys to cover itself. He felt the company needed to document the proper procedures and check the requisite boxes of compliance, the way that everyone else in pharma knew you were supposed to. You ensure your speakers don't have a black mark on their license; you allocate the money cautiously, to avoid the appearance of a quid pro quo; you don't pay fees that far exceed the norm; and you make sure a few legit people are there for the dinners. You *definitely* don't leave a paper trail that shows you tracking your speakers to make sure they're writing enough scripts. It was really pretty simple to avoid the hot water.

Even Burlakoff opposed the idea of an ROI report, though not for legal or ethical reasons. Mainly he didn't want Kapoor on his back about every single speaker and why they weren't writing more Subsys. These doctors weren't robots. It was an art to bribe them, not a science. You didn't need a spreadsheet.

Everyone other than Kapoor seemed to understand something important: there was no need to run this report. Top management was already tracking Subsys prescriptions on a near-daily basis, in their 8:30 a.m. meetings. There weren't that many of them—perhaps two or three dozen a day. It was obvious who the big prescribers were. The same twenty or thirty names kept cropping up. The executives had met many of them. They knew who was on the payroll, usually off the top of their heads, and it wasn't difficult to tell if the doctors were responding to it. Most of them were already doing their part.

Those early results were a testament to Burlakoff's prowess, but they also reflected an industry reality. Doctors who get paid by a drugmaker write more prescriptions for the company's product thereafter. Academics have scrutinized the numbers and proven the trend (surely to the dismay of the industry).

This pattern holds true for opioids specifically, despite widespread alarm over an escalating public health crisis. An analysis of data from 2014 and 2015, in the thick of the epidemic, showed that the more opioid prescriptions a doctor writes, the more likely it is that drug companies are paying him. There is some room for debate about whether the money drives prescriptions or the prescribing brings in the money, but either way the incentive for doctors is clear. If most manufacturers are really trying to avoid a quid pro quo, it's hard to tell: the top tenth of 1 percent of opioid prescribers, according to the analysis, made nine times more money from pharmaceutical companies than the median doctor.

In other words, even if you adhere to "best practices," as Matt Napoletano urged, *all* speaker programs get results that look a lot like bribery. But that's the part you're not supposed to say out loud. It's the truth you're not supposed to put on paper.

Napoletano didn't want to run the ROI report, because he "didn't want to be responsible for having the smoking gun in his hand," Burlakoff said later, gesturing as if holding a pistol. "Why should he do it?"

Napoletano sat in his office, still reeling from the blowup, trying to settle himself, as he talked to Babich. He asked the CEO if he was going to be fired. Speaking as the Dr. Kapoor expert, Babich said he didn't think so—not now, anyway. But he let Napoletano know that he was "in a tough spot, because it's clear as day that Kapoor wants the report run." According to Napoletano, Babich said, "You've got to give him what he wants."

It took a while for Napoletano to fold, but in the end he did. He said he would run the ROI report once, and then he would make sure that no one would ever find it, according to Babich.

The four men gathered in a small conference room in the Insys offices and went through the resulting document line by line. They determined which pain doctors were truly playing ball with them, providing an ROI of at least two to one. They flagged the ones who weren't earning their keep, so they could consider "soft-deleting" them from the program.

All the men had paper copies of the report, but they didn't hold on to them. The documents were gathered in a pile at the end of the meeting, and that was the end of that.

In September 2012, Insys employees from across the nation gathered in the blistering heat for a national sales meeting at a slightly run-down resort in Scottsdale. It was the first time they had all come together since the launch of Subsys. Just six months had passed, but the conference marked the start of a new era. This was Alec Burlakoff's debut as VP, a kickoff to his tenure at the top. The debate about how exactly to run and track the speaker program was still unfolding at headquarters, and it would continue to play out for months, but Burlakoff wasn't waiting. He had a sales force to run, and now there was no one but him to blame if the numbers didn't meet John Kapoor's expectations.

Burlakoff wasn't well known at the time to employees from outside the Southeast region, but that was going to end now. With Kapoor and Babich in attendance, he gave a triumphant speech in a hotel function room. As he spoke, he paced across the front of the room and down the aisle dividing two sets of banquet chairs, to connect more closely with the audience—*his* sales force. Burlakoff's ego had swelled to the point where Tracy Krane said he reminded her of one of those caricatures where the head dwarfs the rest of the body.

The fact that Kapoor had promoted Burlakoff brought him an enormous sense of validation. The younger man had already begun to think of Kapoor as a mentor, someone he badly wanted to please. He could only look up to a businessman who had worked relentlessly to win his fortune, starting from the bottom. He harbored hopes of following Kapoor wherever he went, potentially beyond Insys. Now Kapoor was giving him the stage.

In his speech, Burlakoff pointed to his own career, rising from rep to VP, as evidence that he knew the path to prosperity. He presented a slideshow that included some comic flair and unusually personal touches, including photographs of his wife and family vacationing on a Disney cruise. It had the flavor of motivational speaking, Krane said, "like, 'If you follow my plan, all this can be yours.'"

The reps from the Southeast were exchanging knowing grins. They knew Alec by now. Their colleagues from the rest of the country were getting their first dose.

Even as she shook her head, however, Krane had to admit that the speech was improbably effective. Back at the launch conference six months before, green reps had been picked out of the crowd and put on the spot in front of strangers in training exercises. It felt like an exam. In the months since, reps had been fired left and right. Burlakoff brought an entirely different energy to the proceedings.

He told the reps that he knew there was no way to call on eight or ten doctors a day, a target that company leadership had been pushing. He had seen the routing maps they used to get from office to office. Factoring in all the "windshield time," it was impossible. "I could fire you all right now," he said with a smile, because they had been logging sales calls in their iPads that he was sure they hadn't actually made. A lot of reps, including Krane, felt relieved: it was true, they had been.

Kapoor and Babich were the ones who had been insisting that everyone call on eight to ten doctors a day, and they were right there in the room. They didn't know their new VP was going to contradict them. But that didn't bother Burlakoff. They didn't know sales. That's why he was tapped to run the show. Burlakoff conveyed to his charges that he had been out there on the road, carrying the bag from door to door, just as his reps were. He planned to keep doing it as their VP. He wasn't going to just sit in headquarters writing emails, clueless as to what it was like to execute, he said. (Babich had recently been running sales without having a day's experience in it.) Burlakoff would be out in the field, literally and in spirit. He would also serve as their advocate at corporate and protect them, he suggested. It was a promise he would keep. A message he would often deliver at headquarters was *You can't do that to my reps.*

Burlakoff told the sales force that if they worked smart, choosing the right targets, big things were in store for them. "He was trying to motivate the greed in everybody," Krane said. "He wasn't doing it by fear. It was relaxed. He made you feel like you were a winner, like you were going to be number one."

Just before his promotion and move to Arizona, Burlakoff had met someone who would turn out to be an important figure both in his life and in the story of Insys. The two met at Rachel's, a well-known "gentlemen's club" and steak house in West Palm Beach, Florida, not far from his home in Lake Worth.

Advertised on full-size highway billboards, Rachel's occupies a large building, visible from Interstate 95 and designed in a fauxpalatial style, with gold columns and statues out front. Palm trees loom over luxury cars in the parking lot. The interior is darkened, no matter the time of day, and it features leather seating and elaborate lighting design.

Burlakoff was no stranger to vices. He was using cocaine at the time, as he would throughout his tenure at Insys, as well as marijuana. Sometimes he took mushrooms or molly. Then there was his history with gambling. He had naked pictures of his wife on his phone. And on occasion he took doctors to gentlemen's clubs.

On this particular late summer night, Burlakoff was dining at Rachel's with a customer—a physician. As the men ate, they watched the dancers.

Sunrise Lee was one of them. She appeared at upper-echelon clubs across the country: not only Rachel's, but VIP's in Chicago, Spearmint Rhino in Las Vegas, Scores in New York. She was an exotic dancer, a stripper.

She approached the two men at the club and Burlakoff paid for her to entertain the doctor, he said. Later, after the doctor had left, she sat down with Burlakoff, saying she would keep him company, even though he told her he was done spending money. She spoke openly about her life and listened intently to him. After a while, he began to think he had encountered a raw talent. She had the gift for persuasion. She made him feel as if they had a genuine connection.

A part of him knew it was ludicrous to believe, like a chump, that the two of them had something special. She was selling him. He knew that. No one could spot a hustle like Burlakoff could. But that was exactly what drew him closer. He didn't know exactly what she was up to, with no cash changing hands, but he felt sure she was playing a long game, and he loved that.

It didn't hurt that she was beautiful. Her roots were unusual and hard to place—a mix of Hawaiian, Filipina, Puerto Rican, and French. Her middle name was Makakelani. She was fit and had long black hair with tasteful highlights and a big dazzling smile that made people feel good.

Burlakoff told her she was in the wrong business. He asked her to meet up with him again soon, in the daytime, wearing business attire, and convince him she could work in his world. He wanted to interview her for a job.

Guys said a lot of things in the club, in Lee's experience. This man she had just met could easily have been all talk. But it was worth finding out. What he was waving around was a ticket to the white-collar world. That was something to take seriously. She was thirty-two and hated being a dancer by this point. The industry had changed. In the wake of the global financial crisis, she said, there were fewer "quality clients" coming into the clubs. The girls were less educated and willing to "do more," she said. Dancers like her from the "old school" were being phased out.

Lee was raising two young boys in joint custody after a court battle with her ex-husband, and she had bottomed out financially. She was developing some business projects, but nothing that was bringing in any income yet. She had recently gone on public assistance, for the first time, to feed her family. It was painful for her to walk into that government building and apply. What Burlakoff was talking about was a chance to change the trajectory of her life. She leaped at it.

Burlakoff and Lee met up repeatedly as he coached her through the application process at Insys and lobbied for her to be hired. A romantic connection began to develop, though Burlakoff was married.

Beneath her winning breeziness, Lee had an inner steel that Burlakoff responded to. She wasn't one of those people he knew all too well from working in Big Pharma, the sons and daughters of prominent families who coasted into good careers. He had always longed to be in a position to hire people who were nothing like that—people who were used to scrapping for what they got.

Lee had walked a difficult road. Her parents had a nasty marriage and divorced when she was little, in Hawaii. Her mother subsequently had custody of Sunrise and her younger sister and brother, but her father had visitation rights. In the story she was told, one day in Hawaii, when Sunrise was three or so, her mother handed off the children to their father at the zoo, where he was supposed to spend a few hours with them, Lee said. Instead, he took off with the kids and never came back.

This was the era when milk cartons featured the faces of missing children, and Sunrise's face was one of them. Her father had taken the kids with him to Chicago. Formerly in the military, he was getting into trouble, according to Lee. For the next few years, Sunrise and her siblings were moved constantly from place to place, left with people they didn't know. Her father gave the kids the idea that their mother didn't love them and later claimed that she was dead, as Lee recalls it. He was a religious man, Catholic, and he would show the kids affection, always telling them he loved them. But he would take off for days without the kids, leaving Sunrise, at six or seven, to look after the younger ones and prepare meals with the groceries he left behind. "My sister is the reason we survived those years," Sunrise's sister said.

Eventually, someone reported the father to the authorities. An unfamiliar woman visited the house one day when Sunrise was about seven—a child-welfare worker—and talked to her about going into foster care. Her father was in the room crying, but Sunrise wasn't too upset and tried to comfort him. She had just seen an episode of *Punky Brewster* that made foster care sound not so bad.

Sunrise was finally reunited with her mother at eight years old, but her home life remained chaotic. She continued doing a lot of the work of caring for her younger siblings. At sixteen, she petitioned to be formally emancipated from her family, and a judge granted the request.

She worked three jobs in high school—at a chain diner, a clothing store, and a Chinese restaurant. A friend told her about how much you could make as an exotic dancer. Sunrise started calculating what she could accomplish with that money. But you couldn't dance until you were eighteen. On her eighteenth birthday, she went to a club for an interview.

When they met years later, Burlakoff identified her as someone with the tenacity to succeed. In his eyes, she was just what Insys was after: "poor, hungry, and driven." What's more, she was the perfect vehicle to demonstrate his belief that you didn't need a certain pedigree to succeed in the business.

Lee's stay in Florida was temporary. She normally lived in Grand Rapids, Michigan. To Burlakoff, that turned out to be ideal. He was looking to install a new manager for the Midwest region immediately once his promotion was announced in a few weeks. He had already gotten away with unorthodox hiring practices by bringing in Joe Rowan as a freelancer, and the bosses loved the results there.

When Burlakoff proposed hiring Sunrise Lee, Mike Babich resisted, even though Alec had left some things out to improve his chances. Babich thought Lee's résumé (which omitted the exotic dancing) was "pretty poor" for a management slot. He didn't even know that she hadn't in fact finished her bachelor of science at Michigan State, as the résumé suggested. Babich had just hired a rep he met at a wedding who hadn't graduated from college, Burlakoff said, so he figured that wasn't an issue.

Babich's view was that Burlakoff could bring on Sunrise as a rep, okay, but a manager? Still, he agreed to meet with her. She traveled to Arizona, where she talked to Kapoor and Babich over dinner at Roka Akor as part of the vetting process. Dr. Kapoor spoke of the trust he placed in Burlakoff, she recalled.

It remained something of a battle for Burlakoff to get Lee hired as a manager, but after he went to bat for her in an email to Babich, his argument prevailed: "This is someone who understands REAL sales, I need someone who will follow my direction and implement accordingly. This girl will do this."

At the national sales meeting that fall, Burlakoff unveiled several leadership changes. Joe Rowan, now full-time, was promoted to fill Burlakoff's old job in the Southeast, his first shot at being a manager. Burlakoff installed another old friend of his, Rich Simon, to run the Central region. The two had met a decade before at Janssen, where they shared a hotel room during a training. Loyalty was one of Burlakoff's most prized values. When you have the opportunity, he felt, you look out for your friends. He expected the same in return. Back at summer camp, when someone in his cabin received a care package from home, Alec would be baffled if the boy shared the food with everyone, such that each kid got one measly snack. When Burlakoff got a care package (and his father would send more of them than the rules allowed, by disguising the box as something else), young Alec would summon his two or three best buddies, and they would "eat like kings," Burlakoff said. The favor would come back around.

At the Arizona meeting, it was the new manager in the Midwest who drew the most attention. Sunrise Lee was introduced to her direct reports. Questions quickly began to circulate about her career background and why she was hired. In her varied work history, Lee had worked in sales, selling a diagnostic test, but she knew that her experience was not up to par with other managers. Her new co-workers were suspicious of her, and she soon became aware of it. Burlakoff assured her that he had her back so long as she took his lead. *If some people are criticizing you, so what? If you produce, it won't matter.*

Dr. Paul Madison would now fall under Lee's area of responsibility because she was the new manager for the region. Madison was the major target in Illinois that the Insys rep Holly Brown had thus far failed to win over. He wrote a significant amount of Fentora, and Insys management had identified him as a top target.

It would be a tricky play to win Madison's business. He was a physically imposing man—nearly six and a half feet tall and perhaps three hundred pounds, with unpredictable moods. People who worked for him were afraid of him and his outbursts, Brown said.

Dr. Madison also had a reputation problem. He had taken over as president of his clinic from a man named Joseph Giacchino. Giacchino had been stripped of his medical license in 2011 after he was recorded soliciting sex from a patient in exchange for opioid prescriptions. But Giacchino still worked in the office alongside Madison, as "administrator," and he was frequently present at the desk when Holly Brown stopped in.

Giacchino had extensive tattoos, multiple ear piercings, and a shaved head. A *Chicago Tribune* journalist had dubbed him "Dr. Millionpills" in a series devoted to his 2010 disciplinary hearing before the state licensing board, which was also attended by the doctor's *Playboy* Playmate wife, formerly married to a cocaine trafficker. None of this was any great secret. Brown had learned "all kinds of unsavory information" about Giacchino and the clinic through Google searches, she said.

In the opioid business, a key principle in this kind of situation is plausible deniability. If you're a drug company selling controlled substances to a clinic like Madison's, you don't want a paper trail showing that top management knows the particulars of what's happening there. A rep can know. Corporate headquarters absolutely cannot.

It is common practice in the drug industry for reps to document what they saw and did at each office visit. They use their laptops, tablets, and phones to input these "call notes" in a central company database. A problem with this system is that inexperienced reps might type something that really shouldn't be set down in black and white. The most damning details in litigation against drug companies have sometimes come from call notes. Purdue Pharma call notes revealed that reps overcame resistance from doctors by pushing the message that OxyContin was less addictive than other opioids, which wasn't true.

In the last couple of decades, a number of major drugmakers have made an important change to their call-note systems. Now, reps don't type anything at all. They just select from a series of drop-down menus, answering queries in multiple choice: *How much time did you spend with the doctor? Which of the following product benefits were discussed?* There is no place for the rep to engage in free writing, no opportunity to accidentally leave evidence of off-label promotion or spell out warning signs about the physician. The genius of the drop-down menu, in other words, is that every possible answer a rep can give is legally clean.

Insys failed to practice such self-protective measures. Before Burlakoff was promoted, when Mike Babich was temporarily running sales, he asked that reps submit weekly written reports on their contacts with top sales targets—at Kapoor's direction, Babich said. Babich received these reports by email, and he said he or his assistant would regularly print them out for Kapoor. In other words, Insys created a system where the paper trail led not only to corporate but directly to the top of the hierarchy.

When Burlakoff was brought to Arizona to take over as VP, Babich showed him these reports, forwarding some by email. Burlakoff was hardly a model of email operational security himself, but he was alarmed. "I almost had a heart attack!" he recalled. "I was like, 'Can Maury delete these from my computer?'" (Maury Rice ran the IT department at Insys.) Just about every report he saw posed problems, Burlakoff said.

The damning material was not always blatant; there were a lot of ways to run afoul of the rules in pharma, some of them probably too subtle for Babich to recognize. No one could miss the significance, however, of the reports that Holly Brown was writing about Dr. Madison, one of which was forwarded to Burlakoff. Again and again, Brown included the following passage in messages to Insys's CEO:

> I call on Dr. Madison once sometimes twice a week. Dr.
> Madison runs a very shady pill mill and only accepts cash. He
> sees very few insured patients but does write some Fentora.
> He is extremely moody, lazy, and inattentive. He basically

just shows up to sign his name on the prescription pad, if he shows up at all.

Mike Babich did not somehow miss this message; he read it. But he had gathered from Matt Napoletano that Madison "was a guy in Chicago we need to get," Babich said. Reps for at least two of Subsys's direct competitors, Fentora and Lazanda, were also calling on Dr. Madison, Brown reported in her emails. Those drugmakers evidently had no problem selling fentanyl to him. What was Insys going to do, just let the competition have a big target in a major city?

Burlakoff's mandate was to land whales like Dr. Madison, regardless of what anyone wrote in a memo. Now he had Sunrise Lee to help him.

Burlakoff and Lee were enmeshed in a relationship of powerful mutual dependence, further complicated by the fact that they were becoming romantically involved. She was dependent on his direction and entirely at his mercy professionally, as she saw it. To hold on to a job that could transform her life, she needed to please him.

Burlakoff meanwhile was placing a big bet on Lee. He knew he was taking a risk, but he truly viewed her as a potential "ticket to stardom," he said later. She was just one manager, but if she became a standout performer, "that's all I needed," he said. A few lieutenants alone could execute his strategy; he wasn't particularly concerned about the forty or fifty reps beneath them. This business was all about the top doctors. Most of them were men. If Sunrise brought in sales, that would also protect him for his decision to hire her. If she didn't succeed, they might both be in jeopardy.

Burlakoff asked Holly Brown to set up an office lunch where she could introduce Lee to Madison. Lee asked Burlakoff for some coaching about what to do on her first ride-along, and he told her, "'SMILE and CLOSE'—It IS that simple." The meeting went very well. Burlakoff said Madison later told him that the first time he met Lee, the doctor said to himself, "I don't know what she's selling, but I'm buying."

For her part, Lee wasn't put off by the clinic that her reps considered "shady" or "sketchy." That language seemed to her like code for an uglier attitude. Dr. Madison was black and his patients were largely unprivileged. They had never been well served by the system. In other words, they were people Sunrise identified with. She later said she thought Madison was helping them when other doctors would not. The authorities might not approve, but she didn't put much stock in that.

At the end of their lunch, Lee gave Madison her business card and said he was welcome to give her a call "kind of off the record," according to Brown. Madison soon invited Lee out for drinks, and they met at a popular hotel bar in Chicago. Sunrise had done just what Alec always preached: she had gotten the target out of the office to develop a rapport after hours.

"She was a legend, bro," Burlakoff said later. He started telling other managers, none too delicately, that she was showing them up.

A few days after the hotel drinks, Lee told Holly Brown that Dr. Madison was going to start writing Subsys, and she ought to devote most of her time and attention to him. When Brown told Sunrise that Madison had indicated his Illinois office was "really under the eye of the DEA," Lee deflected: "I am very confident that Dr. Madison will be your 'go to physician.' Stick with him."

Once Sunrise had established a foothold, Burlakoff moved quickly to enroll Madison in the Insys speaker bureau, using his new clout as head of sales to push the process. At the time, Insys was working with a third-party vendor called SciMedica, engaged by Matt Napoletano, to manage the logistics of the speaker program. Making an effort to come off well with SciMedica, Burlakoff described Madison in one email as a "Subsys thought leader" and hailed his "knowledge, expertise, and ability to provide a credible presentation."

Burlakoff hated the meddling of SciMedica staff, and they issued the checks to doctors too slowly, Insys executives felt. By the end of the year, SciMedica was fired.

Three top Insys executives, including Burlakoff and Matt Napoletano, traveled to Chicago that fall and had dinner with Dr. Madison. They were accompanied by the Insys locals Sunrise Lee and

Holly Brown and another area rep, Jodi Havens. When the sales force got an encouraging response from a leading prescriber, it wasn't uncommon for the upper ranks to head out into the field to let the target know how valued he was. The dinner was held at Roka Akor in Chicago.

Afterward, Lee and the two female reps took Dr. Madison to a racy nightclub called the Underground Chicago, frequently visited by celebrities. They all sat in the VIP area and ordered bottle service. At one point, the two reps turned toward Madison and saw something extraordinary, they said. Lee was sitting on Madison's lap, facing him. Havens described "heavy groping. His hands were all over her, her front and her pants, in her shirt. And they were heavily kissing." (Lee adamantly denies that this happened.)

Around this same time, Mike Babich received an email from an unfamiliar personal account, purportedly sent by a doctor, though it was written anonymously. The email was about Sunrise Lee. It said that she was a "high class stripper" who was "not afraid to do anything for a buck," and it included links to a strip-club website.

Babich went to Burlakoff's office and told him to type in a web address from the email. "Is that Sunrise?" he asked. Burlakoff, shaken, acknowledged that the photographs on the site were of her. Babich told him he could not hide this kind of information from Dr. Kapoor and went to see him. Burlakoff sat there waiting, in some fear that he could be fired.

When Babich returned, however, he was smiling, Burlakoff said. Kapoor had told Babich that if Lee was doing a good job, she could stay; everyone has to make a living and pay for school. "He said, 'Well, if you're a stripper, can you never work again?'" Babich recalled. "He didn't care." The pictures, however, had to come down from the internet. Alec conveyed to Sunrise what she had to do, and she got it done: the photographs went away.

About a month later, a federal grand jury returned an indictment against Paul Madison. Along with a nurse at a surgical center he owned, Madison was arrested and charged with insurance fraud, unrelated to Subsys or Insys. Prosecutors said that Madison had led a widespread billing scheme involving chiropractic services and that he had destroyed records when state regulators were pursuing him. Madison posted bail and went back to seeing patients while he awaited trial.

Word filtered up through the Insys hierarchy. Management was really in a bind now. Just as Madison was showing major potential as a Subsys prescriber, he was charged with a felony in federal court. Worst of all, this was publicly available information.

Matt Napoletano wanted to cut financial ties with Madison. Babich wasn't sure how to proceed, but he knew he needed to talk to Kapoor about it. Insys execs had just wined and dined this doctor—at Kapoor's restaurant—and he was in serious trouble with the law. So Babich set a one-on-one meeting.

Kapoor's response, according to Babich, was that everyone is innocent until proven guilty. If a doctor had a license, then he had a license. He didn't want to break off the relationship with Madison over unproven allegations.

Insys executives not only kept sending reps to call on Madison after he was indicted; they continued paying him to speak on behalf of the company for another two and a half years. Over a three-year period, Madison became an enormous asset to Insys, boosting the fortunes of Alec Burlakoff and Sunrise Lee in the process. He single-handedly prescribed 58 percent of the Subsys sold in Illinois.

In late 2012, in the early months of Alec Burlakoff's leadership, the Insys sales force was driving business at a swiftly escalating rate. The speaker program had gone national, and Burlakoff had followed through on his plan to meet personally with blue-chip doctors and get them on board. Prescriptions were up 60 percent in just three months. It was finally the kind of growth John Kapoor felt that Subsys deserved.

But a different and urgent problem now came to the fore: many of the Subsys prescriptions that Burlakoff's reps were bringing home weren't actually generating any profit for Insys. The byzantine structure of the American health insurance system was getting in the way.

The true end customers for Subsys were not the doctors, nor even the patients, but the insurance companies that ultimately needed to foot the bill. Almost all health insurers required prior authorization before they would pay for Subsys. It was a costly and potent drug. A doctor's prescription wasn't enough. Insurers wanted to know that a TIRF product was truly necessary and that the cheaper generic Actiq wouldn't suffice.

In order to justify a Subsys script, support staff at a prescriber's office had to complete a lot of tedious insurance paperwork, a drain on a clinic's resources. Some especially prolific prescribers had administrative staffers devoting hours and hours to Subsys approvals. For a doctor looking to avoid delays, hassles, and payroll costs, the easier route was to turn to other drugs that insurers wouldn't balk at covering. That represented a serious threat to Insys revenue.

To address the issue, Insys had created a voucher program in which the company supplied Subsys free of charge to a new patient while the prior-authorization process was pending. Essentially, Insys picked up the tab for some period in the hopes that the insurer would start paying down the line; it couldn't risk losing the patient to a competitor. But in the meantime, every script was actually costing Insys money, not earning it. There was also the possibility that insurance would ultimately decline to cover the medication, at which point Insys would find itself holding the bag.

Even the reps, down at the bottom of the hierarchy, had a lot on the line personally. They didn't earn money on a script unless Insys did. If the health plan didn't pay, there was no sale and therefore no bonus. This way, the sales force was incentivized not just to win prescriptions but to make sure the revenue arrived.

In the early days, Insys worked with a third-party vendor called Apricot that helped get Subsys "pulled through"—paid by insurance. But even with this intervention, two out of three Subsys prescriptions were being denied, an enormous roadblock to profitability. Apricot was fired.

But no matter what outfit Insys relied on instead to tackle pull-through, the company was going to face a very simple problem: most Subsys patients did not have breakthrough cancer pain.

The sales force was seeing its best results with pain management physicians who saw few cancer patients, such as Gavin Awerbuch, Paul Madison, and Xiulu Ruan. Meanwhile, nearly all insurers refused to pay for Subsys without a cancer diagnosis, because the medication was indicated for breakthrough cancer pain and no other condition. While doctors were permitted to write Subsys for anyone, that didn't mean insurers had to cover it. And Insys needed health plans to pay; the drug was so expensive that few patients shouldered the cost themselves. Insurers would sometimes make exceptions and knowingly approve a non-cancer Subsys script, but that was relatively uncommon. With Medicare plans, there was typically a strict rule against it, owing to federal regulations.

Insys's branded competitors faced the same challenges, because their business was predominantly off label also. According to Burlakoff, in his time at Cephalon, TIRF approval rates were only 20 to 30 percent. At other companies it was slightly higher, but 50 percent or less was the norm.

Dr. Kapoor, however, never liked hearing from Burlakoff or Matt Napoletano about the way things were at Cephalon, or anywhere else for that matter. His business was his business. He was tremendously disturbed by this issue, which he saw, correctly, as absolutely critical to Insys's success. After Burlakoff's sales team pulled every lever to get a prescription, it should be a done deal. It infuriated him that scripts were denied on a regular basis.

In meetings with top management, Kapoor began turning his relentless scrutiny away from Alec Burlakoff and toward Mike Gurry, the newly hired vice president for managed markets—the point person for insurance issues. Day after day, not long after getting the job, Gurry found himself in the hot seat.

Gurry was a U.S. Navy man, still in the reserves, with high commendations from his superiors. He was forty-nine years old. He parted his sandy hair neatly on one side. His broad forehead and square jaw made his face look almost rectangular and solidly constructed. A central aspect of his job involved negotiating with insurers to try to minimize the policy hurdles to getting Subsys covered. It was a nuts-and-bolts back-office role, and Gurry seemed well suited to it. He was quiet and steady, or at any rate he came off that way. People who worked with him thought he was respectful and a little stiff, a stick-in-the-mud. With the air of a stern upper-middle-class dad, he didn't seem like the type you would find at a strip club with Burlakoff and Babich, and in fact you would not.

In an attempt to address Kapoor's loud and recurrent complaints, Gurry looked into replacing Apricot with another third-party firm. Using outside vendors that serve as "hubs" to handle prior authorizations, or PAs, is not uncommon, but the practice occupies a murky space in the industry. A drugmaker that contracts with a hub provides a benefit to doctors by taking onerous work off their clinics' hands, so it can function like a kickback: *If you write our product instead of the other one, we'll pay for the grunt work.* What's more, any outside vendor hired to handle PAs has an incentive to please its client by getting prescriptions pulled through. There is some motive, then, for a hub to massage the facts in order to fit insurance requirements.

Nevertheless, using a hub is common practice, even at big-name pharma companies, and Insys considered staying with it. Mike Gurry sought out bids from alternative hub vendors that might have better success than Apricot.

Meanwhile, though, he moved to hire someone in-house who would be savvy about what insurers wanted, who could manage the prior-authorization process for him so that he could focus on other responsibilities. This person would serve as the liaison for clinics and reps navigating the PA mess. It wasn't always easy for Insys to find a local person with solid experience, in part because greater Phoenix was not a popular base of pharmaceutical business. But one candidate stood out above the others.

Elizabeth Gurrieri, then in her mid-thirties, had a strong résumé. Gurrieri (pronounced "gur-RARE-ee") had held jobs at a hospital and a major health insurer, Cigna. Better yet, she had worked at a Scottsdale-based division of the industry giant McKesson that provided hub services for prior authorizations. She brought a steady hand to the prior-approval process.

Soon after Gurrieri joined the company, top executives and board members began to consider going a step further than hiring a hub. What if Insys brought prior authorization all the way in-house? That way, the employees seeking approvals would be *theirs.* Insys management could control them, rather than relying on distant third-party workers who served other masters and might just be pushing paper and watching the clock. Insys could ensure that the people charged with this critical task were properly motivated. Kapoor loved that kind of control. Also, it would save money. Contracting with, for instance, Liz Gurrieri's former employer McKesson would have cost on the order of $1.7 million per year, whereas Insys projected that an internal unit with six entry-level employees would cost perhaps $300,000.

One day, Babich walked into Matt Napoletano's office and pulled up a chair, putting his feet up on the desk, and told his head of marketing that the decision had been made to go in-house. Napoletano said he immediately objected.

"Mike, that's not a good idea," he said. "You don't do that."

Napoletano's tone of exasperation was becoming familiar, and Babich was growing tired of the resistance. Napoletano meanwhile resented that it always fell to him to explain industry compliance principles that were widely understood outside the walls of Insys.

Napoletano said that you really don't want to know the details about who is taking the product, especially with a Schedule II opioid. It could easily lead to violations of patient-privacy laws. Another issue with failing to keep an arm's length from the patients is that it implicates the company in any inappropriate prescribing. Having an internal division pushing for questionable patients to be approved for a narcotic—it added up to a serious potential liability. If you pay someone else to do it, you can deny playing a role.

But Kapoor wanted to give it a try. In his fashion, he again started with a pilot program. Liz Gurrieri would ask a dozen doctors to sign up. Their clinics would send a one-page "opt-in form" for each patient. Then Gurrieri would begin trying to secure approvals herself, one patient at a time.

When Gurrieri joined Insys, Karen Hill wrote her a message, though the two didn't yet know each other. Hill was the Florida rep who had worked with Alec Burlakoff at Cephalon and had tipped him off that there might be a job for him at Insys. "We need you now more than ever," Hill wrote to Gurrieri. "Our company is exploding and our main interference is the Prior Approval process."

Indeed, Insys was investing a lot of hope in Gurrieri's efforts to break through the bottleneck. When she started making calls at Insys, on behalf of doctors and their patients, she was a mid-level employee at best, working the phone for less than $50,000 a year. She sat in a cubicle across from the office of her boss, Mike Gurry, and she spoke all day to low-level employees in call centers who worked for pharmacy benefit managers, which administer prescription-drug benefits for health plans. It wasn't glamorous work. But a lot of eyes were on her.

Gurrieri began learning something from just about every phone call, offering Insys a window into how coverage decisions were being made. Most insurers, she now saw firsthand, required a diagnosis of breakthrough cancer pain for approval, which disqualified the majority of Subsys patients immediately. But it was worse than that. Insurance plans would typically only agree to pay if the patient had already tried Actiq, the generic TIRF, without success. In fact, plans often required multiple "tried and failed" medications, including opioids from outside the TIRF class, before they would cover Subsys.

Gurrieri faced a difficult situation. It was the rare Subsys patient who actually had a profile that could clear every hurdle. Meanwhile, she was being monitored from above. It wasn't just Gurry who would come by Gurrieri's desk, either. Dogged by Kapoor in daily meetings about the numbers, Napoletano, Babich, and Burlakoff stopped by regularly, too. Everyone wanted to know how things were going.

Gurrieri could be denied for a number of reasons. Sometimes she would be "third-partied out": she would be told that the insurer needed to hear directly from the doctor's office, as a matter of policy. This was typically a requirement on the books for Medicare plans, which insured a substantial portion of Subsys patients, who tended to be older than average. Other times, the worker she spoke to would tell her, for instance, that she needn't bother calling about Subsys in the future unless drugs X, Y, and Z had already been tried. These little courtesy lessons would prove to be useful.

Gurrieri said that Mike Gurry told her there were things you could do and things you couldn't do and then there was the in-between. She needed to "ride the gray line," he told her, making an ocean-wave motion with his hand.

The solution to the problem that Gurrieri did not work at the doctor's office was simple enough: she presented herself as if she did. She began saying she was calling "with" or "for" or "on behalf of" Dr. Jones.

As for the tried-and-failed hurdles, she claims, Gurry told her that 99 percent of Subsys patients had been on those other pain drugs at some point, whether or not it said so on the form coming from the doctor. She could go ahead and say yes, the patient had tried them. That helped a lot.

At one point, Gurrieri and a newly hired colleague figured out what the insurance giant Humana needed to hear about prior medications to release the money for Subsys. Gurry then asked them to retrieve all the Humana rejections from the file cabinet and try again. This time they had the magic words and hit paydirt. Gurrieri's growing team of "prior-authorization specialists" began to keep track of the magic words for particular insurance plans on a shared computer file and on sheets of paper tacked up in their cubicles.

They also discovered that a diagnosis of dysphagia, meaning difficulty swallowing, was especially helpful for getting an approval. It told insurers that no pill would be a good alternative to Subsys for the patient. And neither would Actiq, which was a lozenge that melted in the mouth, leaving a residue to swallow. Burlakoff recalled that after being told of this nugget of wisdom, Kapoor banged a hand on the table and said, cheerily, "Shit, everybody has difficulty swallowing, right, Alec?"

Gurrieri instructed her team to give the dysphagia diagnosis code on every call. Sometimes it was a lie that made no sense, because the patient in question was simultaneously taking multiple drugs that came in pill form. The proof that the person could swallow was right there in the records. But insurers didn't always catch the contradiction.

Gurrieri's unit came to be called the Insys Reimbursement Center. For the IRC team, using the phone conferred an advantage over sending paperwork. You couldn't get creative with a form full of check boxes. In a conversation, you could misdirect and mislead, bending the truth without completely breaking it, unless necessary. That kind of creativity became, in essence, their central project.

Unlike the schemes of the sales force, all the IRC's work was accomplished right out of Insys offices in Chandler, Arizona. The group was moved to a new building in 2013 when it outgrew the main office, but it was still within walking distance. Executives could stop by to monitor what Gurrieri's team was up to whenever they wanted. Newly hired sales reps and managers who were going through training at headquarters were led over to the new building to see how the unit functioned.

IRC workers had to contend, at first, with the fact that their phone and fax numbers carried an Arizona area code. At times, someone from an insurer would want to contact them, rather than the reverse. That presented a sticky situation, because they didn't want to reveal who they were. There was caller ID to think about as well. The IRC's area code didn't jibe with the story that the call was coming from a clinic in, say, New Hampshire or Alabama. Eventually, Insys set up 800 numbers for incoming calls and faxes, and the person who answered calls at the IRC said only "Reimbursement Center," leaving Insys out of it. That still left the caller ID vulnerability, though.

When the IRC changed buildings, the IT director, Maury Rice, asked for guidance on how to set up the new phone system: How should outgoing calls be displayed on caller ID? According to Mike Babich, he consulted John Kapoor, who decided that the caller ID should reveal nothing. The outgoing number for the IRC was blocked, or it registered as all zeros.

The biggest difficulty of all for the IRC was the stubborn fact that most Subsys scripts were not going to cancer patients. A few insurers had loose requirements, especially early on, tending to defer to licensed prescribers on what medication was needed. Tricare, the government program for military families, and a few other payers didn't require prior authorization for Subsys at all. And then of course there were some patients who actually did have cancer, or at least they had a history of it. Even if they had suffered from skin cancer twenty years before, that was good enough, Gurrieri was told, to indicate a cancer diagnosis to the insurer. But on the majority of phone calls, Gurrieri and her colleagues had to face a question that was hard to get around: Does the patient have a diagnosis of breakthrough cancer pain?

When the true answer was an unambiguous no, the IRC used a little script that came to be known internally as "the spiel." The spiel was a rehearsed bit of wordplay, designed to deceive. It evolved over time, but the objective was always the same: to leave the impression that Subsys was being used to treat a patient's cancer pain, when in fact it was not.

The first version was the crudest. Asked if the patient was being treated for breakthrough cancer pain, the PA specialist would say, "Yes, for breakthrough pain," omitting the word "cancer." The word "yes" was effective; a yes or no was all the other person on the call was looking for, in order to select the right option in a drop-down menu.

Later, the spiel changed: "The physician is aware that the medication is intended for the management of breakthrough pain in cancer patients, and the physician is treating the breakthrough pain." To the person fielding the call, no medical expert, it was a blizzard of words that sounded like a "yes." Again, the omission of the word "cancer" in the final phrase was probably missed. The entire statement was often, in fact, technically accurate. It was also, Gurrieri later said, definitely misleading.

Just two months after the launch of Liz Gurrieri's pilot program, in January 2013, the IRC formally launched company-wide. Turning the pilot into a full-fledged program was an obvious step. The IRC's approval rate was climbing steeply already, to 60 percent or more. Sales reps were encouraged to pitch the IRC to doctors as a time- and money-saving tool and persuade them to "opt in" their patients. In an email to the entire sales staff, Mike Gurry wrote, "This program works!"

Gurrieri sometimes showed the strain of pressure from above. She had a habit of chewing the inside of her cheek, and she quickly lost her patience. But rather than undermine her superiors or leave the company, she became a boss in her own right. In a presentation she drafted with a colleague, beneath the heading "IRC HISTORY," the text read, "(HER-STORY, ACTUALLY)." She was tough on PA specialists around her, sometimes vulgar and cruel. But Gurrieri was a success. She would soon be promoted.

In early 2013, Mike Gurry communicated to her and her colleagues that the upward trajectory of approvals needed to continue. It was a critical juncture for the company.

Dr. Kapoor had abandoned his two previous attempts to take Insys public, during the "pre-commercial" stage when the company had drugs in the pipeline but nothing on the market. Now he had a winning product and saw a new opportunity. He was again plotting to take the company public, and soon—by the midway point of 2013. He and Babich viewed the first quarter of 2013 as pivotal. It would produce the financial results that they would be showing around on Wall Street. Insys hadn't quite gotten into the black yet. The two wanted to be able to tell investors that this was a profitable company. The IRC was a key piece of the strategy to get there.

The top Insys executives decided to fully exploit their decision to handle prior authorizations internally. The company instituted a system whereby PA specialists would receive bonuses based on how many scripts they pulled through. IRC staffers were supposed to be walled off from sales; in theory, they were supposed to be merely conveying information to insurers. Executives were giving them skin in the game. They now had a financial incentive to get to yes.

On a weekly basis, Gurry or another manager would set a "gate"—a number of approvals that the group needed to achieve before becoming eligible for bonuses. These rewards weren't just a token gratuity. PA specialists made around $17 to $20 an hour, with no benefits. Some were first brought on board as temps working with an outside agency. They weren't comfortable white-collar employees with a wide range of career prospects. Bonuses of $100 or $200 a week were meaningful.

If the IRC "broke the gate," the PA specialists would start making money with every approval. Their individual numbers were charted on a dry-erase board in the office. The IRC staff never visited a pain clinic, never met any of the real-life patients represented on that board or on the forms that flowed into their in-box. To them, breaking the gate became a kind of game. They excelled at it.

In early 2013, all the building blocks of Insys's success were finally in place. The gospel of the speaker program was spreading rapidly through the ranks. The IRC team was growing and constantly honing its techniques, delivering a dramatic impact on the bottom line. Every month or two, there was a new IRC benchmark, far above anything Apricot or, more important, Cephalon had achieved—50 percent approval, 60 percent, then 87, and beyond.

Unbeknownst to senior executives, however, a serious threat was developing. It was not coming from Cephalon or any other competitor. It was coming from much closer at hand.

The trouble had started the previous year—before the IRC existed, before Alec Burlakoff had even been tapped to head the sales force. Soon after Burlakoff joined the company as a manager in the Southeast, he traveled to Houston for an introductory ride-along with a sales rep named Ray Furchak. Like most of his colleagues, Furchak was inexperienced in the drug industry, though he had worked in sales of medical devices used with animals.

Then thirty-three, Furchak was part of the original Southeast team, hired by Tony Bryant. He had not yet found a major prescriber and was nowhere near the top of the leaderboard. Burlakoff assured his newly inherited team that he had no intention of firing anyone; he just wanted everyone to make more money. Still, Furchak was concerned that Burlakoff had no investment in protecting them because he hadn't hired them in the first place.

When the two met for the first time for that ride-along, however, they quickly developed a friendly rapport. They talked about how Furchak got into the Ivy League by transferring to Cornell. Burlakoff admired the smarts and maneuvering required. They even talked about smoking weed, after Burlakoff somehow deduced that his sales rep was a fellow devotee.

Furchak wasn't fooled by Burlakoff exactly—he quickly recognized that he was dealing with an operator, maybe a confidence man—but that didn't necessarily mar the collegial dynamic. After a sales call, Furchak ribbed his new boss about his little playacting routines with doctors, made to look spontaneous and genuine but obviously rehearsed. Burlakoff was pleased by Furchak's perceptiveness and chutzpah.

The following day, Ray had occasion to rethink his impressions. He spoke to Tony Bryant, who was now employed elsewhere but still a confidant. Furchak asked his old manager why he hadn't shown him some of the tricks that Burlakoff had used. He described the way Burlakoff had hinted to doctors, without quite urging it outright, that prescribing off label wasn't a worry and might be a good idea. "Well, Ray," Bryant said, "what he was doing is illegal."

As Furchak's concerns mounted, he soon saw that he wasn't alone. Tracy Krane had already asked Burlakoff, when he laid out the speaker-program strategy on week one, "Isn't that illegal?" The new boss's audacity was fueling chatter and debate among the reps of the Southeast. Several of them had become close in the trying early days, pre-Burlakoff, when employees kept dropping out of sight as Kapoor fumed over poor performance. Now the group compared notes about their new boss by phone from their cars as they crisscrossed their huge territories, driving for hours at a time, all of them trying to work out what they thought and what to do about it.

Some of the talk was just gossip. It could be fun to marvel together at Burlakoff's personality: *Can you believe he said that?* On some level, everybody liked the guy. On an evening out, he was the one who got the conversational ball rolling and loosened everybody up. He could be a philosopher, a stand-up comedian, maybe even a life coach. Burlakoff's boasting made people cringe, but privately it motivated them, too: *Hey, maybe I should believe in myself the way he does.*

Burlakoff "planted the seed that he was the godsend to this company," Furchak later said, and he made reps want to live up to his expectations. He had that knack as a manager. It could be thrilling when he singled you out for praise.

There were reps who were making good money, who were in debt but now able to support their families. They didn't know what other prospects were out there for them. Many didn't have prior pharma jobs to compare this with. Not everyone was sure that the new techniques they were learning were even that bad. Mia Guzman remembered her old company treating potential clients to prime skybox seats at big-time sporting events. It was an obvious attempt to win their business. Was a speaker fee any different? Some also felt that they finally had an answer to the confusions and difficulties of the job. With a knowledgeable doctor, Guzman and others had wondered what they even had to offer. Now they had something. Most people were focused on performance, driven not only by bonuses but by a natural inclination to do well at their jobs. No one wanted to fall too low on the weekly sales scorecards. It was embarrassing. It was like getting Cs in school, only everyone's grades were posted on the wall.

Still, these debriefing sessions grew more fraught over time. Some reps had taken the job thinking they were signing up for a bland business-to-business sales position. They pictured boring conference calls and lab coats and fluorescent overhead lights. They didn't connect what they would be doing with the opioid crisis they read about in the news. They thought they would be selling a cancer drug. "I'm thinking I'm going to be calling on oncologists," said Jim Coffman, an original member of the Southeast team. Instead, the reps were sent to see dubious doctors, and they were pressured to flirt and engage in blatant favor trading.

Months after leaving Insys, Tony Bryant remained a part of the conversational circle. When he heard several reps express concern, he advised them to document what was happening—he told them to send emails to themselves about iffy guidance from above—so that if human resources questioned their conduct, they would have evidence that their bosses had directed it. Some reps were coming to believe that just by doing their jobs at Insys, they were becoming complicit in something troubling. The atmosphere took on a charge.

Furchak and Krane spoke often, almost daily. Where they used to discuss what to do to improve their sales, they now debated a quite different question: If this is what it took to succeed, should they be trying to improve at all?

Furchak had a righteous streak to his personality. At a previous job, he felt management had lied to him about what he would be paid. One evening, he said so, to the CEO, with his manager present.

In Tracy Krane, Furchak found a receptive audience. He would get worked up as he spoke. Unbeknownst to Burlakoff or anyone else in management, Furchak was becoming a persistent voice of alarm. By late summer 2012, "Ray was really adamant," Krane said. "He would get fiery. He would say, 'What this company is doing is *wrong*.'"

At one point, Furchak had a particularly intense phone call with Bryant, a person he felt he could trust. "I gotta tell you," Furchak said, "I feel like this needs to be reported."

Bryant knew, from his industry experience, all that can happen to people who go outside the walls and speak against the company that pays them. He told Furchak it would consume years of his life if he came forward. It was likely he would never get another job in the pharmaceutical business. Furchak was already thinking about leaving pharma behind, so that was less of a worry. Bryant acknowledged that if someone was going to take the leap, Furchak might be the right person to do it. He had the character profile required. "I'm a stick-it-to-you guy," Furchak said later.

On top of his ethical objections, Furchak had a less altruistic concern. He was, to some degree, a part of this thing. If the authorities closed in, he wanted to be the one who called them to begin with, not one of the people marched out of the building wearing handcuffs. Most of his co-workers would have laughed it off as a stretch, but he thought of arrests as a real possibility.

In September 2012, just after Labor Day, Furchak took his father to the National Corvette Museum in Bowling Green, Kentucky, on an overnight road trip. It was a gift to his dad, a bonding experience for two men who loved cars. On the trip, he confided in his father about the dilemma he was facing at work. They talked it over at length. It was on that trip that he made up his mind.

It only confirmed his decision when, the very next day, Furchak received an email from Burlakoff sent to all of his reps. It proposed flagrantly pushing the higher strengths of Subsys even as a starting dose, contrary to the boldfaced warnings on the FDA label. Mike Babich and even John Kapoor were copied on the message. One day later, Babich announced Alec Burlakoff's promotion to vice president of sales.

On September 28, 2012, Ray Furchak filed a secret lawsuit naming Insys Therapeutics and John Kapoor as defendants. Furchak's suit was what is known as a *qui tam*, brought under the False Claims Act. In cases of this kind, a whistleblower alleges fraud against the taxpayer and sues on behalf of the government. The term *qui tam* is an abbreviation of a Latin phrase describing a legal action brought by a person "who sues for the king as well as for himself." The Department of Justice reviews each *qui tam*, and if it chooses to "intervene" in the action, it joins forces with the whistleblower—referred to as the relator—and takes the lead role in pursuing the case.

These lawsuits are filed under seal and can stay that way for years, giving the government a chance to investigate covertly. Neither John Kapoor nor the company knew they had been sued. Furchak was barred from talking about it. Often a whistleblower's identity and even the existence of a *qui tam* is kept secret from the public all the way until the moment the case is resolved, usually through a settlement, if the suit is successful.

Qui tam suits are a major enforcement tool in the health-care industry, particularly in pharmaceuticals. Any drug company violating the law is liable to be guilty of defrauding the government, because a substantial proportion of prescription drugs are purchased by the taxpayer; public programs such as Medicare, Medicaid, Tricare, and the Veterans Administration pay for prescriptions written for their patients. This monetary loss gives the United States the grounds to go after pharma, to claw back the money. When the Justice Department extracts a serious financial penalty from a drugmaker, and sometimes a criminal guilty plea, the case usually traces back to a quiet decision, years before, of an individual on the inside, a solitary man or woman who took a big step.

Qui tam suits also represent a serious financial opportunity for whistleblowers: they stand to share in any funds recovered by the government. The whistleblower is, in other words, a kind of bounty hunter. When the False Claims Act was conceived during the Civil War, the legislature adopted this framework, drawing on early English law, to encourage informers to report people who were scamming the Union army through price gouging and other schemes. The statute offers a reward out of a recognition that whistleblowers (and their lawyers) would otherwise have little incentive to undertake an arduous and costly ordeal.

In major pharmaceutical cases, the whistleblower's share, up to 30 percent, can run into the millions or even tens of millions of dollars. In a 2009 settlement concerning off-label marketing at Pfizer, six relators shared a payout of over $102 million.

A surprising number of people in the industry are unaware that they could make money by blowing the whistle. But at larger companies, where employees are more experienced, enough people are in the know that any misconduct can foster an atmosphere of suspicion and competition. Reps who consider filing a suit wonder if someone else already has—the first to file is heavily favored by the law—and people speculate about whether their co-workers might be recording calls or wearing a wire. Top executives have to worry about spies in their ranks and consider the potential consequences of alienating or firing anyone who knows too much.

Ray Furchak said in a later interview that he had no idea there might be profit involved when he began exploring the idea of reporting Insys. He soon learned the term *qui tam* by googling, but he said he went to a lawyer because he thought people at Insys needed to go to jail, not to cash in. According to Furchak, the lawyer replied that a *qui tam* was the best route to take.

After filing suit, while still trying to do his job, Furchak covertly gathered emails and internal documents with a new intensity. Turning over more material would strengthen his case. He stepped up his intelligence work by recording calls. Attempting to draw people out on the phone, he pushed the envelope, prodding them for details, asking them to recap something they'd said when the tape wasn't running.

Furchak struggled with how to conduct himself at Insys. Going along meant criminal activity, as he saw it, but defying direction might raise suspicion or get him fired. Staying on the inside was clearly the best way to spy. Discussing his case with anyone would jeopardize it. On some of the calls he recorded, the other people on the line sounded wary, as though they were onto him. It was a lonely position to be in.

Furchak became fearful, to the point of paranoia. He stored his growing digital trove on a computer and on external drives, and he emailed it to multiple accounts. He wasn't really thinking about backing up data in case of tech problems, he said. He was thinking, "If something happens to me, this will be found."

He worried that Burlakoff in particular could be vindictive if he found out. Furchak's material cast suspicion on Kapoor and Babich, but he worked much more closely with Burlakoff, and most of his damning specifics implicated him. The sketchy rumors about the Burlakoff family ties to organized crime had begun to circulate. Even if they weren't true, it wasn't difficult or far-fetched to imagine Alec being enraged. "We work on loyalty here pal," Burlakoff once wrote in a typo-ridden text message to a doctor he felt had betrayed him and Insys. "Waxh your fuckn back and grow a set of eyes in the back of your head . . . you don't EVER fuck with a burlakoff!"

Burlakoff evidently didn't always follow the self-protective measures he preached. Furchak's legal complaint cited Burlakoff telling him in writing to ensure that a speaker was "writing more and more subsys to justify these programs." Neatly summarizing the quid pro quo, Burlakoff wrote in a text, "Speakers should be writing 1 a day."

Joe Rowan, who had stepped into Burlakoff's place as manager of the Southeast, at one point set up a phone call between Furchak and the Florida rep Karen Hill so that he could get some advice and coaching. Furchak saw an opening. Hill had worked with Burlakoff and Rowan at Cephalon, and, according to Burlakoff, she was used as a conduit for messages that he and Rowan didn't want to spell out themselves. Reps picked up on the dynamic.

As Furchak prodded her along, Hill taught him, on tape, how to identify the prescribers who would take the deal if you laid it out to them, the "guys that wanna play ball." It could be any doctor, she said, not only a pain specialist; a script is a script, and "the company does not give a shit where they come from." You look for doctors who are doing a lot of procedures or establishing a new clinic, she said, or the "speaker whores" who will take cash from any company. "All those guys are money hungry," she said. Hill suggested that he look for men who were going through a divorce, because they're "hurting for money big time." If you float the idea of being a paid speaker to a doctor, she said, and "there is a light in their eyes that goes off, you know that's your guy."

Ray Furchak filed his complaint before the advent of the Insys Reimbursement Center, so his suit didn't capture the insurance fraud that later routinely occurred at Insys headquarters. As a rep far from the Arizona offices, he had a limited view of what was happening at the very top. But his legal complaint did provide evidence that, at a minimum, his boss was pushing off-label promotion and kickback schemes and had just been rapidly promoted to run the sales force.

Furchak's case presented a real opportunity not just for him to expose Insys, but for the Department of Justice to make a statement in the face of the growing opioid epidemic. When the DOJ had struck a deal with Purdue Pharma in 2007, after a massive investigation, many observers felt profoundly disappointed by the outcome, especially the families of people who had fatally overdosed on Oxy-

Contin. Presiding over the sentencing, the judge said, "I do not doubt that many of our fellow citizens . . . will deem it inappropriate that no jail time is imposed. It bothers me, too." The financial penalty represented less than a year's worth of OxyContin sales revenue. Senator Arlen Specter, the Pennsylvania Republican, remarked that fines like that are not a true deterrent but instead "expensive licenses for criminal misconduct."

Furchak had handed officials at the Justice Department another chance, albeit with a much smaller company, to send a signal to the industry, to pursue a penalty with teeth.

When Ray Furchak and his legal team finally met with lawyers for the United States, months had passed and Insys's fortunes had dramatically improved, buoyed by the speaker program and the IRC. Insys had by then fired Furchak, citing weak sales. First he was put on a performance improvement plan, or PIP, a common measure in the industry that serves as a warning and a final chance to correct course. Furchak ultimately got the call from Joe Rowan and HR a few weeks before Christmas 2012. Rowan wouldn't be heeding Burlakoff's advice against firing reps. Underperformers had to go. Furchak and Tracy Krane were terminated on the same day.

When Furchak's meeting with the Department of Justice finally arrived, it wasn't what he had expected. He thought he had Insys dead to rights, that he had uncovered something huge. But he didn't sense a lot of gratitude or enthusiasm from investigators. A few weeks later, he was told the government was declining to intervene in his lawsuit. He didn't even get a real explanation.

For the Justice Department, going after a pharmaceutical company—or any national corporation, for that matter—means taking on an opponent that isn't going to fold easily. Outstanding, expensive defense attorneys are likely to be hired. The case will involve a protracted investigation and a significant investment in resources, funded by the taxpayer. Although the Justice Department prefers not to discuss it openly, there is plenty of illegal conduct in health care that never gets prosecuted, owing to limited government bandwidth and the daunting burden of proof. The DOJ declines the majority of the *qui tam* cases it sees.

An attorney familiar with the Furchak decision later said that, callous as it may seem, the Justice Department views *qui tam*s like business ventures. If they are going to invest the years it takes to bring a case, they want to get a sizable return. When Furchak filed his suit, Insys was growing, but it wasn't hauling in revenue on a Big Pharma scale. Even if the company was defrauding the government, how much were the ill-gotten gains, the money the United States could potentially claw back?

Furchak's attorneys told him he could continue with the case, but the chances wouldn't be good and the government wouldn't be sharing the costs. He would also have to find a different lawyer. Furchak did what most people do in this situation: he dropped the case. In March 2013, his legal complaint was quietly unsealed by a federal judge in the Southern District of Texas, making it a public record. But the media took no notice. Insys had escaped unscathed.

The following month, the company gathered for several days at the Arizona Grand Resort & Spa in Phoenix for another national sales meeting. The mood ran high. The theme of the meeting, borrowed from a best-selling business book by Jim Collins, was "Good to Great," suggesting the next phase for the company.

A Texas sales rep likened the conference to a college frat party. At the kickoff and send-off meetings, which took place in the evenings, there was considerable drinking. People who had just met coupled off at night. There was a lot of buzz about what was coming soon: an IPO. Everyone's stock options were about to be worth something.

In May 2013, fourteen months after the Subsys launch, Insys Therapeutics debuted on Nasdaq, with the ticker symbol INSY. Kapoor had reached a longtime goal, after multiple failed attempts. The IPO marked an end to shoveling money into an uncertain venture all on his own. Beginning with an initial $1 million to seed the company in 2002, he had lent cash to Insys over and over, in addition to holding nearly all the equity. On the eve of the IPO, the company owed about $60 million to trusts he controlled. With the offering, by agreement, that debt would be instantly converted into equity—personal wealth.

Institutional investors arrived at a valuation of $8 a share, lower than Insys had sought. But that meant that Kapoor's debt translated into a greater number of shares. He emerged with a larger chunk of the company than anticipated, about three-quarters of it, giving him added motivation to drive up the share price in the future.

A litany of damning evidence implicating the company and its senior executives sat in a courthouse in Texas, provided by Furchak and made public two months earlier. It was available online to anyone who thought to hunt around. But at Insys, there weren't a lot of worries.

An array of Insys employees would later travel to Manhattan to celebrate Wall Street's embrace of the company. Alec Burlakoff didn't join them. Insys had just been treating the President's Club—the top performers in sales—to a luxurious getaway in Costa Rica, and Burlakoff was lingering there for a few days with his family. But Kapoor and Babich didn't miss the rite of passage in New York, the opportunity to ring the opening bell. An array of Insys employees appeared onstage at the Nasdaq MarketSite in Times Square for the photo-op ceremony. The CEO and the founder stood together near the center, the protégé towering over his boss. They smiled widely and cheered.

When Alec Burlakoff preached the importance of lavishing doctors with speaker programs and VIP treatment, he would point to his elite reps as models to emulate. Not long before the champagne moment of the IPO, he wrote to his sales force, "The below 5 names mentioned at the top of the company's rankings literally have their entire business driven by basically one customer. . . . They found a customer to 'own,' and they packed the proverbial suitcase and moved in." One of the standouts listed was his old friend Joe Rowan, and in Rowan's case the crucial doctor was of course Xiulu Ruan, down in the Gulf Coast city of Mobile, Alabama.

Rowan's courtship of Dr. Ruan had not only helped earn him a promotion and propel Burlakoff to the VP position; it had established a critical beachhead for future operations. Given that Ruan co-owned his perpetually crowded clinic, Physicians Pain Specialists of Alabama, or PPSA, with another whale, John Patrick Couch, it was a particularly valuable piece of turf. John Kapoor and Mike Babich were personally familiar with the two men and had closely watched their prescribing habits from the beginning. Dr. Ruan was one of the dozen prescribers Insys had flown to Arizona to serve on its advisory board, even before the Subsys launch.

In spring 2013, when Rowan was taking on more responsibility as a manager and needed to appoint a successor to call on Ruan, he consulted the doctor on the decision. Rowan first offered to hire Ruan's girlfriend. Ruan had a different proposal. For several months he had been making advances on a young woman with long brown hair and dark eyes named Natalie Perhacs, who visited the clinic as a rep selling respiratory equipment, such as CPAP machines for sleep apnea. Simultaneously, Ruan was making efforts to help her get a new position as a drug rep. When he invited her to dinner or asked personal questions, she would always politely rebuff him. But if Dr. Ruan got Perhacs the Insys job, she would be forced to visit his clinic several times a week and ingratiate herself to make a living.

Ruan was fifty years old, and Perhacs was twenty-seven. She was the daughter of an attorney from Birmingham, a few hours' drive to the north. She knew nothing about pharmaceuticals, she said later. Dr. Ruan sent her a Wikipedia link about fentanyl so she could prepare for her Insys interview.

Perhacs got the job. She would be calling on Ruan and Couch both; the rep for Couch had recently left. She scheduled speaker programs for each doctor about once a week, following direction from above. Ruan's standing appointment took place at a local restaurant called Osaka, which he claimed ordered special food from its suppliers at his request. Dr. Couch favored Fuego, an upscale Mexican place, or else Wintzell's Oyster House. Often, at these programs, the audience consisted of their own office staff, who weren't licensed to prescribe Subsys and had already heard about it. For a while, one nurse who was new to the job didn't realize the doctors were being paid for these meals she attended. She thought it was just about the free food and drink.

Like the swarm of other reps who fed on the clinic, Perhacs began acceding to Dr. Ruan's brazen requests for favors in hopes of winning his business. When Ruan asked, other reps would bring his cars in for maintenance, take his dog out for walks, pick up his relatives at the airport. Perhacs helped out with car auctions he participated in. She wrote at least one rave review online for his practice, posing as a patient under an alias, at his request. She joined his health-products pyramid scheme.

Meanwhile, Perhacs had to contend with the problem of Ruan's personal affection for her. She became friendly with a nurse-practitioner at the clinic, Justin Palmer, and would groan to him about Ruan's flirtation, Palmer said. She would slip into his office and say, "Please hide me."

Natalie was caught up in the hectic and outlandish world of the Mobile practice, where tidbits like these barely registered on the gossip radar. One sales rep who frequented the place, Lynette Lord, described the prevailing atmosphere as "*Wolf of Wall Street* in a pain clinic."

Dr. Couch, who founded the clinic in 1997, was handsome, with well-groomed sandy hair and movie-ready eyes. He was skilled at medical procedures, employees said, such as implanting pain pumps or performing nerve block injections. He maintained the appearance of a successful physician, with a country-club membership and kids in private school. But by the time Natalie Perhacs met him, he had lost interest in being a doctor, according to employees. "He was just done," Justin Palmer said.

Couch had struggled for years with addiction to drugs and alcohol, with a history of drunk-driving convictions beginning in high school. After Ruan became a partner in the practice, Couch took some time off to go through rehab. At least one staffer said he saw used needles in Couch's personal bathroom at the office. (Couch later said he was never an IV drug abuser and denied there were any such needles.)

When Insys entered the picture, Couch had gone through a contentious divorce and was involved in another relationship so stormy that he twice pursued legal action to stop the woman from contacting him, he said. Couch owned a Porsche with a vanity license plate: "PAIN MD." He frequently hit on female reps, employees said, closing the door to his personal office for long stretches while they were inside. Couch would bring a guitar to the clinic, put his feet up on his desk, and play a few licks. He played and sang in a band that performed out on the Causeway, east of the city center. The group was called Midlife Crisis.

People who worked for Couch said they would have to practically drag him out of his office to see patients, whom he treated, at times, with open contempt. He would throw prescriptions at them. According to Palmer, Couch sometimes lamented privately to him, "All we do is write narcotics," as if opioids were a force of nature the doctor couldn't control. So many of them came from his prescription pad that some doctors in the city called him "the Candy Man."

Office visits at the clinic were routinely billed as if the doctors had handled them, but the nurses did most of the work and in some cases all of it. (A former longtime patient of Couch's failed to recognize him in a room.) The physicians were supposed to at least sign off on prescriptions for tightly controlled narcotics, because the nurses could not legally write them. But Justin Palmer grew tired of waiting for Couch to show up while patients got fed up with the delays, he said. Palmer started forging Couch's name on prescriptions on a regular basis. Just about everyone in the clinic knew it, he said. Thousands of scripts were issued in Couch's name in his absence— when he hadn't arrived yet in the morning, or while he was out of the state or country.

Palmer had struggled with opioid addiction in the past himself, as he said he told Couch in his job interview. He was clean when he started work there. But one day, Palmer found some leftover Dilaudid, a potent opioid, in an exam room and he shot it up, even though he knew where it would lead. Before long, he was using IV drugs taken from the clinic on a daily basis, in escalating doses. "Pills couldn't touch me," he recalled. "I was so far beyond that." Palmer started using at work with his co-worker Stacy Madison. Both of them were treating patients all the while. Palmer would walk around the clinic sweating profusely, a telltale sign. One day, an employee found him passed out in a recliner in the office with a needle in his arm. It was reported, and Couch suspended him for two weeks, with pay.

Palmer said it was obvious that a third nurse at PPSA, Bridgette Parker, who suffered from painful back problems, was also misusing narcotics, and that he spoke to Couch about it. Parker had only recently become a nurse-practitioner, and she felt at sea making the kinds of decisions she was called upon to handle. (She later said the doctors should not have given her so much responsibility.) Parker would sometimes follow the boss's lead and initiate prescriptions for

Subsys or its competitors, but she later had trouble answering questions about TIRF drugs and their purpose, describing them as strong but "no different than any other medication." Her problems with addiction grew worse over time. A staffer recalled seeing Parker have trouble operating a door handle. Co-workers would look after her when she was "dopesick" and try to get her through it, encouraging her to seek help.

With Couch often checked out, Dr. Ruan began to take the dominant position in the partnership. It was just as well. Ruan was cut out to run a business, not follow someone else's lead. He was almost unbelievably arrogant, with no tolerance for being questioned, and he had little aptitude or interest in reading social cues to get along. He was more accustomed to behaving as if everyone worked for him, or holing up alone to pore over medical journals.

He was a legitimately knowledgeable physician, and he gave some patients excellent care, employees said. Few people could understand him when he carried on about the science of medicine—partly because of his accent, but also because of the technical jargon he used, making no allowances for an inexpert audience. He boasted of his "world record" number of board certifications.

The doctor seemed oblivious to the impressions he left in his wake. He would deny raises to his employees on the grounds that he couldn't afford it, a staffer said, but then he would show off his new Rolex to them and brag about how much it cost. He held a large "open house" party at his lavish residence, displaying a crowd of fancy cars in the driveway. Medical providers from across the region were there, including people who referred patients to him. He paid no mind to the fact that making that much money at a pain clinic—or any practice, really—would raise some eyebrows.

Ruan didn't engage in the typical social pastimes in Mobile. He didn't belong to private golf clubs or Mardi Gras societies. He wasn't a follower of the local religion, college football. His major hobby outside work was cars. Ruan was amassing a fleet of luxury vehicles, some of them extremely rare sports cars. He came to own a Saleen, three

Bentleys, two Lamborghinis, and two Ferraris. He accumulated so many collectible cars—eighteen, eventually—that he secured a warehouse and set it up like a showroom, with the impeccably maintained vehicles neatly aligned at the same angle, behind velvet ropes, with placards describing each one and plenty of room to walk around and have a look. (Despite showing off these toys to others, he went to some lengths to shield them from his estranged wife during their divorce proceedings.)

Ruan was forever obsessing over how to squeeze the maximum profit out of the clinic, employees said. He wasn't shy about applying leverage. The key principle that Ruan understood was that he and Couch wielded enormous power. Of their two clinic locations, Ruan worked primarily out of an unattractive brown one-story building on the western outskirts of the city, occupying a commercial lot adjacent to a Shell station. Driving by on Airport Boulevard, you could easily miss it. But the two doctors owned one of the largest pain practices in the Southeast, with some eight thousand active patients. Ruan and Couch advertised on TV and on full-size billboards. Alabama was number one in the nation in the rate of opioid prescribing, and the clinic was a major supplier. That opened up an array of financial opportunities.

Companies like Insys saw Couch and Ruan as just the kind of targets they were looking for. "We were always looking for guys with a business sense," a former senior Insys manager said.

But the way Ruan saw it, two could play that game. If he and Couch turned from one drug to another in their prescribing habits, pharma companies thousands of miles away felt the impact. The same was true for companies selling urine testing, compound creams, back braces, home-health services. Reps and their higher-ups in all these fields descended on Mobile in force, to genuflect to the doctors, especially Ruan.

"It was a gold mine, just because of the volume of patients," one medical-equipment rep said. The rep would throw a barbecue for the clinic's employees twice a year in their parking lot. He collected a lot of his income through the practice. He couldn't afford to lose his hold on it.

Reps jockeyed to earn coveted access to the employee entrance so they could "get back" without getting stuck in the crowded waiting room. Everyone was angling for some face time with the doctors so they could pitch their products. Or perhaps they could offer a thinly disguised kickback that narrowly topped the one Ruan had just secured from the competition. Reps would float schemes, side hustles: *I hear you're looking to upgrade your computer system, get your medical records squared away. I know a guy.*

Alec Burlakoff visited the clinic a few times. He said that it wasn't a pill mill, exactly. It was "a factory."

The typical pill mill takes all comers and accepts cash. Sometimes it's cash only, which prevents scrutiny from insurers. (It also helps you stay under the government radar. The Medicare authorities aren't likely to come after you if you aren't billing Medicare.) Ostensibly the fees at a pill mill are collected for the doctor's time, but really the transaction is more concrete: money in exchange for a prescription.

Couch and Ruan's practice generally didn't accept cash and required a referral from another clinician. The policies helped project the image of a legitimate operation, which in some respects it was. There were some "pill seekers" around, but a lot of people came there just looking for help. The doctors were well educated, had the latest equipment, and performed procedures, rather than solely handing out scripts. They also used security guards to keep order in the waiting room and prevent crowds from spilling outdoors. (People would sometimes buy and sell prescription drugs in the parking lot, but that was difficult to stop.)

Instead of collecting a mere $200 or so for an office visit, Couch and Ruan treated each patient as a profit center, an opportunity to bill for tests and procedures in-house, or to refer out to some other provider who would cut them in on the business. They reinvested to grow their factory, buying new machines that added lucrative capabilities.

On Ruan's initiative, the two doctors took the profit-center concept a crucial step further. They set up a pharmacy that was physically attached to their own clinic. C&R Pharmacy, named for Couch and Ruan, eventually occupied a wing of their clinic building on Airport Boulevard. One entrance to the pharmacy was inside the clinic. The pharmacy was technically managed by an independent entity, but Couch and Ruan collected 75 percent of the profits. Patients were strongly encouraged to fill their scripts at C&R, nurses said. When the pharmacy first opened, the operators of a Rite Aid next door to the other location of the practice stopped letting the clinic use their parking lot, one staffer said; the Rite Aid had suddenly lost a lot of business, because Couch and Ruan were steering their patients to their own pharmacy.

What it amounted to, for the doctors, was a kind of double-dipping. Where a typical pill mill makes money only on the appointment fee, Ruan and Couch found a way to take in cash for the actual drugs. Their pharmacy billed over $572,000 for Subsys in a single month. Very few pharmacies even carried Subsys, a niche medication packaged in large boxes that needed to be stored securely. Patients had almost nowhere else to go but C&R to fill their scripts. In addition, having the medication on hand meant that the doctors could write more Subsys and live up to their end of the speaker-program bargain, without hassle for the patients or interference from an outside pharmacy. (Under federal regulations, pharmacists have a responsibility to ensure that a controlled-substance prescription was issued for a legitimate medical purpose.)

Combining the incentive of the speaker program with the profits from C&R, Insys and the two doctors formed a collaboration that snowballed in value for everyone involved. At the sales rep Natalie Perhacs's previous company, her salary was just over $30,000 a year. At Insys, she easily cleared that amount in a single month, owing almost entirely to Ruan and Couch.

She made President's Club and was invited to speak from the stage at an Insys national sales meeting, where her incredible earnings were announced to the whole company. She spoke of how she was now able to support her mother, who was divorced and suffered from cancer. Ultimately, Perhacs earned some $700,000 at Insys in less than two years.

———

Kathy Burns worked for the city of Mobile, Alabama, as a horticulturalist. She would take care of the greenery lining the parks and the roads. When she first moved in with her husband, Tim, she would work in her own garden, out in back of the house, late into the night, pulling weeds by the light of a headlamp.

When Kathy, then fifty-one, first went to Couch and Ruan's practice in May 2012, complaining of lingering pain from a car crash years before, she was honest with the medical staff: she told them she had abused narcotics before. But they took her on. Whether you were legitimately suffering from terrible pain or you just hungered for the medicine—and with Kathy it was hard to tell which it was at any given time, her husband said—the clinic was a place you could go when you had run out of options. It was often the end of the road for patients set adrift by other doctors.

Just before Perhacs took the baton from Joe Rowan in early 2013, Dr. Ruan put Kathy Burns on Subsys. She didn't have cancer, and the insurer put up some resistance, but the Insys Reimbursement Center got it through. In the ensuing months, the clinic warned her about her overuse of Subsys and other narcotics; she kept using up her supply early. Her husband would sometimes pick up her Subsys spray bottles at C&R, several boxes' worth—unless they'd run out of stock—and then "she would go through them like water," he said. She was warned by Ruan or his medical staff at least three times.

Normally, a pain specialist might terminate a patient after repeated violations like this, ideally with a plan in place for addiction treatment. One university student who was studying how pain doctors approach discharging patients sent a cold email to Ruan and other doctors to inquire about their policies, as a survey of sorts. Ruan replied, to a stranger, "In literature, physicians used to say zero tolerance, but in reality we fire patients rather infrequently. We always give folks one more chance. In private practice the more you fire, the more revenue you lose. . . . Another interesting thing is when one patient tests positive for street drugs"—a typical cause for termination—"that gives you more reason to do more frequent urine drug screens, which pays three times more than an office visit. So there is incentive for taking care of risk individuals."

While being seen at PPSA, Kathy Burns lost interest in her gardening, along with everything else. She went from 145 pounds down to 110. Her husband, Tim, would hide her medication from her, leaving only enough for that day, but somehow she always found it—in a locked file cabinet, in his truck while it was parked at work. Then she started squirreling it away so he couldn't monitor what she was taking. He came across medicine hidden under the grounds in the backup coffee can.

Tim would find his wife passed out, unresponsive, on the floor or on the couch. Once, she had multiple fentanyl patches stuck to her and Subsys spray bottles strewn around her body. He had to call an ambulance for her several times.

Dr. Ruan received a letter from Kathy Burns's insurer asking him to verify, with a signature, that Kathy was prescribed Subsys for a diagnosis of breakthrough cancer pain, which she was not. Ruan signed it. C&R Pharmacy billed about $150,000 for the Subsys that Kathy was prescribed. Finally, after fifteen months, the insurer denied a Subsys claim for her. C&R could no longer bill for her prescriptions—a blow to Insys's bottom line but also Dr. Ruan's. Nine days later, he fired her as a patient.

Kathy died the following year, of heart disease. She was still misusing prescription drugs, and she wasn't the same woman she had been a few years before, her husband said. He woke up on the couch one day and found himself surrounded by the terriers that usually slept in bed with Kathy. He knew right then that something was wrong.

The engine was thrumming at Insys. In the second half of 2013, following the IPO in May, managers and their reps were bringing blue-chip doctors on board nationwide. On Sunrise Lee's turf, Gavin Awerbuch in Michigan and Paul Madison in Illinois were producing; Joe Rowan had Ruan and Couch in Alabama, and Steven Chun was starting to come through in Florida; Rich Simon had picked up a whale in Texas, Judson Somerville. All three of those managers were promoted as the sales force expanded, creating new layers in the hierarchy. All three were Alec Burlakoff's recruits. Employees marveled at the way Burlakoff seemed to be everywhere at once: traveling almost weekly; blasting out emails late at night (whether motivational or irritated); working out before dawn; entertaining doctors who had flown into Arizona by setting them up at nightclubs or strip clubs for an evening out.

At the Chandler office, the top executives were enjoying themselves. Mike Babich was romantically involved with multiple women at the company during 2013. Matt Napoletano at some point had affairs with two employees himself. For his part, John Kapoor grew close to the New Jersey sales rep Sue Beisler, who had gotten his number back at the launch conference. Their relationship became physical at one point, she said. Napoletano once saw them embracing and kissing on patio furniture outside an Insys house party in Arizona.

Beisler began writing Kapoor emails that gave him a direct view of what was happening out in the field. She complained that the speaker money "being *thrown*" at certain doctors was giving their reps an unfair advantage. She mentioned that one Manhattan doctor was "getting $2500 a pop to eat at fancy steakhouses in NYC *often*," adding, "I don't even think anyone goes to his 'programs.'" Kapoor never replied to these messages.

All the while, Subsys was gaining ground fast on Fentora, the "900 pound gorilla" of the branded TIRF market, as Babich called it. At launch in early 2012, Kapoor and Babich had tried to steer clear of directly challenging Fentora to a fight, knowing they were outgunned in resources and head count; instead, they focused on taking market share from the generic TIRF products. But those days were over. By October 2013, Babich was telling the sales force, "I never in my wildest dreams thought we would become 'the man' so quickly. . . . In the last 6 or 7 weeks you have slammed Fentora."

It turned out to be a banner year for IPOs, the biggest since 2000, and health care in particular was a hot sector. Even in a bumper crop, Insys stood out. Everyone's piece of the company—from Kapoor's majority stake down to every sales rep's little slice—quadrupled in value.

But as the year went on and Insys's fortunes climbed higher, the company became fixated on a new worry, centered on Ruan and Couch's practice in Alabama. In the midst of a highly profitable partnership between the drugmaker and the Mobile doctors, an interloper had appeared.

Back in the spring, before the IPO, Mike Babich had crossed paths with executives of an upstart company called Galena Biopharma. They were the new faces at a regular meeting where the handful of TIRF manufacturers gathered in the course of jointly administering the TIRF REMS program, the FDA-mandated safety protocol for the product class. Galena had recently acquired the U.S. license to market the drug Abstral, a Subsys competitor. Abstral, a sublingual tablet, had previously sold poorly in America. It was one of "the peon products" that Subsys had swiftly conquered, as Babich put it—the minor players in the TIRF class that together accounted for less than 10 percent of the market. But Galena saw potential in Abstral and was hiring up a sales force to "relaunch" it later in the year.

Babich was clearly not too worried about Galena mounting a challenge. In a text message to Matt Napoletano, he wrote, "Galena is at the rems mtng, can't wait to buttfuck them too."

However, the Insys team began to pick up some sketchy but concerning intelligence about its new competitor. Galena was smaller than Insys, in both head count and market share, but the company was bringing on reps with more experience, at higher base salaries. This was enough to prompt some talk among Insys employees about the prospect of changing teams. Some of the gossip appeared on the Insys page of the online industry message board at cafepharma.com. Many people at the company monitored the site, from the rank and file to upper management, partly because Insys employees often posted there anonymously. Kapoor learned of the Galena chatter.

Galena had a pipeline of oncology products that looked promising, including a potential blockbuster—a vaccine to prevent the recurrence of cancer in certain breast cancer patients. The company attracted some hires who were looking to get in early at a company on an upward trajectory. Galena was publicly traded and garnering buzz in publications for niche investors, the kind of TIRF-world spotlight Insys had grown accustomed to having to itself. In the fall of 2013, when Galena was relaunching Abstral, its stock rose significantly.

Kapoor and Babich were mindful that where they had once been the underdog, dizzying growth had put them in a new position. Competitors such as Galena "are not aiming for Fentora or Actiq," Babich wrote to the sales force in a "state of the union" message that fall, "they are coming straight at us." He adopted a swaggering pose. The challengers, he wrote, "don't have a chance in Hell!!!" But as time went on, it became clear that the leaders at Insys were worried.

Almost immediately after Galena relaunched Abstral, Natalie Perhacs was notified by her superiors that Xiulu Ruan had given patients some scripts for the drug. She took the news seriously. "I was told Dr. Ruan had never written one," she wrote in an email to Joe Rowan. "I was wrong."

"Get him," Rowan replied.

It wasn't just Ruan. In pockets across the country, Galena was gaining traction, often with doctors Insys was paying handsomely. This did not go unnoticed. It was the kind of thing that enraged Kapoor. He saw it as an act of betrayal for a doctor to take Insys money with one hand and prescribe a competing product with the other. Burlakoff and his minions in sales were supposed to prevent it. The theme of one national sales meeting at Insys was "Protect Your TIRF."

Burlakoff sent out a distress call in November, noting in a message to Babich and others that Abstral "DOUBLED their script count in one week." He forwarded a list of the prescribers responsible.

Babich replied, "We need to refocus on stopping this asap." He added, "I thought we owned the high decile folks? Lot of big names on there." Number one on that list was Xiulu Ruan.

Insys was getting word that Galena was actually taking a hit on many of these early prescriptions, footing the bill through a generous patient-assistance program. Galena's successes, in other words, might have been bought at great cost.

Burlakoff pointed this out when Kapoor challenged him for answers to the Galena problem. But Kapoor told him, "Alec, you don't fucking get it." Every Abstral script represented a gain in market share that could have belonged to Subsys, and once patients tried Abstral, they might stick with it. That couldn't happen.

Insys began to stamp out Galena fires everywhere it could. But down in Alabama, the Abstral prescribing stubbornly persisted. The need to put a stop to the defection became an obsession up and down the Insys ranks.

Natalie Perhacs saw the Galena rep showing up at the Mobile clinic over and over, encroaching on her territory. His success represented a threat to her newly prodigious income, but the situation was even more dire than that. Natalie knew that everyone above her at Insys was watching what happened in Mobile. She felt her job was at stake. "Dr Ruan and Dr Couch are way down," Burlakoff warned her. "Can you assist please. . . . This was the topic of conversation today with Dr Kapoor and Mike."

Perhacs confessed her anxiety about the pressure from corporate to her new regional manager, Karen Hill, who had stepped into the role when Rowan moved up. "I do not know at this point what other angle to take," Perhacs said in an email. "I cannot stop Dr. Ruan from writing [Abstral] and I know they expect me to be able to."

The Galena threat was not as dire as executives made it out to be. The Mobile doctors were both still among the top ten Subsys prescribers in the nation in the last quarter of 2013, even with Abstral cutting in. Natalie Perhacs, a beginner sales rep in her mid-twenties, was single-handedly bringing in better than $100,000 per week in net sales for the company. But her bosses didn't like the look of the trend line.

The core problem was not that Subsys patients in Mobile were being switched to Abstral, though that did sometimes happen. The main concern was that when Ruan and Couch decided to put someone on a TIRF drug for the first time, more and more often it was Abstral that they were choosing. This was new business that Insys executives thought they deserved.

At the clinic, Couch and Ruan's nurses, who spent the most time with their patients, sometimes had trouble discerning why their bosses were prescribing Abstral versus Subsys in any given case. In fact, often the nurses didn't know why a TIRF drug was being added to a heavy regimen of opioids at all. After seeing a patient, the nurse would generally go to the doctor in his individual office, which sometimes required waiting in line behind other nurses, then summarize the situation, outlining a treatment plan. Frequently the proposal was just to continue with the same medications. But sometimes the doctor would reply that he wanted to add some new branded product to the mix. The same drug name would keep coming out of the doctor's mouth for a while; there always seemed to be a "flavor of the day," one nurse said. It might be Subsys, then suddenly Abstral, then Subsys again—sometimes all to treat the same person.

It was left to the nurses to explain these moves to patients, who were apt to get upset by a change to a regimen that had been working well. "I couldn't give them a good reason," the nurse-practitioner Bridgette Parker said.

There was a "big push" from Dr. Ruan to prescribe Subsys after he became an Insys speaker, one of his nurses said. That part at least made sense. With Abstral, it was a little more mysterious what was motivating Couch and Ruan, especially to Natalie Perhacs, who urgently wanted to know. Galena wasn't paying the doctors to participate in a speaker program, much to Ruan's annoyance. Ruan had told Galena employees that they ought to hire him to speak, framing it more as a demand than a request. He told one of them how much Insys was paying him, an undisguised implicit threat.

But a Galena manager, Dave Corin, replied that it wouldn't make sense to pay Ruan to speak, because Ruan and his partner were evidently the only people in the area interested in prescribing TIRF drugs. There was no one else for them to speak to.

The Insys team worked to gather intelligence about what was driving Ruan and Couch's newfound devotion to Abstral, but it was a tricky task. They couldn't just ask the competition about their tactics, obviously. But raising the subject directly with a doctor such as Ruan came with its own risks. On the one hand, part of the point of putting doctors on the speaker payroll, in Burlakoff's teaching, was to set up a dynamic where you could "hold them accountable" for doing their part—you could "own" them, as Babich said—and earn the right to brazenly challenge them: *What the hell are you doing with Abstral? We're paying you every week.*

But someone like Ruan was a different beast, because he knew his own power. If Insys questioned him, he was apt to exaggerate what Galena was doing for him in order to squeeze out better incentives: he would drive up the price of his own loyalty. Or, conversely, he might keep the specifics of his relationship with Galena under wraps, hoping to use the uncertainty to his advantage.

The Insys team found themselves in the fog of war. They came to believe any number of theories, many of them false. It took them some time to arrive at perhaps the most important detail: Ruan and Couch owned a piece of Galena.

Dr. Ruan felt he had missed a big opportunity to get in early as an Insys investor. Insys had become an instant hit on Wall Street, and he paid attention to news like that. He had hoped that Insys would offer him stock in the early days, seeing as he was an adviser, but it didn't happen. Now Galena seemed to represent a second chance for him. An article on the investing website Seeking Alpha touted Galena under the headline "Is Galena Following in the Footsteps of Insys with Abstral?" Dr. Ruan read it.

When Ruan told the Galena team that they should hire him as a speaker, he said he wanted to be compensated in stock. After being rebuffed, he looked into buying shares himself. Ruan knew that he and Couch were major players in the small niche of TIRF drugs, and he saw an opening. They could turn Galena into a winner virtually all by themselves. "This is the product we can play a big role," he told Couch in an email.

Galena's share price rose rapidly from November 2013 to the following January. During that period, Couch and Ruan purchased more than $1.3 million in Galena stock, individually and through their business. The nurse-practitioner Justin Palmer, who thought Abstral was better than Subsys and figured the doctors knew what they were doing, decided to buy a few shares himself.

The two doctors and Palmer began pushing Abstral to patients to help the company meet sales goals, and they thought they were going to profit handsomely off the stock, Palmer said. Ruan and Couch became an enormous proportion of Galena's business. They were eventually responsible for approximately 30 percent of the Abstral prescribed in the United States over an eighteen-month period.

Natalie Perhacs finally decided to ask Dr. Ruan directly why he was prescribing so much Abstral. In his fondness for Perhacs, Ruan was straight with her. He told her he had invested in Galena. Ruan swore her to secrecy, she said. But by late January 2014, her manager, Karen Hill, had learned the truth. Soon, Insys's top executives knew it too.

———

For Insys, Ruan and Couch's divided loyalty wasn't the only concern. There was also the matter of inventory. C&R was having trouble keeping Subsys in stock, even with some business being lost to Abstral. The pharmacy managers just couldn't keep up with the amount of Subsys the doctors were prescribing. C&R staff couldn't simply buy more Subsys, because their distributor was restricting their supply.

In the era of the opioid crisis, C&R was tripping alarms.

A medication typically travels along a three-step supply chain—from the drugmaker's shipper to a wholesale distributor and finally to retail pharmacies. With controlled substances, the entire chain is tightly regulated. Since the beginning of the opioid epidemic, drug distributors—including all of the "big three" of McKesson, Cardinal Health, and AmerisourceBergen—have paid hefty fines and settlements for failing to notify the Drug Enforcement Administration of "suspicious orders" of controlled substances from particular pharmacies, as required by law. Under mounting scrutiny, distributors have put in place monitoring systems in which controlled-substance orders from a given pharmacy that exceed a monthly threshold, or "cap," are put on hold and, barring some innocent explanation, reported to the DEA.

C&R was regularly hitting these thresholds with its distributor. As a pharmacy manager told the doctors, "We have prescriptions for more Subsys than Amerisource will sell us."

Galena was struggling with the same issue: C&R would run out of Abstral owing to thresholds, according to a former Galena senior sales executive. But the Insys team had a shaky grasp of where Galena stood. In December 2013, Natalie Perhacs, reporting from on the ground in Mobile, told her manager she had learned that Galena was shipping Abstral directly to C&R Pharmacy, cutting out the middleman—the distributor—and resolving the inventory problem. "They literally have unlimited supply," she wrote in an email. This wasn't true. Ruan and C&R did press Galena for a direct-ship arrangement, but the legal department at Galena nixed the idea.

Still, Perhacs's piece of mistaken intelligence rocketed up the chain of command at Insys, causing a commotion at the home office. When the message reached the top, Alec Burlakoff, of all people, was the voice of caution. He told Babich and others that if Insys were to counter Galena by shipping direct to C&R, it would be an act of self-sabotage. "This will destroy us," he wrote.

Burlakoff had been told repeatedly by the head of trade and distribution at Insys, Dion Reimer, never to offer direct shipment to a customer. Reimer was tremendously uncomfortable with the idea, Burlakoff said. "He didn't like the optics." With a Schedule II narcotic, it was just too dangerous to try to circumvent measures designed to combat an epidemic. Burlakoff knew that Ruan and Couch were interested in direct ship, but he respected Reimer's experience and opinion. He figured that the final word was no.

On February 13, 2014, John Kapoor and Mike Babich flew from Phoenix to Mobile. They had rooms booked for the night at the grand Battle House Renaissance Mobile downtown, the premiere hotel in the city, with a lobby featuring a domed skylight three stories high, inlaid with stained glass. The two men had traveled to Alabama to meet with Ruan and Couch for dinner that night.

Kapoor was the executive chairman of the board of a company traded on Nasdaq, a business mogul. Entrepreneurs were always trying to get some face time with him in the hopes that he would invest in their ventures, and Babich would have to fend them off. It was far out of the ordinary that Kapoor would fly to another city just to meet with two customers. He had sales reps, regional managers, and a head of sales he could have dispatched. He could also have sent Babich alone, his CEO.

But word had traveled up the hierarchy that Ruan and Couch wanted to meet with "the top people," Babich said. Ruan was keen to have Dr. Kapoor in particular come to town. Reps and managers wouldn't do anymore. Not even Ruan's friend Joe Rowan could fend off Galena. So Kapoor answered the call, a fateful decision. Before the meeting, Karen Hill told Perhacs, "Hopefully with a little help from above we can land this."

Insys had made reservations at the Ruth's Chris Steak House in town, a favorite of the doctors, and secured a private dining room inside. Rowan had helped line up the meeting and joined the group. The restaurant featured a dark interior, with leather banquettes, intricate wallpaper, framed paintings, and heavy curtains.

The doctors were direct, as usual. Ruan had already communicated to Insys that his pharmacy was looking to order Subsys direct to get around the problem of suspicious-order monitoring. Now he and Couch made clear that they had another motive. Through the pharmacy, the two were making more on Abstral than they were on Subsys, they said. The doctors had brought with them to dinner a man who helped manage the pharmacy, and he presented comparative data to illustrate the issue. If Insys wanted to win this battle with Galena, speaker programs weren't enough. Kapoor and Babich had to compete on price.

The Insys men raised the notion of direct shipment, according to Babich. (Burlakoff, who had said that going direct with C&R would "destroy us," was nowhere to be found at this dinner. The bosses went ahead without him.) Kapoor and Babich expanded on their proposal: By eliminating the middleman and shipping straight to Alabama, Insys would save the 8 or 9 percent cut that the distributor would normally take for itself. Kapoor and Babich's idea was to split that savings down the middle with C&R. Everyone at the table would make more money, and Amerisource wouldn't keep shutting off the tap because of the DEA.

It was an extraordinary offer. Kapoor and Babich were shouldering a major risk just to please two prescribers. Still, Couch and Ruan were unimpressed. They pushed harder, looking for better terms. In the end, Insys caved. By the time the deal was struck and put on paper, Kapoor and Babich had handed over the entire 8 or 9 percent. Insys wouldn't make any more money on a Subsys prescription than it had before. There was no plausible business reason for them to make the deal at that point. Except for one: to give the doctors an incentive to choose Subsys over Abstral. For Insys, that was good enough.

14   "LETS GET A FEW MORE"

In the middle of the battle for Couch and Ruan that winter, a new challenge had presented itself at the Insys headquarters. In December 2013, two months before the steak dinner in Mobile, the company had received a subpoena from the U.S. Department of Health and Human Services Office of Inspector General, demanding a broad range of documents related to the sales and marketing of Subsys.

Unbeknownst to the higher-ups, two new whistleblowers in the lower ranks had come forward and filed *qui tam* suits under seal against the company. Since government authorities had taken a pass on Ray Furchak's legal complaint, leaving him baffled and outraged, the company had gone public and quadrupled in value. Many more patients were now being exposed to Subsys, without knowing about the deals their doctors had struck with the manufacturer. This time, with the complaints adding up and Insys a growing force, investigators were taking a deeper look.

The first of the new whistleblowers to take action was Mia Guzman, the Florida sales rep who had joined the company with Tracy Krane in the earliest days. (Despite their ongoing friendship, Krane wouldn't learn that Guzman had blown the whistle for five more years. Guzman was forbidden from discussing it.)

By the time she filed suit, in August 2013, Guzman had been fired, like Krane before her. In Burlakoff's version of events, a whale in Guzman's South Florida territory told Babich on the phone that summer that he hadn't seen Guzman in months. Babich was out-raged at this lapse with a VIP customer. He stormed into Burlakoff's office and said that in the next hour, Alec had to fire either Guzman or her manager, Joe Rowan. Burlakoff wasn't going to fire his good friend Joe, so Guzman had to go. But Burlakoff didn't like the idea of it. Guzman was pregnant. It would look bad. And she wasn't the type who would just roll over. "I'm telling you, this girl is tough as nails," Burlakoff said. "She's going to frickin' destroy us."

When Guzman was told over the phone that she was being ter-minated, with Burlakoff and Rowan on the call, she said, "Are you sure you want to do this?"

Just weeks later, she filed her whistleblower suit.

Guzman had grown disgusted by not only the marketing tac-tics but the atmosphere of sexual exploitation at the company. Her complaint quoted X-rated remarks that Burlakoff had made about a female doctor in a text message thread with her and Rowan.

Guzman had been quietly collecting evidence for months. Back at the national sales meeting at the Arizona Grand Resort the previ-ous spring, in one of the "casitas" where managers were housed, Guz-man was surreptitiously recording with her iPhone when Joe Rowan and Karen Hill led a kind of off-the-record coaching session in the dark arts of pharmaceutical sales. There was no smoking-gun remark about the speaker program, but there were plenty of dubious tips on cozying up to doctors, grounded in Rowan's and Hill's long careers in the industry trenches. Rowan repeatedly warned that you had to be careful with what you put in writing in this business because there might be consequences: "Talk about scary, man, to have an attorney come—a U.S. Attorney—come to your door. It's not real cool."

A U.S. Attorney's Office would end up listening to those words, over and over.

When the subpoena arrived at Insys, the board of directors held an emergency meeting. They still had no in-house counsel, but they received advice at the meeting from an outside lawyer with industry experience, Leslie Zacks, whom they had on retainer. Zacks advised

Kapoor, Babich, and the rest of the board on how to cooperate with the government investigation in a way that would placate prosecutors and minimize sanctions. This would be an expensive and protracted endeavor—it would go on for years—but it was "critical" to be proactive and root out wrongdoing at Insys, Zacks indicated, according to his notes for the meeting.

The typical next step for a drug company in this situation is to engage a law firm for an internal investigation. Before federal agents present you with a damning email, you want to demonstrate that you're already on top of it and be able to tell them, for instance, that the person responsible has already been fired. The firm's attorneys often lead a series of meetings with the government, not the other way around, and they bring PowerPoints and artful spin along with them. These lawyers, often from the same handful of elite firms, investigate employees on the one hand and serve as the company's advocate on the other, a dual role that's part internal-affairs cop and part defense counsel. Insys followed the industry playbook and made the move, quickly hiring one of the world's preeminent law firms, Skadden, Arps, Slate, Meagher & Flom, to conduct an internal probe.

For Insys employees, mostly inexperienced, it was hard to know what to make of the subpoena. There was no question it was ominous, but how ominous?

Announcing it in an internal memo, Babich warned everyone that they might be approached by federal agents, even at home. He told them that because a "document hold" was now in place, they shouldn't destroy any digital or paper files. That didn't sound good.

Matt Napoletano said "there was a lot of anxiety," including his own. Napoletano knew that Insys was out of bounds, and he had seen a government investigation unfold at Cephalon. According to Burlakoff, Napoletano would advise him to "slow down" what he was doing. "I've seen this movie before," he said.

But Napoletano was the anxious type. Burlakoff didn't see the subpoena as such a big deal. He wasn't usually included in top-level legal discussions, such as the emergency board meeting with Zacks, and he wasn't feeling pressure from Kapoor to rein it in, he later said. He often feared for his job, but not for overstepping; he was afraid he might be fired because sales weren't good enough. Burlakoff was annoyed that because of the subpoena he wasn't allowed to delete voice mails, so his mailbox filled up. He wasn't worried about the FBI digging through his phone. He considered himself "under the auspices of Dr. Kapoor," who could use his vast wealth and Subsys profits to navigate out of trouble.

As Burlakoff saw it, could anyone name a successful pharmaceutical company that *hadn't* been investigated? It was part of the business. That message propagated out to managers and reps, and not just from the head of sales: *The company is taking care of this. Focus on doing your job.*

A subpoena like the one Insys received, if it leads anywhere, usually leads to a financial settlement, years down the road. The drugmaker ends up paying millions—occasionally billions, with a blockbuster drug—to "resolve" the allegations, with or without admitting guilt, and perhaps submits to new restrictions. Because no trial takes place, the underlying evidence never gets a full airing. When the settlement is announced, a spate of media coverage mars the company's reputation. But it might be a one- or two-day news story. Investors are typically unsurprised by the settlement—they've been aware of the investigation through public filings—and to them it registers as good news for the company: the costly ordeal is over, the dark cloud lifted. It's not uncommon to find that just as the Justice Department is announcing its success in holding the industry accountable, the accused company's share price actually rises.

Insys disclosed the subpoena in a press release on December 12, within days of receiving it; being a public company required some transparency. The stock fell precipitously, from approximately $15 to $11. Within about a month, however, the share price had recovered completely. A few weeks later, it was approaching $20, a record high. The rebound didn't go unnoticed among the company's close associates. When Dr. Ruan was talking up the Galena stock to others, posing it as the next Insys, he noted that the Insys subpoena hadn't put a dent in its market value.

On December 27, Mike Babich was interviewed on CNBC. The network was spotlighting the best-performing initial public offering in the country for 2013: a little-known pharmaceutical company called Insys Therapeutics. Babich wasn't a natural on TV—his demeanor was wooden and seemed rehearsed—but still, this was great press. The CNBC interviewer made no mention of the government investigation that had just been announced two weeks earlier. Instead, he said, "Tell us what it is that has investors so excited."

A few months later, Babich would exercise options and cash out over $21 million of Insys stock in a single day. The boy from the South Side of Chicago, it appeared, would never again have to worry about money.

At the emergency board meeting, Leslie Zacks had discussed the fact that at his urging the company had commissioned an outside firm earlier in 2013 to audit the Insys speaker program "to ensure [it was] not a kickbacks program," according to his notes. (Napoletano was said to have pushed for this move.) The audit was still ongoing, but it had turned up some serious problems, Zacks reported. According to a prosecutor and Zacks's notes, Zacks told Kapoor and the board that it would be best to put a stop to the speaker program at least until the audit was completed. But the speaker program was the keystone of Insys's sales strategy. The recommendation was not approved.

In the weeks following the subpoena, the Insys brass was consumed not with their defense but with devising a strategy to win back Ruan and Couch from the clutches of Galena. When Kapoor and Babich traveled to Mobile to strike their deal with the two doctors in February 2014, they were fully aware that their company was under investigation by the U.S. government.

A few months later, a young Insys rep based in Michigan, Brett Szymanski, drove to the outskirts of the city of Saginaw, as he had countless times before. He was bound for the clinic of Dr. Gavin Awerbuch. Szymanski was another pharma rookie hired before the Subsys launch after seeing an online job ad. But owing almost entirely to Awerbuch's prescribing, Szymanski had become an Insys superstar, the number one rep in the country, a fixture at company-sponsored President's Club trips. He sometimes collected bonus checks in the six figures, for a single quarter.

As he approached Awerbuch's clinic, Szymanski saw a fleet of law-enforcement vehicles parked outside. Szymanski turned the car right around and got out of there.

It was May 6, 2014. After executing a search warrant and secretly recording office visits, federal investigators in Michigan had arrested Awerbuch, accusing him of illegal drug distribution for prescribing Subsys "for no legitimate medical purpose."

When the news broke, the Insys stock took an immediate hit. Inside a week, it lost around a third of its value. *The New York Times* published an article about Insys that mentioned Awerbuch's arrest and drew on anonymous company sources to probe Insys sales practices. "Doubts Raised About Off-Label Use of Subsys, a Strong Painkiller," the online headline read.

Insys's reputation and market value had weathered the subpoena, but this new crisis had a darker cast. A doctor was the target, not Insys, which would seem to make the threat more remote. But Awerbuch was facing possible prison time in direct connection with Subsys. The criminal complaint, a public record dissected in media reports, also made it clear that Insys leadership could not plausibly claim that Awerbuch was some obscure physician they'd never heard of. He was far and away the number one Subsys prescriber in the nation to Medicare patients, writing more than six times as many scripts for them as his next closest competitor (Dr. Ruan in Alabama). Awerbuch alone accounted for over 20 percent of Medicare's spending on Subsys through February 2014.

The public-relations problem was serious enough, but to many inside Insys the situation was even more dire. They knew that when it came to the company's relationship to Awerbuch, the public didn't know the half of it.

Insys had been courting and grooming the doctor for more than two years. Szymanski had turned him into a Subsys prescriber early on, and the company had brought him to the first speaker-training event in Chicago in the summer of 2012. His numbers had taken off after Burlakoff was promoted and hired Sunrise Lee to oversee the Midwest. About two weeks after becoming VP, Burlakoff had traveled to Michigan and taken Awerbuch out to dinner, joined by Szymanski. Burlakoff was following through on the "plan of attack" he had pitched to Babich and Kapoor, getting out in the field and personally connecting with top targets. Over dinner, after developing a rapport through personal chatter, Burlakoff had what he called The Conversation with Awerbuch: Insys was willing to give him regular speaker programs, Burlakoff said, but he needed more "experience" with Subsys. The more Subsys he wrote, the more often he would get paid to speak.

Some people would be more delicate and euphemistic in framing this kind of proposal; that way, everyone could pretend they weren't engaging in naked corruption. But Burlakoff believed you have to summon the chutzpah to be direct and risk burning the relationship. He wanted doctors to be "crystal clear" about the expectations so that Insys could then "hold their feet to the fire."

Awerbuch thought the suggestion that he needed more clinical experience to be a speaker was ridiculous; he had been prescribing TIRF drugs for many years and already had a number of patients taking Subsys. But Awerbuch didn't say any of that. He agreed.

The following day, Burlakoff sent an email about Awerbuch to colleagues: "Expect a nice 'bump' fellas." The bump materialized immediately.

Lee helped cultivate Awerbuch as a customer in the years that followed. She developed a bond with Awerbuch's wife, whom she met in Arizona, at Roka Akor, when the doctor's wife accompanied him to an Insys speaker-training event. She invited Lee out onto the family's pontoon boat, on the lake by the Awerbuch property in West Bloomfield. Burlakoff visited the house for a barbecue. Lee thought the Awerbuchs were a good family, and that Dr. Awerbuch cared for his patients. The doctor would praise her to Burlakoff, saying she "lit up a room."

When Awerbuch started producing big numbers, Lee told Brett

Szymanski to keep scheduling programs for Awerbuch, as many as three a week if possible: "I need him to be as busy as he wants to be." The programs started out legitimate, but they became a farce. Sometimes it was just Awerbuch and Szymanski having dinner and ordering meals to go for their wives so that the receipt would make it look like a dinner for four. Szymanski wrote made-up names on the sign-in sheets.

Awerbuch was prescribing so much Subsys that the assistants in his clinic were having trouble keeping up with the prior-authorization paperwork that the Insys Reimbursement Center needed from them, on top of their other responsibilities. It was becoming a full-time job for a woman in his office named Kourtney Nagy, which Awerbuch found frustrating. Insys executives came up with a solution. They had recently created a position called area business liaison, or ABL, on the recommendation of Rich Simon, who had heard of the practice at other drug companies. When top reps and high prescribers couldn't handle the volume of administrative work, ABLs would fill the gap. Insys would hire Nagy as an ABL. That would relieve Awerbuch of the need to pay her. It would also make her a company operative inside the clinic, helping ensure that Subsys scripts were well taken care of. "Mike Babich described this hire as 'strategic,'" Burlakoff wrote to HR. Nagy became an Insys employee.

As the relationship with Insys deepened and the speaking fees accumulated, Awerbuch's medical decisions became ever more corrupted. He already knew that federal agents had their eyes on him, but he thought of the Insys team as friends he couldn't let down, not with all they were doing for him. He had to find patients he could put on Subsys.

One patient, a middle-aged woman suffering from depression, was taking a raft of medications, but she said they weren't helping her with her chronic pain. Awerbuch tried Subsys on her. He could justify it on the grounds that other treatments had failed her. But Awerbuch ordered a mental-health battery that showed she had somatization disorder, a condition in which patients complain about physical pain that is really psychological in nature. "It was basically telling me that her pain was in her head," Awerbuch recalled. He took her off some pain medications but not others. He kept her on Subsys so that he wouldn't lose favor with Insys.

The patient's life was spiraling out of control, she said later. Her marriage was coming apart. She drove under the influence of Subsys. She totaled her car. "I was so out of it," she said. "I didn't know what was going on." At her daughter's baby shower, surrounded by family, she kept passing out. "Life with me was unbearable," she said.

In September 2013, Burlakoff directed his top managers to use their "god given talent" to "find the next Dr. Awerbuch." He added, "It's the Dr. Awerbuchs of the world that keep us in business, lets get a few more."

When Awerbuch was arrested, Insys executives scrambled to protect themselves. In a "clarifying statement," the company said, "Insys does not sell directly to physicians. Insys only sells Subsys through DEA approved wholesalers who monitor and track prescribing activity."

In the wake of the subpoena, a small compliance team at Insys was now working with Skadden attorneys on the internal investigation, and they went to the Insys Reimbursement Center to pull Awerbuch files for review after he was charged. One IRC staffer, Patty Nixon, began having panic attacks and vomiting before work, she later told *The Wall Street Journal*. She had processed many of the opt-in forms that poured in from Awerbuch's office. Almost none of his Subsys patients had cancer. Nixon routinely misled and lied to insurers to get them to pay for the drug.

In the wake of the Awerbuch news, Sue Beisler, the New Jersey rep who had been involved with Kapoor, wrote to a friend, "Yup. Fucked." When the friend tried to assuage her concerns by saying that the arrest was bad for the doctor but not for Insys, Beisler replied, "The thing is they bribed the shit out of that guy to write."

Awerbuch and his wife tried to contact Sunrise Lee following the arrest, but the compliance team had instructed her to cut off all communications with the doctor. She felt that Awerbuch was being targeted unfairly, that the charges were "B.S.," and she didn't like that Insys seemed to be abandoning him.

The company wasn't distancing itself completely, however. When the Awerbuch news broke, Alec Burlakoff and Rich Simon already had a trip to Michigan planned; they were supposed to arrive within a week. Even after the arrest, Burlakoff asked Brett Szymanski to set up a meeting with Awerbuch. Burlakoff knew it was a dicey idea to meet with a man who had just been accused of illegally prescribing Insys's opioid product, so he ran it by the company's new general counsel, Franc Del Fosse, he said. In the end, Burlakoff, Simon, and Szymanski went ahead with the meeting.

The three men from Insys met Awerbuch at a casual diner in metro Detroit, in the afternoon. According to Burlakoff, they were there to comfort him and hear him out. "We were friends," he said. "We had a relationship. We wanted to let him know that it wasn't just about business and see if we could offer any support."

They were also trying to make sure the doctor kept his mouth shut, as Paul Baumrind saw it. Baumrind, a special agent at the FBI, was the case agent on a criminal investigation of Insys, which was being run out of the U.S. Attorney's Office for the District of Massachusetts, in Boston. He was one of the agents who had questioned Awerbuch in downtown Detroit on the day of his arrest, when Awerbuch immediately agreed to cooperate. The agent was taken aback when Awerbuch told him, a few days later, that Burlakoff was headed to town and wanted to meet with the doctor. Within hours, Baumrind coordinated with agents at the FBI Detroit office: they were going to wire up Awerbuch. Baumrind coached the doctor, in a hurry, on what to say.

At the diner, Burlakoff noticed that Awerbuch wasn't interested in pleasantries. The doctor steered the conversation directly into uncomfortable territory. Burlakoff recalled him saying, "Listen, I'm in trouble because I wrote a lot of Subsys because you guys were paying me to speak."

Burlakoff suspected a trap, and he played dumb: "Dr. Awerbuch, it's really unfortunate to hear you talk that way," he recalled saying. "My understanding is that you wrote Subsys because you thought it was the best possible medication for your patients at the time."

Awerbuch continued to press, saying he didn't have any money, his assets were frozen, and he couldn't see patients. He kept asking things like "What are you guys going to do for me?" and "Can you get me a lawyer?" Burlakoff tried to fend off the alarming questions, looking to mollify the doctor without committing himself or Insys to anything compromising.

For their part, Rich Simon and Brett Szymanski said very little. At one point, Awerbuch pointed at Burlakoff and said to them, "Why is *he* doing all the talking?"

Awerbuch was not an ideal covert operative. Baumrind had "war-gamed" the meeting with him, but Awerbuch got off track. He showed his nerves, spoke too much. And he was none too subtle.

When the three men from Insys left the meeting and got in their car together, the atmosphere was tense. Szymanski knew Awerbuch best out of the three of them and remarked that he was acting really strange. Szymanski said he thought the doctor was recording them.

Burlakoff felt sick. He thought he was going to throw up and asked Brett to pull over. He'd had the same instinct, he said later—that Awerbuch was wired up. From the car, Burlakoff called Mike Babich. As Szymanski remembered it, Alec said on the phone, "We may have been recorded, but we didn't say anything bad, and I bought him lunch, but I paid for it in cash."

To some inside Insys, the fall of Awerbuch, coming on the heels of the subpoena, felt like a watershed moment, the beginning of the end. It seemed like only a matter of time until everything unraveled.

The leadership team, however, stayed the course. Kapoor's primary concern about Awerbuch's arrest, according to Babich and Burlakoff, was the loss of business. Awerbuch was their top guy. Babich said he and Kapoor reviewed the criminal complaint together, which gave evidence that Awerbuch had been writing Subsys for completely inappropriate people, including undercover officers who were posing as obvious drug seekers with mild pain.

Kapoor took the news in stride, Babich and Burlakoff said. He wanted to know where all of Awerbuch's Subsys patients were going to go, and to have reps call on those offices to make sure the doctors kept them on the medication. After the meal with Awerbuch, Burlakoff had also called Kapoor, he said, and assured him he was "in the war zone," doing everything he could to hold on to Awerbuch's patients, including meeting with the doctor who planned to take over his practice.

Rather than fire Brett Szymanski for running sham programs with Awerbuch, Insys promoted him to management. Burlakoff pushed for the move, arguing that Szymanski was persona non grata as a rep in local doctors' offices in Michigan, so it was better to get him out of the field, into a less visible role. Kapoor approved the promotion, Babich said.

Kapoor had hired a general counsel and a compliance director, Danielle Davis, and he was authorizing huge expenditures for Skadden's internal investigation. To some degree, he was taking corrective action in response to a government probe, and compliance did improve in certain respects. The tried-and-failed cheat sheets came down from the cubicle walls in the IRC. However, when Davis, working in conjunction with Skadden, presented Kapoor and the rest of the board with extensive evidence of wrongdoing at the company, at a meeting in August 2014, it is not clear what he did about it.

Davis was in her early thirties and had never worked in the pharmaceutical industry; she had worked in compliance in the casino business. She knew people at Insys before getting the job and was hired after coming along on a company outing to a golf tournament and meeting Mike Babich. Davis was able to enact some changes at Insys, but she was a mid-level employee and she was essentially "powerless," according to Babich. Davis "became afraid to bring up certain issues," as Babich saw it, because she knew that "there were certain employees that were untouchable," including Szymanski and Natalie Perhacs.

In a text message to Mike Babich shortly after the Awerbuch

episode, Rich Simon complained, "We are becoming a company that is scared to go for the kill in my opinion with all of these compliance sissies." He offered himself as a "scapegoat" if consequences were coming. Babich assured him that "no changes r contemplated," adding, "If we can maintain 45 mill a quarter or so, we will all be heroes again!"

Burlakoff was openly combative with Davis and others who tried to rein him in. He complained loudly that compliance discussions were a hindrance and a waste of his time and boasted that he had the support of Babich and Kapoor.

The previous fall, a horrifying event had rocked Burlakoff's family. His brother shot his wife dead on the street in Boca Raton, Florida, and then drew fatal gunfire from arriving police, evidently on purpose. Some at Insys thought that Alec's conduct became more erratic thereafter. He was traumatized and coping with the fallout in his personal life, but he felt that at work he behaved just the same.

Danielle Davis believed that Mike Gurry, Elizabeth Gurrieri, and Burlakoff should all be terminated. None of them were at the time. In fact, Burlakoff was forever threatening to resign—agitating for more money and complaining about changes that threatened sales—but the bosses kept reeling him back in. He even submitted his resignation in November 2014, but Babich wouldn't accept it. ("He knew he couldn't do what I did," Burlakoff said.)

After the subpoena, the IRC kept finding clever ways to mislead insurers, and the speaker program continued to be a kickback vehicle. The speaker budget wasn't cut; it was quadrupled, to a level far out of line with the company's peers. Mia Guzman had been told in the early days to stay away from the Florida doctor who held a stake in a strip club next to his clinic. In fall 2014, the same doctor was invited to an Insys speaker-training event in San Diego, and the company began paying him to speak.

Sales staff were being told by senior management on conference calls that the company was cooperating with the government investigation. For many, the inference was that whatever they were now being instructed to do was legal. *What company would keep committing crimes while under subpoena?*

———

Matt Napoletano was not handling the legal scrutiny so calmly as the others at the top. To those around him, he appeared to be coming apart at the seams, torn up about his role at Insys and intensely worried about what would become of him and the company. On the one hand, he was locked in a "power play" with Burlakoff, as Babich saw it; Napoletano wanted the credit and money he felt he deserved for his part in the company's success. On the other hand, he tried to distance himself from everything Insys had done wrong to achieve that success. He posed himself as the good guy countering Burlakoff—and to a certain degree, he was—but he resisted acknowledging that that wasn't the whole truth.

Napoletano was haunted by the fact that he had agreed to draw up the return-on-investment report, the one that had laid out the kickback scheme on paper. According to Babich, Napoletano was "out of control" in the office, scaring people around him with his anxiety about where things were headed. People saw him holed up in his office at the computer, staying late, and wondered what he was up to. Burlakoff thought maybe he was "covering his tracks." One day, Napoletano was heard raging in his office: "We're all going to go to jail."

According to Napoletano, when he aired his compliance concerns to Danielle Davis, Babich quickly found out and challenged him, saying "we're still a team" and telling him that he and Burlakoff needed to work together and "get on the same page."

"Look," Napoletano replied, "if he was even remotely in bounds, I could get on the same page, but he's not."

"Then you don't want to be here, do you?" Babich said.

Mike Babich and Kapoor decided it was time for Napoletano to go. For Babich, the remark about everyone going to jail was the last straw. The company was in trouble, sure, but there was still a job to be done, and Napoletano was unwilling or unable to do it. He was asked for his resignation.

In the battle between Matt and Alec, Alec had won.

———

Inwardly the company was in turmoil, but outwardly Kapoor, Babich, and Burlakoff were being rewarded for forging onward. By the time Napoletano left, prescriptions for Subsys had recovered from the pronounced dip that followed Awerbuch's arrest. Market share had never been higher, at nearly 40 percent, eclipsing not only Fentora in total scripts but even the generic alternatives, which were much cheaper and thus easier to get covered by insurance. Insys was increasing the price of Subsys significantly each year, and revenue was on the rise. The stock was on its way back up too. By the end of September 2014, the share price was back to pre-Awerbuch levels.

John Kapoor hadn't sold any of his or his family's holdings, so his Insys money was all paper wealth. But the shares under his control were worth around $1 billion by the end of the year. Alec Burlakoff was exercising his options at every available opportunity, eventually reaping more than $5 million on top of his salary. At one point, he walked into a dealership, pointed at a Porsche worth some $110,000, and said, "I want this car." It was a gift for his wife. The dealer snapped to attention, happy to help, but explained it would take some time to get the model he wanted delivered. "No," Alec said, "I want *this* car." He paid for it in cash, and the Burlakoffs took it home that day.

If Burlakoff thought there wasn't a great deal to worry about, he wasn't alone. A December 2014 report from Jefferies LLC, a firm that evaluates Wall Street investments, extensively discussed the Awerbuch arrest and the bad press surrounding Insys's financial relationships with doctors. Drugmakers' payments to physicians were now public knowledge, owing to a newly implemented provision of the Affordable Care Act referred to as the Sunshine Act. A front-page *New York Times* article had just used the new data to establish that many of Insys's twenty most highly paid doctors in late 2013 also happened to be its top prescribers, and that five of them had faced legal or disciplinary trouble. The company's attempts to distance itself from Awerbuch were now complicated by the revelation that Insys had been sending him a steady flow of checks right up until he was arrested.

But Jefferies surveyed some twenty-two high prescribers of TIRF drugs, the week after the damaging *Times* story, and found the results encouraging for Insys. None of the clinicians had any intention of reducing their Subsys scripts in the next six months, and ten of them planned to prescribe more of the product, despite being fully aware of the recent media coverage.

"What *New York Times* article?" Burlakoff wrote, buoying his sales force. "You can't stop this company!"

The Jefferies report also noted that Insys had received a second federal subpoena, from the U.S. Attorney's Office in Boston, publicly signaling a potential criminal investigation of the company, not just a civil one. However, the report concluded, based on past experience, "we're pretty sure that the worst outcome for Insys is some sort of fine."

Concluding with a measured optimism, Jefferies rated Insys a "buy." As it turned out, over the next half year, the investor community was even more enthusiastic. From a split-adjusted share price of about $20 when the report was published, the Insys stock would climb to a high of $46 in the summer of 2015, giving the company a market cap of more than $3 billion.

On May 8, 2015, federal and local authorities in Alabama conducted a so-called trash pull outside the home of Dr. John Patrick Couch, with the help of sanitation workers. Garbage left in bins at the curb is deemed abandoned property and can be searched without a warrant. The investigators found discarded letters documenting two recent payments to Couch for speaking on behalf of Insys Therapeutics. They also recovered two Subsys spray canisters and packaging for the medication. Couch did not have a prescription for Subsys.

Within two weeks, law-enforcement agents descended on the clinic and residences of Dr. Couch and Dr. Xiulu Ruan. The two doctors were arrested on federal conspiracy charges, following a lengthy investigation. With their practice out of commission, the street price of opioid pills in Mobile shot up, according to one user.

Since John Kapoor and Mike Babich had met with the doctors over dinner the year before, the battle between Insys and Galena for Ruan and Couch's loyalty had continued. Insys got lucky when it emerged that Galena and its then CEO, Mark Ahn, had apparently engaged in a pump-and-dump scheme; Galena secretly paid agencies to write and publish bullish articles on investor websites to boost the Galena stock, according to a Securities and Exchange Commission order, before Ahn and other insiders reaped millions of dollars unloading their own shares. The sell-off and revelations tanked the stock, enraging one of its major investors: Dr. Ruan. His and Couch's prescribing of Galena's drug soon plummeted. Ruan demanded that Galena replace Ahn as CEO, a request that the company took seriously given that he was a top customer. (Ahn was out five months later, with no severance pay.) Galena won back some business after the company struck a performance-based rebate agreement with C&R Pharmacy. The deal amounted to an illegal kickback to Couch and Ruan, prosecutors later alleged.

When the doctors eventually went to trial, facing a litany of charges, Christopher Bodnar and Deborah Griffin of the U.S. Attorney's Office for the Southern District of Alabama prosecuted the case. One late night at the office reviewing the evidence and putting together a timeline for the trial, Bodnar had a eureka moment. A few weeks after Gavin Awerbuch was arrested in Michigan, Galena's top sales executive had given Ruan a heads-up by email, making sure he knew that it was Insys, not Galena, that was implicated in the Awerbuch case. Attached to the message was a photograph of the one page of the Awerbuch criminal complaint most likely to catch Ruan's attention: the chart of the top ten Subsys prescribers to Medicare patients. Although names were redacted, Ruan and Couch were easily identifiable, and both were in the top five. Galena's message to Ruan, in other words: *Be careful with Subsys. The feds are paying attention.*

What Bodnar noticed, late that night, was that Ruan began redirecting his Insys speaker fees to charitable giving the very next day. Sensing trouble, Ruan "ran away from that money as fast as he could," Bodnar later said in court. Nevertheless, Insys kept paying Ruan and Couch for speaker programs, and the two kept signing scripts for Subsys.

At the doctors' trial, Tamisan Witherspoon, a forty-two-year-old woman, stepped up to the witness stand in a courtroom three stories high, a couple of blocks from the hotel where Kapoor and Babich had stayed in downtown Mobile. She had approached the government at the last minute, volunteering to testify. When Witherspoon first went to PPSA, for back pain stemming from a botched hernia surgery, she was the wife of a minister, active in the church and in the schools, where her children were all strong students. She lived in a neighborhood of plush lawns, wrought-iron gates, and attractive homes set back from the street. She had never had a sip of alcohol, let alone tried any illicit drugs, she said. She didn't follow the news and had never heard the term "pill mill," had no conception that pain medications might be something to approach carefully.

Witherspoon was already taking an opioid prescribed by her previous doctor, without difficulties, but she still had pain. At her initial visit to PPSA, she was given a 600-microgram prescription for Subsys, six times the recommended starting dose.

In an interview years later, she recounted what happened next. "From the first day I took it," she said, "I wanted it all the time."

At first Subsys was a wonder drug, relieving her pain and giving her a euphoric energy to do all the chores she had been putting off. Then she became its slave, taking more than she should. She would ask her children to hide the Subsys from her and then scream at them to tell her where it was and start tearing up their bedrooms. Her husband took away her car keys because she was passing out at stoplights. Her daughter would carry her to bed at night, unable to rouse her. Her marriage headed toward a final collapse. She moved out eventually, to a bleak apartment complex.

Testifying against the doctors in court, Witherspoon described a powerful moment of reckoning, in her final appointment at PPSA. In November 2014, she waited in the exam room at Ruan and Couch's clinic until the nurse Bridgette Parker came in to see her. Immediately Witherspoon could see that something was off. Parker was incoherent, Witherspoon said. She was "babbling" and "going in and out." The nurse slumped her head against the desk for several minutes. Witherspoon recognized the state that Parker was in, because she had been there herself, she said, from taking Subsys.

Witherspoon tilted her head toward the ceiling and began to pray. Looking at Parker, the woman who was supposed to be helping her, she felt she was looking in the mirror, and she was ashamed of what she saw. Before a hushed courtroom, Witherspoon recalled, "I started to cry, because I realized that she was in trouble and so was I."

Couch and Ruan's arrests were another gut check for Insys insiders. While the initial charges didn't implicate Insys, it seemed apparent that the company's extensive ties to the two men would be uncovered. Alec Burlakoff was on vacation in California with his wife when he read the news, and the color drained from his face. But when he called Mike Babich, according to Burlakoff, the CEO said, "Alec, grow up. Stay in your lane." Neither investors nor prescribers were turning on Insys, and Babich was sticking to the line that troubles like these were commonplace in the industry. Burlakoff wasn't so sure anymore.

This kind of dispute was playing out throughout the ranks, because the company was in a bizarre position that was difficult to read. In the first half of 2015, Insys was both climbing to new heights and threatening to collapse—at the same time.

The company appeared to be accumulating a war chest that would allow it to push other promising drugs through the pipeline to FDA approval, including several based on a spray-delivery platform. Subsys sales reached a peak that year, with net revenue of $329.5 million, up from just $8.6 million in 2012, the year Subsys launched—a phenomenal trajectory. Under Burlakoff's reign, a sales engine that had produced around $1 million per month was now generating that amount on a daily basis. Perhaps more extraordinary, net revenue from Subsys had more than tripled since 2013, the year Insys announced it was under federal investigation.

According to the market-intelligence firm Evaluate Pharma, the 2015 numbers put Subsys in the top five of all opioid products in sales. Insys had fought its way into the big leagues. Employees who had taken the risk of coming to a startup and banking on stock options were reaping a payoff. Kapoor's stake, at the peak, was worth more than $2 billion.

Meanwhile, witnesses from around the country were being subpoenaed to come to the ninth floor of the John Joseph Moakley United States Courthouse in Boston to appear before a federal grand jury investigating the inner workings of Insys. The witnesses included top prescribers as well as former and even current employees. Grand jury proceedings are shrouded in secrecy, but witnesses are generally not legally bound to keep silent, and word was leaking out about who was being summoned and what was being said.

In Arizona, company defense attorneys were all over the office, and federal investigators were contacting former staff, igniting gossip and worry within. Employees looked over their shoulders and tried to go about their business. Dr. Paul Madison was still being paid to speak for Insys. Elizabeth Gurrieri was still supervising the IRC. "Do you think I should delete this?" Gurrieri wrote to a fellow manager in the unit, attaching internal documents from years past, including one that spelled out "the spiel."

"OMG DELETE!" her co-worker responded.

Some investors had been smelling trouble for some time and were selling the stock short, betting on a big decline. One of them had tipped off the independent financial journalist Roddy Boyd, who specializes in exposing corporate fraud, hoping to interest him in publishing an article that would drive down the Insys share price. Boyd has a devil-may-care confrontational approach and dug in eagerly and deeply. In April 2015, he produced the first in a series of hard-hitting reports. *The New York Times* had already shined a light on the company's payments to questionable doctors and potential off-label promotion, but Boyd was the first to delve inside the Insys halls and name names. He interviewed Burlakoff and Sunrise Lee, and revealed that Lee had worked as an exotic dancer. He also unearthed some details, in later installments, concerning the curious origins of Insys's phenomenal insurance-approval rate.

Boyd's first article jolted the Insys stock. But sales were still climbing, and again investors shook off the hit and drove up the company's market value.

A new legal blow soon landed, however. Across state lines from the Boston investigation, in the District of Connecticut, a forty-two-year-old advanced practice registered nurse, Heather Alfonso, pled guilty in June 2015 to violating the Anti-Kickback Statute by accepting $83,000 from Insys for sham speaking events in exchange for writing more Subsys. Alfonso had only recently started working in pain management and prescribing controlled substances when Insys came along. Whereas Couch and Ruan were already bringing in millions of dollars, Alfonso's salary was about $80,000. She had five children, and her significant other didn't work full-time.

Insys sometimes targeted "mid-level" clinicians such as nurse-practitioners and physician assistants—who are less commonly hired as pharma speakers than doctors—recognizing that speaking fees would make a more meaningful impact on their income. According to Babich, Matt Napoletano knew about Alfonso's family finances and had zeroed in on her as a potential speaker. Alfonso later acknowledged that she was driven by greed, but she added that she "had come to rely on that extra money" from the company "and needed it to live."

Alfonso was the first prescriber accused of a crime in connection with the Insys speaker program. With Gavin Awerbuch, the charges involved only his prescribing; the money that Insys was paying him didn't enter into the case, which gave Insys a little bit of wiggle room to distance itself. With Alfonso, the wiggle room was virtually nil. A kickback takes two.

Her prosecution was a relatively uncommon event in the industry. Even when the government accuses a drugmaker of paying kickbacks to health-care providers, the person on the receiving end rarely faces legal action. In a *New York Times* article about the Alfonso guilty plea, legal experts speculated that prosecutors might well have a bigger goal in mind; perhaps they were looking to flip Alfonso—to gain her cooperation in the investigation into Insys.

As if that weren't worrying enough for the Insys executive suite, the Alfonso case carried a special significance. It would be very difficult for Insys to pose the Alfonso bribes as the work of a distant sales rep gone rogue. One of the reps who had arranged Alfonso's bogus speaker programs was Mike Babich's wife.

Babich had met Natalie Levine after she came to Insys headquarters to be trained back in the spring of 2013, when she first got the job as a rep based out of Boston. She had a more impressive résumé than the average Insys hire. Levine was a graduate of the University of New Hampshire, with a master's degree in counseling psychology from Boston College and experience as a social worker in a psychiatric hospital, on a locked ward. She was a striking woman, twenty-nine years old, with a winning self-deprecating manner and an empathetic way about her. It was easy to imagine her connecting with people in crisis. She and Babich started dating "formally" in December 2013, he said, when she was still a rep at Insys.

"I really was terrible at the job," Natalie Levine said of her early days. "I sucked." She almost never even made it past the front desk at a clinic, no matter how much she smiled, no matter how much food she brought for the staff. Meanwhile, a rep for a territory next door to hers was an all-star. (It likely helped that one of his top prescribers was his father.) At the national sales meeting the month after Levine was hired, her eyes widened when her colleague was presented with a giant bonus check onstage. It wasn't just the amount but the physical check itself that was giant—the kind that Publishers Clearing House gives out to the surprise sweepstakes winner.

In the summer, Levine finally had a breakthrough with a physician's assistant named Christopher Clough, at a pain clinic in New Hampshire. Levine was in the exam room when Clough wrote his first script for Subsys, to a man in his early thirties who was ill with cystic fibrosis and didn't have long to live. Clough had inherited the patient from a doctor in the practice who had started him on Subsys a few weeks before. Levine asked the staff to let her into the exam room before Clough entered, because she knew the patient was coming in for his next appointment. For some reason, they allowed it.

Levine asked Clough almost immediately whether he'd want to be an Insys speaker, and he leaped at the chance. She was thrilled to get her first real bite on the end of the fishing line. Clough texted Levine right away to ask her out to dinner. He was nearing forty, a decade older than Levine. He was friendly but peculiar, patients said, almost childlike, with a poor sense of what was appropriate to a given situation. He talked about his personal life with his patients. "They all knew my mom was dying," he said later.

One woman, Melissa Perusse, accompanied her husband to an appointment to express her grave concern that the Subsys he was taking was too much for him—he was addicted, she felt—and to ask Clough about reducing or stopping it. According to the couple,

Clough joked that the man was being "a baby" by bringing his wife in. (Clough said he did not recall this.)

Clough was going through a divorce with a woman who worked in the same practice, which was fodder for gossip around the office. Natalie Levine would hear him out about his problems. She fit the role of the love interest in a romantic comedy, the one who is sweet and goofy and approachable for the awkward male protagonist—and just happens to be dazzlingly pretty. The two went out for dinner or ice cream and he would pay, he said. He bought tickets to a World Series game at Fenway Park and brought her along with him and his relatives.

Many of Clough's speaker programs were nothing but dinners for two with Levine. The other names on the sign-in sheets were forgeries. Who forged the signatures is disputed, but Levine said she always insisted that Clough do it, partly because if she was going to do something she knew was wrong, "I needed someone else to have skin in the game, too." When Levine's manager at Insys accompanied her on a ride-along to Clough's office, he stayed in the car, because he didn't want to be a "male threat" to Clough, Levine acknowledged.

Clough wrote approximately 84 percent of the Subsys prescribed in New Hampshire between 2013 and 2014. Of his roughly 400 patients, he tried writing Subsys for at least 138 of them. Only a handful had cancer. A medical expert later reviewed seven of Clough's patient files and concluded that he did not manage the patients "with any pharmacological or other skill whatsoever."

"Christopher Clough was infatuated with Natalie Levine," said Jessica Crane, who assisted Levine at Insys as an area business liaison. "And the majority of time it was Natalie kind of using that relationship against him to manipulate him." Crane had been hired because Levine was swamped with paperwork. Prescriptions were pouring in from Clough and from two other frequent speakers in her territory. One of those other speakers was Heather Alfonso, soon to be convicted of a felony.

In a photograph from a purported speaker program in May 2014, Levine and Alfonso can be seen posing together with others, smiling broadly, at the Empire restaurant in Boston. The restaurant is located a block and a half from the U.S. Attorney's Office, where an investigation of Insys was already under way.

Natalie Levine left Insys in the fall of 2014, having earned over $400,000 in commissions. She didn't tell Christopher Clough that she was engaged to Babich. Clough texted her four or five times after she quit. She never replied.

"I knew the speaker program was unethical, and it's something that I wasn't raised to do," Levine said later, explaining why she resigned. "I just didn't want to be part of that anymore." Another reason she left the job, she said, was to move to Arizona to be with Babich. They soon married, and she took his name.

Much later, in court, Natalie Babich was on the witness stand facing hostile questioning about this sequence of events. You were "uncomfortable with what was going on with Insys," an attorney asked her, so you left and then moved in with the CEO? Wasn't he "in charge of everything that was going on in the company"?

Natalie paused for a moment, casting her eyes to the side, before answering carefully. "He was the CEO, yes."

In the months after Heather Alfonso pled guilty, Mike Babich sensed a chill in the air at Insys headquarters. Skadden, the law firm Insys had engaged, was probing the Alfonso matter internally, but Babich was kept out of those discussions. The company was besieged with litigation, facing a mounting pile of document demands after settling an investigation by the State of Oregon into its marketing practices. One settlement with a government entity portended more. Patients or their families had begun to sue. Sales were as good as they had ever been, but the Insys stock finally began to fall.

In the late summer of 2015, instead of getting phone calls from John Kapoor six or seven times a day, Babich was hearing from his boss only occasionally. Babich began to realize that he wasn't being invited to meetings that he knew were taking place. It wasn't difficult to figure out. Some of these meetings were held in a conference room right outside Babich's office, and others took place in an office immediately next to his. He could hear Kapoor's voice through the wall.

At Insys, Babich had always been the guy everyone turned to when they needed to read or anticipate Dr. Kapoor. Nobody else in the office had seen him operate for so long. Babich had been by his side since he was in his twenties, more than a decade earlier, back in Lake Forest, Illinois. He could read the cues.

In early November 2015, Babich got a call from Dr. Kapoor inviting him to have a drink at his Scottsdale restaurant, Roka Akor. "I knew it was D-Day in my world," Babich recalled.

Babich was at Roka first, and he saw how uncomfortable Kapoor was when he walked in and joined him. At the restaurant where Babich had first met Burlakoff, where Insys had regularly hosted doctors, where the two men at the top had met countless times, Kapoor came around to the point.

According to Babich, Kapoor told him, "Every company goes through its struggles, and when things like that happen, there's always a fall guy. You're going to be the fall guy."

As scrutiny mounted and Insys began to crumble, Alec Burlakoff was harboring his own worries about where he stood. In 2015, his relationship with the company was deteriorating, though he didn't fully understand why. The previous fall, when compliance wanted to see him fired, he had been given a bigger title and more responsibility instead. But he told Babich he wanted a new contract to come with his new role, and after being promised he would get it, he said, he was strung along for months and finally told that it wasn't going to happen.

Burlakoff left the company in a fury in the summer of 2015, just as Babich was being gradually frozen out. Burlakoff was infuriated still further when Insys cut ties with him entirely in December, terminating an agreement that was still providing him income and benefits, in a letter citing an unexplained "material breach." By this time, Insys was in deep legal trouble, and Burlakoff figured he was being sacrificed. "They made a decision they were going to fuck me," Burlakoff said later.

As Burlakoff had anticipated, the case against Dr. Couch and Dr. Ruan soon brought repercussions for Insys. When investigators combed through medical charts, email accounts, and financial records connected with the Mobile clinic, the words "Subsys" and "Insys" kept coming up. The trail led to the front door of Natalie Perhacs, the Insys rep hired at Ruan's personal request. In February 2016, Perhacs pled guilty to conspiring to violate federal kickback laws.

She was the first Insys employee convicted of committing a crime at the company, but it was hard to believe, for anyone familiar with the facts, that she would be the last. Perhacs had been brought onstage the year before to give a speech at a national sales meeting and hailed as a success story. Burlakoff knew as well as anyone that Perhacs had only done what she was told. She was a pawn on the Insys chessboard. From Perhacs, the logical path for investigators was up the chain of command.

Burlakoff was filled with fear and rage at the way things were pointing. He had been advised by an outside lawyer connected with Insys that he needed a criminal attorney, which terrified him. He and Babich were now out at the company, as were numerous people Burlakoff had hired, including Sunrise Lee.

Meanwhile, John Kapoor was still running Insys. After firing Babich, Kapoor had taken over the job of CEO himself.

Burlakoff suspected a setup. People close to him worried about what he would do about it. He was a person of dramatic emotional weather, raised in a volatile family. As his relationship with Insys and Kapoor deteriorated, he spoke darkly of feeling that he was being targeted in some way. Lee said that in 2015, Alec showed her a gun he was keeping in the glove compartment of his car. "Nothing he said" that day "was making any sense," she recalled. Burlakoff said later that he was threatened by Dr. Kapoor, that he feared for his safety.

True to his Mob-inflected code of conduct, Burlakoff verbally lashed out at people he felt were turning on him. He sent threatening text messages to a New Jersey sales rep, Michelle Breitenbach, and Insys paid for personal security for her, according to a lawsuit she filed.

"Fuck you bitch," Burlakoff wrote in a text message to Karen Hill, accusing her of disloyalty and lies. "Hope you die. You are in fact done! Done!!!!!" He continued, "Die Karen. You betrayed me!"

In the spring of 2016, Alec spent a month brooding alone in a rented house on a lake in Connecticut. Burlakoff had chosen the spot because it was near his old summer camp, which he viewed as a lost childhood idyll. "I am facing where my EGO took me," he wrote in his journal. He wanted to put Insys behind him, but on some level he knew that was impossible. Lawyers and journalists were contacting him. What he had done was not just going to go away.

Burlakoff couldn't stand sitting back and waiting for the investigation to close in on him. He decided to make a bold move. He would go to the government and talk. The problem, he said, was that his criminal attorney was opposed to the idea. So Burlakoff fired him and went ahead with the plan, without a lawyer.

To arrange the meeting, he called the Massachusetts attorney general's office and left a message. This was a mistake; he had contacted the state instead of the feds. That's how little understanding he had of the forces he was up against. Federal authorities in Boston had been zeroing in on him for two and a half years. Paul Baumrind and another lead agent, Scott Wisnaskas of HHS–OIG, had stood within arm's length of him, on surveillance. But Burlakoff still had never met any of the investigators nor learned their names.

When Burlakoff's message got through to the U.S. Attorney's Office in Boston, in May 2016, it caused a major stir. K. Nathaniel "Nat" Yeager was the prosecutor who coordinated the government's response. At the time, Yeager was the head of the office's vaunted health-care fraud unit. He had been working on the Insys case for years. Yeager was in his late forties, tall with silver hair and a long face. He wore rimless glasses and an expression of near-permanent skepticism. Yeager hadn't made an early-career stop at an elite law firm defending corporations. From the beginning, he had played offense, prosecuting crime at the state and then federal level. The phrase "prosecutorial zeal" seemed made for him.

With news of Burlakoff's approach, Baumrind got to a phone and called Burlakoff, who said he could be in Boston the next day. Baumrind, the same FBI agent who had prepped Dr. Awerbuch to wear a wire, scrambled to gather the Insys team, numbering six or seven people at the time. They needed to prepare for a situation unlike any they had ever seen. A target of a major investigation was voluntarily coming to them—without an attorney.

When Baumrind met Burlakoff in the lobby of his Hilton hotel near Boston's Logan International Airport to pick him up, the FBI agent told him gently that he needed to pat him down and suggested they go to the restroom for privacy. As Baumrind searched him for weapons, Burlakoff was near tears.

It was late afternoon on the Friday of Memorial Day weekend by the time the interview began. Agents had to call home and cancel plans. Yeager wanted a limited number of people to be in the room, a fishbowl-style conference room. With a wall of glass providing a view in from the rest of the office, a wider group of agents positioned themselves at nearby desks, pretending to work on other things, so they could listen and see Burlakoff live.

Burlakoff sat at the head of the table, with Baumrind to his right and Yeager and Wisnaskas to his left. The FBI agent advised Burlakoff of his rights, making clear that he could leave at any time, and then turned things over to Yeager. The prosecutor had been wringing his hands over the legal delicacy of the situation. Yeager had decided to record the meeting and be completely upfront. As soon as he introduced himself, he immediately told Burlakoff that his office was investigating not only Insys Therapeutics as a company but "a number of individuals, including yourself." Burlakoff said that he wasn't aware that he was personally under investigation. He kept talking anyway.

Alec knew he was a born storyteller, with a gift for maneuvering and manipulating and shaping the narrative. He had information to offer, and he thought he could use that leverage to talk his way out of trouble. The idea was to take the pressure off himself and redirect it to the top of the chain of command. Burlakoff thought Kapoor was throwing him "to the wolves" to save himself, and he seemed to be getting away with it; Kapoor was still running the company years into a federal investigation. Burlakoff saw this meeting as a chance to turn the tables. "I know it's unhealthy," he had written in his journal the month before, "but I'm still wanting justice/revenge."

Burlakoff made no secret, in the interview, of his "resentment" and "hatred" for Dr. Kapoor, saying that "it's going to be written all over my face," so he might as well acknowledge it. But he also framed what he had to say as a truth that the government needed to know.

Burlakoff was getting the impression that Kapoor was "just going to walk away," he told Yeager, and "to me, that's just—that's not justice, that's not justice at all."

For nearly five hours, Burlakoff spun a tale in which there was plenty of misconduct at Insys but he himself did nothing illegal. He implicated Kapoor and Babich but kept himself out of the picture. With great emphasis, he told the story of Kapoor and Babich overriding his objections in order to strike "a corrupt deal" in Mobile with Couch and Ruan. Instead of the slippery half acknowledgment Yeager was accustomed to hearing in white-collar cases—*looking back now, I can see how I showed poor judgment*—Burlakoff outright denied doing anything wrong.

Yeager put a piece of paper in front of him. The document showed that Insys paid Judson Somerville—the Texas doctor Rich Simon had helped cultivate—$124,000 in speaker fees in 2013. Insys had an annual cap of $100,000 in place, but when Somerville was nearing the cap, Burlakoff won a battle in the office to bump up the limit to $125,000. In December of that same year, the state medical board ordered Somerville to stop prescribing painkillers, determining that his practice of medicine constituted a "continuing threat to the public welfare." Three of his patients had died of drug overdoses in 2012, within days of receiving prescriptions from him.

"So you're telling me," Yeager said to Burlakoff, "that he didn't write because you guys were paying him?"

Burlakoff paused for several seconds. "He—"

"Wait, I want you to think about it," Yeager said.

"I am. I know. I'm—"

"Stop, wait, wait, stop for a second—"

"I don't want to put on an act, though," Burlakoff said, "and I don't want to think. I want to *talk*."

Somerville didn't prescribe for the money, Burlakoff told Yeager. He wrote the medication because of how Insys made him feel. For him, it was "the coddling and the attention and the opportunity," Burlakoff said. Somerville was paraplegic, following a bicycle accident. His Insys rep arranged for an accessible van that accommodated his wheelchair to bring him around town, according to Burlakoff.

"These doctors . . . need to feel a little something about themselves," he said. "They need to feel like they're doing good." Speaking for Insys changed things for Dr. Somerville, Burlakoff said. "He was on stage. He was in a wheelchair, but he was on stage. He was the *man*. And I came in and flew in to see him, and Babich came in, and everybody came in, and that, again, that makes me a cheesy salesman, but that doesn't make me a criminal."

Nat Yeager was not won over by this story. Burlakoff had charisma; Yeager had evidence.

The prosecutor presented Burlakoff with emails and texts he had sent and received, messages he didn't even remember. And Yeager wasn't showing him his best material. Yeager's emotions aren't difficult to read, especially when he's frustrated or angry. Confronted with unethical conduct, he doesn't wear his outrage lightly. If Burlakoff was hoping to woo his audience with his amoral charms, he came to the wrong room.

At a meeting the previous year, Skadden attorneys representing Insys had given an elaborate presentation to the government regarding their efforts, handing Yeager a list of Insys employees who had been terminated. They were looking to please him, assuring him that the bad apples had been thrown out. Yeager immediately remarked that Burlakoff wasn't on the list.

"Why? What do you think of Burlakoff?" a defense attorney asked him.

"What do I *think*? I think he committed crimes—that's what I think," Yeager said. "That's why we're here."

Now in a room with Burlakoff for the first time, Yeager told him, "I think all you're doing is, quite frankly, continuing to lie to federal agents."

"I never lied in my life," Burlakoff said.

Eventually, Yeager had seen enough. He called an end to the interview. Virtually nothing that Burlakoff had said had any value to the investigation because it was so tainted by his dishonesty.

Burlakoff knew that the most important sales pitch of his life had failed. While Baumrind was driving him back to the hotel, he told Burlakoff, "Don't even talk to me." It was a solemn ride. Burlakoff went up to his room and called his wife.

"It's fucking over. It's *over*," he told her. "It's going down. It's all going to fall apart."

Seven months later, just after 6:00 on the morning of December 8, 2016, Mike Babich heard banging at the door of the house he shared with his wife, Natalie, in Scottsdale, Arizona. He had been up until 4:00 a.m. with their newborn baby, their second child, who had just come home from the hospital. It took Mike Babich, a heavy sleeper, some time to wake up and look out the window. He saw more than a dozen federal agents with their weapons drawn, yelling, "Open the door!"

"My wife held my 10-day-old son, imploring them to put their guns down, that she's holding a 10-day-old baby," Babich said. "The next thing I remember is I was outside handcuffed, outside of my home." Paul Baumrind was there. He advised Babich of his rights and took him into custody.

The team of agents on the Insys case, from ten agencies, had fanned out across the country in the preceding days, working with local authorities in preparation for a timed arrest across three time zones. They didn't want to give anyone a chance to flee.

Sunrise Lee had seen her kids off to school and gone back to bed. She was out of work and sleeping a lot at the time. Insys had fired her the year before. After she roused herself to answer the incessant knocking at the door, she saw two agents. Suddenly several more appeared, coming from both sides. Her first thought was embarrassment about the neighbors. She was a mom with a nice house in the suburbs.

Mike Gurry, the executive who formerly oversaw the IRC, happened to travel to Illinois from his Arizona home a day or two before the planned arrest, forcing agents to switch gears. He was taken into custody at a Chicago hotel.

Investigators knew that Rich Simon was out of the country,

in Costa Rica. They started the process of extraditing him, but he turned himself in.

Joe Rowan lived at the water's edge on a bay in Panama City, Florida. He was still working at Insys. He thought he'd survived the company's purge of employees who were caught up in the investigation and was poised to rise in the ranks. Some agents closed in on him by land and others by sea, on a police boat.

Several people came to the door of Alec Burlakoff's house in the high-visibility vests that utility workers wear. He was living in Charlotte, North Carolina, at the time. They told Burlakoff and his wife they were from the cable company and needed to dig a trench on their property. Burlakoff told them it wasn't a good time; he was worried the feds would show up at any moment. He had just heard about other arrests by text message. The workers were insistent and asked him to come around and meet them in the backyard, where one of them showed a badge: "FBI. You're under arrest." More agents poured into the house.

The Department of Justice had charged six top executives and managers of an opioid manufacturer, accusing them of leading a nationwide conspiracy of bribery and fraud. This was an unprecedented event. The news that felony charges had reached all the way to the executive suite of a publicly traded drugmaker jolted the pharmaceutical industry. It was one thing for the DOJ to force a company to cough up shareholder money and face sanctions. This was something else.

Among those closest to the story, however, the conversation turned immediately to who had *not* been arrested. Mike Babich had been the chief executive for almost the entire alleged conspiracy, but insiders knew the title was misleading. While Babich had been seized at gunpoint in Scottsdale, no one had come to the door of John Kapoor's house just a few miles away. The founder and current CEO, who still controlled a majority stake in Insys, had gone untouched.

It was just what Alec Burlakoff had feared. In his worldview, wealth meant influence, and influence always carried the day. If you had enough of it, there wasn't any trouble you couldn't muscle your way through.

Kapoor had allegedly told Babich, "You're going to be the fall guy." That is exactly what seemed to be happening. Prosecutors had nearly reached the top and stopped one rung short.

Less than two months before the arrests, *Forbes* magazine had published a rare interview with Kapoor. It was a special issue dedicated to the so-called Forbes 400, "The Richest People in America." Kapoor was less wealthy than he had been when the Insys market value peaked, but *Forbes* still had his net worth pegged at $2.1 billion. The print edition had five "covers" spread across its opening pages, one of them showing Donald Trump and another featuring Kapoor.

The *Forbes* reporters, Matthew Herper and Michela Tindera, didn't write a flattering profile of a conquering business titan. The article opened by recounting the death of an off-label Subsys patient, a thirty-two-year-old New Jersey woman named Sarah Fuller whose autopsy showed a toxic level of fentanyl in her blood. Her family's attorney, Richard Hollawell, helped push her story into the limelight, in his relentless and vocal crusade against Kapoor and the company. *Forbes* recounted Kapoor's history of regulatory difficulties and focused on the growing body of litigation surrounding Insys.

Kapoor distanced himself, in the interview, from everything that had gone wrong at the company. "My involvement is I am an investor," he told *Forbes*. "As an investor I'm on a board. As a board member and an investor you are involved, but you are not involved in day-to-day operations, and that's where the problems come in."

Any number of people who worked at Insys headquarters, or even attended a national sales meeting, could tell you that this was a disingenuous remark. Babich and Burlakoff had been on a conference call with Dr. Kapoor nearly every morning at 8:30, often combing over prescriptions from the previous day. For his colleagues, the idea that Kapoor wasn't a part of day-to-day operations at Insys was galling.

Now, with Kapoor surviving the wave of arrests, the government seemed to be buying it. One quotation from the *Forbes* story, featured on the cover, looked prescient. "In my career," Kapoor said, "my plan has always been: I am the last guy standing."

Foes of Insys grew increasingly cynical as time went on, resigned to the idea that Kapoor would walk. Former employees recalled that he rarely sent emails and almost never sent text messages. Well into the smartphone era, he still carried a clamshell-style cell phone, making texting difficult. Maybe there just wasn't enough of a digital trail to prove a case against Kapoor. Or perhaps, as Burlakoff thought, he was just too powerful a person for the government to go after.

Then, at dawn one day in October 2017, ten months after the arrest of the six executives, several SUVs entered a gated community in Phoenix and drove up a mountainside road. They ascended nearly to the top, to a house with a circular swimming pool, surrounded by undeveloped desert peaks. Federal agents climbed out of their vehicles at about 7:00 a.m. and knocked loudly on the door. No one answered, so they showed a badge to a security attendant in a small booth outside the residence. He gave them a key to the front door. They entered with their guns drawn and split up to search the house.

Paul Baumrind went to the right and up the stairs, where he confronted John Kapoor midway, on a landing. Kapoor was wearing headphones, and he was dressed in workout clothes reminiscent of another era, with short shorts and long socks pulled up. He looked shocked to see a man inside his house wearing an FBI jacket and carrying a gun.

According to Baumrind, Kapoor said, "I thought this had gone away."

In recent decades, it has become increasingly uncommon for the United States to bring criminal charges against top corporate executives, and even more uncommon for the government to win a conviction. In the pharmaceutical industry specifically, it's especially rare.

On the one hand, major drug companies have been credibly accused of committing crimes on a consistent basis for thirty years, and they have regularly admitted to doing it. According to a 2018 research report by the consumer advocacy group Public Citizen, drugmakers pled guilty to federal crimes at least forty-eight times from 1991 to 2017. If you include civil settlements that involved no admission of wrongdoing, the numbers become much larger still. Pfizer, GlaxoSmithKline, Novartis, Bristol Myers Squibb, Teva, Merck, Johnson & Johnson, AstraZeneca—these marquee names all paid to settle Justice Department investigations between 1991 and 2017. In fact, they did so at least six times *each*. Repeat offenders are the norm.

Meanwhile, however, the individuals who have overseen the illegal conduct in the industry have rarely been held to account. In the rare instances when executives have been singled out and successfully prosecuted, they have typically faced financial penalties and, at most, home confinement and community service. Public Citizen's researchers were able to identify only a single executive in the industry, Marc

Hermelin of KV Pharmaceutical, who had been sentenced to jail time. He served fifteen days.

In the Insys case, prosecutors were acting in accordance with the so-called Yates memo, a 2015 public memorandum to Justice Department attorneys written by Sally Q. Yates, then the deputy attorney general. In the wake of widespread outrage over the failure to jail top bankers implicated in the global financial crisis, Yates announced in the memorandum a policy of prioritizing individual accountability in white-collar crime. "Corporations can only commit crimes through flesh-and-blood people," Yates said at the time.

The Boston U.S. Attorney's Office was already headed in that direction, in multiple investigations. With Insys, prosecutors there went a few steps further. Among other charges, the defendants stood accused of racketeering conspiracy under the Racketeer Influenced and Corrupt Organizations Act, or RICO. The law, enacted as part of the Organized Crime Control Act of 1970, is more commonly invoked against Mafia families and violent gangs. The government argued in court that Kapoor and the other defendants had turned Insys Therapeutics into "a criminal enterprise from top to bottom."

The RICO Act is a potent tool for prosecutors that can bring lengthy sentences. The Insys defendants were facing the prospect of years in prison, not fifteen days. The maximum sentence for each of the seven defendants on the RICO count was twenty years.

By pursuing top executives and pressing weighty charges, federal prosecutors in Boston were also opening up a new front in the government's efforts to combat the opioid epidemic. Insys was by no means a major player in the opioid crisis in numerical terms, as defense attorneys for the executives would often point out. Prescriptions for Subsys represented a tiny fraction of the overall prescription-opioid business. Insys's medication didn't exist when the epidemic began, and it was too specialized and expensive, too subject to gatekeeping by insurers, to be doled out millions of times and flood the streets the way that OxyContin had. The defense posed the prosecution as a political move, an attempt to make a splashy statement about pharma's role in the epidemic when in fact Insys had not materially contributed to the public health crisis.

In an important sense, this criticism was accurate. Justice Department officials of course believed that the Insys defendants had committed crimes, but to judge only from decades of corporate guilty pleas, lots of drug executives oversee criminal activity and are never arrested. Prosecutors were looking to set a new precedent and send a signal to the industry.

The health-care fraud unit in Boston knew as well as anyone that Insys's tactics were of a piece with those of the opioid business as a whole. Insys executives didn't write the playbook of painkiller marketing. They adapted it and pushed it to extremes, straying further outside the lines, heedless of image management.

As Burlakoff said, nothing that Insys did was truly new. Its leadership didn't invent targeting decile 10 opioid prescribers and pushing higher doses. They weren't the first to promote off label, nor to insert themselves into insurance decisions and fudge the facts to get to yes. And they didn't come up with using speaker programs as a pretext to set up a quid pro quo.

Had the U.S. Attorney's Office in Massachusetts settled for prosecuting Insys as a company, the investigation would have proceeded largely outside public view and ended in a plea bargain conducted in secret. In a brief hearing, lawyers for the company—and not the Insys executives themselves—would have stood up in court and pled guilty to an "information," a dry document outlining the charges, and accepted significant financial penalties, stricter monitoring, and a deferred prosecution agreement, a form of corporate probation. Given the severity of the conduct, the company would have agreed to divest Subsys to a third party, but Insys wouldn't have been barred from doing business with government programs. In a press release, federal officials would have hailed the victory and announced that the settlement "sends a strong message to pharmaceutical manufacturers" selling opioids. It would have produced a blip in the news.

We know this because the Justice Department did, in fact, pursue Insys as a company, in parallel with the case against its former executives. And all of that is exactly what happened.

Had that been the end of it, there would be good reason to doubt whether the "strong message" would be heeded. As the journalist

Barry Meier pointed out, if the DOJ sent a strong message in its case against Purdue Pharma in 2007, why did drug distributors—beginning that same year—send enough pain pills to West Virginia over a five-year period to supply every man, woman, and child with 433 of them? Why did Purdue itself keep committing crimes for another eleven years, by its own admission? If the Justice Department sent a strong message in its prosecution of Cephalon for off-label promotion, resolved in 2008, why was the founder and CEO awarded $14.5 million in compensation that year, and why were the company's financials so attractive three years later that it was acquired for $6.8 billion, by the industry giant Teva Pharmaceuticals?

Indeed, if the Cephalon case was a forceful deterrent, why did the Insys story happen at all? A major element of the Insys sales strategy was to simply import the old Cephalon playbook. The leadership recruited Cephalon alumni to make it work: Matt Napoletano, Alec Burlakoff, Joe Rowan, Karen Hill, along with several key managers and reps beneath them, had all worked for the direct competitor. According to Burlakoff, more effort was made at Cephalon to check the boxes and create "the optics" of legitimacy, but "we were bribing doctors through the speaker program at Cephalon."

Back in 2011, when Kapoor and Babich had interviewed Napoletano for a job, they naturally asked him about his experience at Cephalon. Over the decade that Babich had known his boss, Kapoor had expressed a liking for Frank Baldino Jr., Cephalon's charismatic founder and longtime chairman and chief executive. The two Insys men would discuss Baldino and his company, their future competitor, when they periodically visited industry conventions. (People were always surprised that Kapoor, worth hundreds of millions, would deign to walk the floor of a trade show, learning about little start-ups and hearing their pitches, but that was his way.) Like Kapoor, Baldino was a science type, an entrepreneurial tinkerer, who started his company from nothing and never gave up control.

According to Babich, during the interview with Napoletano, Kapoor wanted to talk about Baldino, who had died at fifty-seven the previous year, and how he had built Cephalon. Kapoor viewed the company as a success story despite its regulatory and legal troubles.

At one point, however, Kapoor asked Napoletano, "Well, what about the fine?"—the $425 million settlement that Cephalon had paid. As Babich recalled it, Napoletano replied by describing Baldino's reaction: "He smiled, he wrote the check, and they moved on, and they kept doing what they were doing. . . . It's a fine; everybody pays fines."

The top men at Insys had good reason to believe, when they came under investigation, that one day the company would probably write a check and then their careers would go on. An FBI special agent on the case, Vivian Barrios, described their outlook: "Likely what's going to happen is the company will get a slap on the wrist and I'll walk." If they were looking at the precedents, she said, "they weren't wrong, right?" If the financial penalty was likely to be severe—worse than a mere slap—all the more reason to push for profit in the meantime so that Insys could afford it.

"No one thought that they would be arrested," Paul Baumrind said.

The fact that Kapoor and the others now faced criminal charges profoundly altered the dynamics. Insys Therapeutics and its new leadership would have liked to put the whole fiasco in the past, to keep a lid on the unsavory details through a negotiated settlement. But Insys could only settle a case brought against Insys, as a corporation. When it came to Kapoor and the other former executives, Insys had no say in the matter. The defendants were individuals, and they were facing a far worse prospect than paying out shareholder money. Their freedom was at stake. John Kapoor couldn't use money to end the ordeal. Either he would have to plead guilty to a felony, which would almost certainly mean prison time, or he could fight the charges, exposing himself, and the whole drug industry, to the public reckoning of a trial.

True to form, Kapoor chose to fight. And so, for the first time, the justice system pried open a window onto the way potent and addictive painkillers have been marketed and sold in the midst of an epidemic.

To truly send a message this time, the U.S. Attorney's Office in Boston would of course need to win. That would be more difficult than it might appear to a distant observer. Given Insys's casual approach to operational security in emails, text messages, and internal documents, the details outlined by the government appeared to paint a damning picture. But in hearings during the run-up to trial, the judge, Allison D. Burroughs, expressed deep skepticism about the indictment, calling it "a crazy way to charge a case." She suggested that prosecutors consider streamlining the case to avoid a dismissal. The government subsequently asked the grand jury for a new indictment that boiled the charges down to a single count of racketeering conspiracy. Everything now hinged on proving one charge. There would be no partial victory or partial defeat.

Proving a RICO conspiracy can be complicated. Prosecutors must show that the defendants agreed to commit specified offenses—the RICO "predicates"—through "a pattern of racketeering activity." It is the agreement itself that is the crime, rather than any resulting illegal acts. In the absence of a written contract laying out a criminal scheme, an agreement is an abstract concept, subject to interpretation by jurors. Showing that there was endemic fraud and corruption at Insys wouldn't be enough to convict; the government needed to demonstrate that these individuals conspired with one another in particular ways. It isn't easy to penetrate a corporate hierarchy and prove criminal intent on the part of specific people, especially at the top. There, executives are somewhat insulated from the nitty-gritty, and they tend to be represented by the best defense counsel money can buy.

The health-care fraud unit in the U.S. Attorney's Office in Boston is highly regarded and tries an outsize share of the major cases nationwide in that arena. The Insys criminal case could have been tried in any number of federal districts, but Boston had the resources and expertise.

In the years leading up to the Insys case, however, the Boston office suffered some significant defeats in health-care cases, particularly when trying individuals. In 2012, an off-label marketing case against a company called Stryker Biotech and several of its executives all but fell apart in the middle of the trial; while the company pled to a misdemeanor, the government dismissed charges against the accused employees. Shortly after the release of the Yates memo in 2015, the Boston office caught the attention of the industry when it brought criminal charges against W. Carl Reichel, the former president of Warner Chilcott's pharmaceuticals division, in a case that resembled the Insys prosecution; Reichel was accused of conspiring to pay kickbacks to doctors through a sham speaker program. The company had pled guilty to substantially the same conduct and Reichel's internal emails appeared incriminating, but his 2016 trial ended in an acquittal. Observers speculated that the verdict might have hinged on the judge's instructions to the jury. The judge had indicated that a defendant cannot be convicted of bribery under the Anti-Kickback Statute "merely because he sought to create a business relationship or create a reservoir of goodwill that might ultimately affect" the decisions of the person receiving payments. This was a worrying precedent for the Insys prosecution.

As the Boston trial approached, numerous other Insys-related prosecutions unfolded nationwide. The Insys story became a sprawling scandal, drawing widespread media coverage and spinning off a galaxy of criminal and civil litigation.

In addition to numerous medical-board disciplinary actions against doctors, more than a dozen practitioners were charged with crimes in connection with Subsys, a stunning number. At least nine other former Insys employees around the country were also prosecuted, in addition to the seven indicted together in Boston. The general pattern was that an investigation of an Insys whale would lead to charges against not only the initial target but also the Insys sales rep and perhaps a manager involved in funneling speaker money to the whale. Most of these cases were brought by U.S. Attorney's Offices in other jurisdictions, not in the District of Massachusetts, and there was less coordination among the districts than there could have been. But the overall effect was an investigation reminiscent of a takedown of a Mafia family or a drug-trafficking operation: it proceeded from the bottom of the pyramid to the top—from the doctors and reps out in the field to middle management and toward the executive suite—

and along the way the authorities squeezed people for information about those above them.

The Boston office gained a major edge when some employees and prescribers pled guilty to felonies and agreed to cooperate in hopes of leniency. Prosecutors collected a range of insiders who were now legally obligated and motivated to talk. These included Gavin Awerbuch in Michigan; Heather Alfonso, the Connecticut nurse-practitioner; Natalie Perhacs, the Alabama sales rep; Karen Hill, the sales manager; and Elizabeth Gurrieri, who had reported directly to the defendant Mike Gurry when she managed the Insys Reimbursement Center.

However, one of the problems the Boston team faced in their efforts to convict the men at the very top—Kapoor, Babich, and Burlakoff—was that in bringing charges against almost the entire senior management team, they left themselves a limited pool of knowledgeable insiders to draw on as witnesses. Prosecutors can't just present a case to the jury with a PowerPoint presentation; they need people on the inside to tell the jury what happened. And a lowly sales rep out in the field, for instance, wouldn't have the access necessary to implicate Kapoor.

One name stood out as a possibility: Matt Napoletano. He had escaped being charged, likely saved by the documented fact that he repeatedly objected to the worst excesses at Insys. But Napoletano would make for a problematic star witness for a number of reasons. Perhaps foremost among them, he tended to deflect blame rather than own his role in misconduct. He could be granted immunity—he would have to be, because otherwise he was sure to invoke the Fifth Amendment—but even if he admitted to his involvement, "he did everything in his power to justify that what he was doing was legitimate," Baumrind said. That human tendency, common as it is, could create an opening for the defense to attack his credibility, burying him in documents and questions that undermined his self-portrait. On the government side, some felt that Napoletano was not going to get the prosecution across the finish line.

Close observers of the case speculated about the possibility that some of the seven Boston defendants would turn, that the wall around

Kapoor would collapse. Perhaps they would plead guilty one by one, leaving Kapoor as the lone defendant. But the seven were banded together in a joint defense agreement, allowing their attorneys to coordinate strategy, and as the months passed and trial approached, they all stood firm. A prosecutor on the case said that there are a lot of important cases in the district that are never even brought by the government "because the defense bar circles the wagons and nobody cooperates" and "you just can't get there."

By the summer of 2018, with the long-delayed trial set to begin the following January, Alec Burlakoff had come to understand how badly he had damaged his legal standing by approaching investigators without a lawyer, two years before, and giving a recorded statement riddled with lies. He had gift wrapped a body of evidence that would hurt him at trial. Burlakoff had also come to grapple with the idea that his rationalizations—that bogus speaker programs are commonplace in pharma, that he had only done what the bosses wanted—were just that, rationalizations. Even if they were true, they were inadequate.

Burlakoff had a new attorney, George Vien, a prominent Boston lawyer well liked around the courthouse. Vien would turn up in court in a sweatshirt and joke around when he was off duty. That summer, Burlakoff and Vien had a lengthy meeting, one in a long series, to go over evidence. Burlakoff was exhausted by the end of it. Vien walked his client to the elevator and shifted into his most serious mode, catching Burlakoff in a weakened state. The lawyer looked him in the eye and said, "You're going to plead guilty. You're going to tell the truth." His client crumbled. They soon went together to meet with the prosecution.

Burlakoff was looking for a deal, but that didn't mean he would get one. Investigators he had lied to were far from sure they wanted to give him a cooperation agreement. It would mean stomaching the idea of going to bat for him with the judge to recommend leniency, should his assistance prove valuable. And it was a tremendous risk to put Alec Burlakoff on the witness stand. The defense would paint him as a liar, a manipulator, an architect of wrongdoing at Insys, a psychologically unstable figure driven by a desire to save himself and take revenge on John Kapoor. Months of negotiation ensued as Burlakoff essentially auditioned for the role of government witness.

During that period, in September 2018, Fred Wyshak joined the prosecution team. A burly man in his mid-sixties with white hair and little interest in diplomacy, Wyshak was a major player in the Boston office, where he had worked for decades, outlasting bosses appointed by five presidents of the United States. "He's the cock of the walk around here," a courthouse beat reporter said.

Wyshak had zero experience in the health-care arena, but he had a lengthy history with racketeering cases. He had spent the vast majority of his long career tackling organized crime and is widely credited as a driving force in dismantling the Mob in New England. He and a longtime partner, Brian Kelly, started prosecuting James "Whitey" Bulger's violent Winter Hill Gang in the early 1990s, and the project kept building and spinning out offshoot cases. They exposed corruption in the FBI informant program, which did not win them too many friends in government. They finally put away Bulger himself.

In Wyshak's big organized-crime cases, the "bread and butter" of the prosecution, he said, was to get someone on the inside to turn state's evidence: "If you want to be successful, you want to have an insider."

It wasn't long after Wyshak joined the Insys team that the government turned its big insider, profoundly changing the landscape of the case. With two months to go before trial, Burlakoff struck a cooperation agreement and pled guilty to racketeering conspiracy at a November 2018 hearing at the federal courthouse in Boston. Kapoor's defense counsel publicly scoffed at the deal, saying in a statement that the government's "embrace" of Burlakoff, a known liar, was "a sign of desperation."

Standing before the judge, Burlakoff looked considerably older than he had a few years before, his widow's peak more pronounced, with more gray hairs. But he looked relieved too. Burlakoff knew that the evidence was stacked against him and that he could reduce his potential sentence considerably. He also liked the idea of standing up out of the crowd of defendants and being the first to take responsibility. But those weren't the only considerations. Burlakoff still saw the world in terms of alliances and betrayals. He bore no animosity, he said, for any of his co-defendants—except for one. "Standing by their side would have meant that I had to stand by Kapoor's side," he said. "That would never, *ever* happen." In theory, Burlakoff wouldn't have liked the idea of being a "rat," but he was picking up hints that Kapoor and the others were plotting to hang the blame on him. "You're not a rat if the other guy is already giving you up," he said.

Burlakoff viewed Kapoor as a mentor who had let all his charges down. "We wanted to do for him," Burlakoff said, adopting the language of a Mob movie. "We counted on him. We were kids. We were young." Burlakoff said he felt for the real victims, the patients, and that he wanted to finally do the right thing and own up to his conduct. But he also needed to tell the world that it wasn't all his fault.

Prosecutors believed that they could corroborate Burlakoff's account with evidence. Wyshak felt he could handle Burlakoff as a witness, that the risk was worth it. Earlier that same year, in a Mafia trial, Wyshak had put his faith in a pivotal witness who testified that he had taken part in about fifty murders. The seasoned prosecutor was accustomed to the idea that if you need a witness to take you inside an alleged criminal conspiracy, you're going to have to tolerate some flaws. He and Burlakoff were a match.

With Alec Burlakoff cooperating, the pressure on the other defendants increased significantly. He had information about people both below and above him in the hierarchy. Joe Rowan was his old friend, Sunrise Lee his former lover. Mike Babich, too, was in a perilous position. The two were close enough that Burlakoff had attended Babich and Natalie Levine's wedding and had visited the couple at the hospital just after the birth of one of their children. (He brought with him a comically enormous teddy bear.) More to the point, Burlakoff could put the jury in the room at corporate headquarters with Babich and Kapoor, describing high-level meetings and decisions.

Babich was also facing a situation that was legally irrelevant to him but nonetheless awkward, and it was coming to a head imminently. Christopher Clough, the New Hampshire physician's assistant, had been indicted in connection with the speaker fees he received from Insys. His trial was set to begin within weeks. The star witness was going to be Babich's wife.

Natalie Babich had routinely conducted sham speaker programs and falsified paperwork in order "to keep Chris paid," in her words. She had already pled guilty in 2017 to her involvement in the speaker-program kickback scheme, agreeing to cooperate with the investigation. For more than a year, Michael and Natalie Babich—happily married, by all accounts—were in a bizarre circumstance in which they were essentially on opposite sides of a legal saga. Natalie was obligated to tell the government what she knew about misconduct at Insys, even while Mike was facing trial and maintaining his innocence. Natalie couldn't be compelled to testify against her husband in Boston, due to the legal rule of spousal immunity. But by testifying against Clough and describing the direction from Insys management, she would indirectly implicate him in open court.

Less than two weeks after Burlakoff entered his plea and days before the Clough trial, Mike Babich made a move. He flew to Boston to speak to investigators in a meeting held at the offices of one of his attorneys. It had been two years since his arrest, and it was his first time speaking to the authorities. For all that time, he had held his ground. The trial was set to begin the following month.

Babich "ran the room," Paul Baumrind said. He started from the beginning and told the whole story of his relationship to his former mentor, the man who had sent him to business school and tapped him as a CEO, the man responsible for the fortune he had made at Insys.

The meeting, a "proffer session," was the prelude to a deal. Babich would plead guilty to conspiracy and mail-fraud charges rather than face trial. After Burlakoff came forward, Wyshak later said in court, "Mr. Babich realized that the handwriting was on the wall." The former CEO became a cooperating witness, dealing a tremendous blow to John Kapoor's defense.

In the period after Kapoor had ousted Babich and continued on at Insys as CEO and as a director, Kapoor had assembled a massive three-ring binder that he toted around with him. Inside it was evidence of the corrective action the company had taken under his direction. It was the proof that he and Insys were on the right path. Kapoor was convinced that the Department of Justice would engage with him, that together they would review that binder, and that in the end they would arrive at a settlement. Even if the sanctions were painful, a settlement would represent some measure of redemption, an outcome that would afford him some dignity. It would also comport with his ardent conviction that even if his company had gone off the rails, he was a person who had committed no crimes. He earnestly believed that, and he thought anyone would come to the same conclusion. His arrest was a rude surprise.

After that day, he wasn't the same person. He still extended himself for remarkable acts of generosity; he reached out to a server at one of his restaurants whose child had been born severely premature, just after Kapoor's arrest, and pledged to cover all his medical expenses. But those around Kapoor had trouble recognizing the man they had known. Gone was the scientist who took great pleasure in minor breakthroughs. Gone was the virile clenched fist of unquestioned authority. In the long run-up to the criminal trial, he lost interest in the world. He aged considerably, became confused. The acts of betrayal by Alec Burlakoff and Mike Babich and the government's willingness to enable them only brought him lower. Instead of coming to court poised to fight, he would come in battered and staggering.

The trial of the Insys executives began in late January 2019, in the cold of New England winter. A chilling wind blew outside the federal courthouse, which sits by the water on Boston's Inner Harbor. Even under cloud cover, natural light poured into the common areas and hallways of the courthouse through a floor-to-ceiling wall of glass giving out onto the icy bay.

On the day of opening statements, the gallery was packed, and the proceedings were simulcast to an overflow crowd in another courtroom. In the weeks to follow, the trial would be interrupted for a day, in February, by the suspicious absence of a juror who had worn a New England Patriots sweatshirt and then happened to call out sick on the day of the team's Super Bowl victory parade. In March, a fifteen-inch snowfall provided another day off. Nobody involved in the trial anticipated that it would last as long as it did.

The tension sometimes reached an excruciating pitch, yet a certain camaraderie took hold in Courtroom 17 as the weeks rolled on. A core group of people reconvened day after day, spending over three months in a room together. The jurors used their own guarded elevator bank and had lunch brought to them so that they wouldn't cross paths with anyone else. But the rest mixed freely, regardless of their stake in the outcome. Lawyers, federal agents, court reporters, journalists, defendants and their relatives—everyone held doors for one another, griped about the weather and the uncomfortable seats, debated the merits of the cafeteria, became familiar with one another's snacking habits and rotation of semiformal clothes. Everyone talked about how Juror No. 1 almost never took off her coat.

Many of the attorneys, on both sides, came from the same insular legal world in Boston, centered on the courthouse, and had known one another for decades. A common elite legal career path is to serve as a federal prosecutor, then leave for a more lucrative job in private practice representing clients who want insight into the opposing team. The white-collar defense bar is therefore filled with former prosecutors, and big trials often pit onetime colleagues against each other. In this instance, the judge herself formerly worked in the Boston U.S. Attorney's Office, alongside lawyers on both sides. Brian Kelly, Fred Wyshak's longtime partner in prosecuting organized crime, was on John Kapoor's defense team, handling civil cases. The beat reporters covering the trial were familiar with most of the cast, and vice versa. To visit the proceedings was to enter a long-standing social ecosystem, a world in which the defendants come and go and everyone else remains.

Judge Burroughs, nominated by President Barack Obama in 2014, presided over the case with a sense of humor and a notable intellectual humility, openly airing her own uncertainties about the best course of action. Burroughs was simultaneously handling a landmark affirmative-action case involving Harvard University (a nonjury trial in which she ultimately ruled that the school did not illegally discriminate against Asian American applicants) and didn't disguise her stress, at moments, over the workload.

Burroughs showed a deeply held belief in the rights of the accused. Strong feelings about opioids and pharmaceutical marketing created difficulties in selecting eighteen jurors and alternates out of an initial pool of some three hundred people. "When I heard what the case was, I gasped," one woman said, tears welling in her eyes. Her father had been addicted to prescription pills and died of an overdose, she said. She was struck from the jury pool. But Burroughs pressed other people to set aside their biases, giving stern civics lectures about the bedrock principle of the presumption of innocence. Once the trial began, Burroughs showed an ardent protectiveness for the jurors, treating them as the most important people in the room.

At the final pretrial conference, Judge Burroughs asked the assembled cast of attorneys if there were really going to be five defendants at trial. Speculation was still circulating, with days to go, about whether anyone would follow the lead of Burlakoff and Babich and become a cooperator. But no one did. On the eve of trial, the parties had to devote some time to discussing how everyone was going to fit in the courtroom.

The five who went to trial—John Kapoor, Mike Gurry, Rich Simon, Joe Rowan, and Sunrise Lee—were an odd group, with widely divergent roles and levels of seniority. Sunrise Lee had been advised and pressured to plead guilty multiple times, over many months, but she refused. So Lee, hired to "SMILE and CLOSE" after a chance encounter at a strip club with Alec Burlakoff, was going on trial alongside the immensely wealthy founder of a drug company. Meanwhile, testifying for the prosecution would be a vast array of their former colleagues, the most notable among them being the longtime marketing head, Matt Napoletano, testifying under immunity; Alec Burlakoff; and Mike Babich.

Leading the defense, stacked with talented white-collar attorneys, was Beth Wilkinson, one of the most sought-after and well-connected lawyers in the country, a Washington power broker. She was lead counsel for John Kapoor. A former Assistant U.S. Attorney, Wilkinson helped prosecute the Oklahoma City bomber Timothy McVeigh and was the first person to win the Justice Department's highest honor twice. Judge Merrick Garland officiated at her wedding. The law firm Wilkinson founded set up a command center for the trial that occupied much of a floor at the InterContinental Boston, a large hotel sheathed in glass, a short walk across a bridge from the courthouse.

Wilkinson could be seen holding forth at the center of conversation in the hallways outside the courtroom in a stylish bright-colored blazer, encircled by taller male attorneys in nearly identical drab suits. Jurors seemed to like Wilkinson even when she was at her most fierce and combative. When she asked Alec Burlakoff, during his testimony, if he ever discussed cross-examination with the government, he drew some laughs from the jury with his response: "I expressed my anxiety to be cross-examined by *you* specifically."

On the government side, Nat Yeager, with his years-long tenure on the case and experience in health-care fraud, had a deep command of Insys minutiae and the folkways of pharma. He did little to disguise his emotions from the jury, often shaking his head in disgust at the tactics of the defense and raising his voice when he had a chance to rebut.

Fred Wyshak enraged the defense with his interruptions but appeared to connect with the jury. Wyshak is about as famous as an Assistant U.S. Attorney can be—the 2015 Whitey Bulger film *Black Mass* features a character with his name—but he comes from Boston and speaks like someone the average juror might know from the neighborhood. He portrayed the defense's arguments as nitpicky technicalities that he was going to counter with some straight talk, with a tone of *let's cut the BS.*

A third prosecutor, a younger man named Dave Lazarus, developed a rapport with nervous witnesses and served as the government's specialist in the Insys Reimbursement Center. As he worked his way through his precise questions, he ticked them off in his notes with the flick of a pen. Lazarus delivered the prosecution's opening statement and boiled the allegations in the case down to a simple formula of one plus one equals two: "bribing doctors, conning insurers, making money."

The government's case, stretching from January 29 to April 1, could be characterized as a show of overwhelming force. It underscored that despite the protections afforded to the accused—to say nothing of the vast resources of a defendant such as Kapoor—a criminal prosecution in the United States is not really a fair fight. In any criminal proceeding, the state is the heavy favorite. When the government prioritizes a case, as it did here, it can bring staggering resources and tools to bear. The Insys prosecutors, unlike the defense, had the power of the badge and could draw on the work of ten investigative agencies. Paul Baumrind of the FBI estimated that the team of Insys investigators had traveled to forty-six states. Federal agents had interviewed the government's witnesses numerous times. Defense counsel had access to written summaries of those interviews, but they had never actually met many of the witnesses before they walked into court and were sworn in.

Most important of all, prosecutors were able to leverage the power of the state to pressure or compel almost anyone they wanted to testify at the trial, whether through a subpoena, a cooperation agreement, or an order of immunity. Four people were at the center of the critical decisions made at the company: Babich, Burlakoff, Napoletano, and Kapoor. The government made deals with three of them in an effort to convict the fourth.

The government focused its case on eight Subsys whales, linking them to the defendants with a barrage of witnesses and documents. Dr. Steven Chun in Florida was one of these whales. The jury learned that after Tracy Krane had failed to bring in enough scripts from him and was fired, she was swiftly replaced with a former Cephalon rep who was close to the doctor, a man named Dan Tondre. Insys then upped the ante by hiring the doctor's then girlfriend, Aqsa Nawaz, the young woman he had brought along to dinner with Krane and Burlakoff. Nawaz had also met Kapoor, before she was hired, when she came along with Chun on a trip to Arizona to meet with the Insys founder.

Nawaz, still in her twenties, was called to the witness stand herself, looking reluctant to be there. It was apparent from her testimony that her relationship with Chun had been troubled and that meanwhile her Insys bosses had pressured her to exert her influence over him. She testified that Chun (who had not been charged with a crime) had forged the signatures of purported attendees at his speaker dinners. Finally she said that Dr. Chun had been addicted to opioids himself—in particular, to fentanyl products like Subsys. "I saw the effects of it," she said. She began to cry.

Two of the featured prescribers, Gavin Awerbuch and Heather Alfonso, testified themselves and told the jury about the crimes they had committed.

"I am embarrassed and ashamed to talk about it," Awerbuch said, pausing to collect himself while the courtroom waited in silence, "but I pled guilty to two felonies." Awerbuch was slender and short, his head barely visible over the top of the witness stand. He came across as a defeated man. The doctor had done volunteer work in his career, had taken care of a quadriplegic, had worked in clinics for the indigent. Hundreds of his patients had written letters of support for him to the judge in his own case. He appeared competent, intelligent, and completely lost. Over the course of his career, the doctor seemed to have become, little by little, so corrupted that he could no longer see how corrupt he was.

As Nat Yeager led him through a series of patient charts, Awerbuch clearly remembered some of the patients on a personal level. He admitted that he had violated his Hippocratic oath and his duty to these people he knew. Trying to prescribe Subsys whenever possible, he zeroed in on patients whose charts might make them look, to an outside investigator, like legitimate candidates for Subsys—when he knew they were not. "In my own heart, I know," he said.

In some cases, he said, they should not have been taking any opioid at all. The litany became appalling: some of them could have been on Motrin, he said; that woman needed mental-health care, not Subsys; this man was doing all right without Subsys, and it could have gotten him in "real trouble"—his sleep apnea increased the risk that he would "stop breathing," and he had severe memory problems and could easily have taken a double dose by mistake.

Why did you do it? Yeager asked, over and over, for almost every patient. At one point, Awerbuch threw up his hands and dipped his head for a moment, as if to say, *You're going to make me say it again?* He did it to keep the speaker money coming.

But it became clear that for the practitioners who took the deal with Insys, there was more than greed at work. With Awerbuch and Alfonso, and with the physician's assistant Christopher Clough, who had taken the stand in his own defense in his separate trial in Concord, New Hampshire, a common psychological thread seemed to emerge from their testimony. There was something peculiar about these top "targets," something miscalibrated or absent in their social understanding. Questioned about a previous investigation and reprimand of her license, in the grave atmosphere of the courtroom, Alfonso was blasé: "Like, that whole period was just a bad scene." Clough blurted things out with odd inflections. He corrected a patient who had testified in his trial, almost eagerly saying that the prognosis for her arthritic condition was worse than she understood: "She's not going to recover." All these clinicians, the evidence showed, had been inexcusably reckless with the lives of people who trusted them. But they seemed less like criminal masterminds than easy marks.

Most doctors have no tolerance for talking to sales reps, Alec Burlakoff said. Those doctors were a dead end for people in his position. The trick was finding the small percentage who don't maintain the same kinds of defenses.

In pain management, patients present complex problems. Often a lot is going wrong for them at once, some of it psychological or vague. It's hard to know where to begin. There is no test to assess pain that does not rely on subjectivity, on what the patients say. They might be exaggerating their symptoms to get narcotics, or they might legitimately need a high dose because they have built up a tolerance, through the body's natural response. Perhaps they should be weaned off opioids entirely; for non-cancer chronic pain, that's what many doctors would advise. But that is a difficult road. The patients might get scared or angry and never come back.

If you're a doctor, the sales reps all want something from you. So do the patients. The easy way out, and also the lucrative path, is to just give in. Just sign your name—to insurance forms you don't read, to treatment plans your employees come up with, to speaker agreements that pad your income, and of course to prescriptions for opioid painkillers. If you go that route, the reps will compete for your attention and treat you as important, and your practice will flourish. It takes a certain fortitude to be responsible. Insys found people who were weak.

To prove the insurance-fraud element of the alleged conspiracy, the critical witness was Elizabeth Gurrieri, who had started out working the phones alone to get scripts "pulled through" and then managed the growing call center known as the IRC. She too had pled guilty to a felony—conspiracy to commit wire fraud—and was cooperating in hopes of leniency. Gurrieri depicted the IRC as a hotbed of dishonesty and deceit where virtually the entire aim was to get insurers to pay for prescriptions they wouldn't pay for if they knew the truth.

Because Gurrieri reported directly to the defendant Mike Gurry, the only hope for Gurry's attorney, Tracy Miner, was to distance him from Gurrieri and keep the blame squarely on her and her underlings. She and the other "prior authorization specialists" worked, for most of the IRC's existence, in a separate building, and it seemed possible that Gurry was not fully up to speed on what was happening there, that Gurrieri got carried away in her fiefdom. Little that went on in the IRC appeared covert, judging from internal records and the testimony of Gurrieri and several corroborating witnesses. But there wasn't much documentary evidence that tied Gurry to the scheme.

Gurrieri was asked, "The things that you did that led to your pleading guilty, do you know whether Mike Gurry knew about them?"

"I *know* he did," she replied, perhaps with more zeal than the prosecutors would have liked. Her tone suggested that she didn't want to go down alone.

The jury heard the audio of numerous phone calls made from the IRC. They saw the corresponding paperwork. The cascade of falsehoods and misrepresentations became numbing and tedious, and the courtroom gallery thinned out. But later in the trial, the government called former patients of paid Insys speakers to the stand. Some of those phone calls riddled with lies, it emerged, were about these patients now entering the courtroom one by one. Insys employees had gotten on the phone to make sure the company got its revenue every time these men and women got another prescription for Subsys.

Presented with documents and recordings about themselves, designed to dupe their insurers, the patients corrected the record. *No, I didn't have trouble swallowing. No, I've never tried that drug they said didn't work for me—never heard of it. No, that's not my signature; some-*

one actually spelled my name wrong. No, I didn't have cancer. Yes, I became addicted to Subsys. It completely ruined my life.

The defense succeeded in blunting some of the impact of the patients' testimony, bringing out discrepancies and confusions and implicitly distancing the defendants from them. Most patients had been on multiple pain medications at once—Subsys is meant to supplement longer-acting opioids—and their memories were flawed. It wasn't simple to assess what role Subsys had played. Still, there was no use denying that these people sitting before the jury had suffered and that *someone* at Insys had paid their dubious doctors and lied about their health. Given the array of guilty pleas, the defense couldn't "look the jury in the face," as one of Kapoor's attorneys put it, and argue that nobody did anything wrong.

Late one afternoon, with little time left in the day, a twenty-eight-year-old woman from Michigan, Kendra Skalnican, stepped up to the witness stand. Skalnican was the patient of Dr. Awerbuch's whom federal agents in Michigan were so struck by when they interviewed her in her darkened home, the one who seemed like a shell of the young woman pictured on her driver's license.

In court, she wore a pink blouse and a black jacket, with barrettes pinning back her light-colored hair. She had steeled herself all day for this moment. In a prep session with the government, she had excused herself and vomited in the bathroom. The hours ticked by while the trial ran behind schedule and she tried to calm herself by looking out at the harbor view. She had come to Boston alone, leaving a newborn with family at home, because relatives couldn't afford to travel with her.

Awerbuch had testified about Skalnican earlier in the trial, though she was unaware of it. Her urine had tested positive for cocaine, he said, and it was clear she was taking too much Subsys. "I should have stopped it immediately," Awerbuch said.

On the witness stand, Skalnican spoke in a reedy high pitch, with little inflection. She seemed to be expending great effort to steady herself. "That was way too strong of a medication for me to be on," she said.

On cross-examination, Beth Wilkinson confronted Skalnican

with some evidence that she had overused opioids before Subsys, and that she had signed agreements at Awerbuch's clinic consenting to off-label treatment and stating that she wouldn't take more medication than prescribed. Wilkinson's tone was gentle, but anyone could see what she was implying—that this young woman was partly to blame for her fate. Skalnican began to cry. When Wilkinson looked up from her notes and belatedly noticed what was happening, she quickly wrapped up her questioning.

A few moments later, the day was over, and the jurors stood up to stretch. The judge started telling them about the schedule for the rest of the week. Counsel on both sides chuckled over an inside joke. Few people paid any attention to Skalnican as she stepped down from the stand and made her way through the gallery to leave by the rear door. Her mouth crumpled as she tried to hold back her sobs until she reached the hallway. As she wiped her hand across her right cheek, tears slicked her face.

19   DIRTY LITTLE SECRET

When Nat Yeager stood up and said, "United States calls Michael Babich to the stand," there was an audible commotion in the gallery as heads turned to look at the rear door. The jurors watched carefully as Babich entered and approached the front of the room. Tall and solid, with a full face and close-cropped brown hair, he wore a blue suit with a pink tie and raised his right hand to be sworn in.

Some former Insys employees out in the field formed an impression that Babich was essentially a puppet, a weak figure that Kapoor knew he could easily manipulate. But even as Babich's testimony left no doubt that Kapoor was the one in charge, Babich came across as his own man. He seemed like someone who could take the reins in a meeting despite being surrounded by people older and more experienced than himself. He was an impressive presence in court, exhibiting a polished self-presentation and the demeanor of a leader.

Yeager led Babich through the entire history of his relationship to Kapoor, from his first interview for a low-level job in Lake Forest, Illinois, to the day in Arizona that Kapoor forced him out as Insys CEO. Babich showed himself to be a natural storyteller. Some of the narrative—about the pre-Insys years, for instance—was barely relevant in strict legal terms, but the jurors grew to understand something critical: the dynamic between the two men. It became virtually impossible to believe that Babich, the thirtysomething protégé working under a brutally demanding boss, could somehow lead a nationwide conspiracy against Kapoor's wishes or while he wasn't paying attention.

"How is it that you used your speaker programs to achieve success?" Yeager asked.

"We achieved some success with certain doctors by bribes," Babich said.

The FBI agent Paul Baumrind, sitting in the gallery, felt his pulse rate rise. After more than five years of investigation, the CEO was confessing under oath.

Asked if the Insys leadership cared whether a doctor they hired to speak was a respected clinician, Babich said flatly, "No, we didn't."

Babich's testimony that Kapoor had told him he was going to be "the fall guy" made the headline in the next day's *Boston Globe*. Babich recalled telling Kapoor in response that in that case he wanted to pack up his office and leave the company immediately, "and you won't see me again." But here Babich sat in the courtroom across from Kapoor, perhaps fifteen feet away, implicating him in a criminal trial. Kapoor sat still, betraying little emotion. He had developed a hint of an elderly hunch. He looked diminished.

On cross-examination, the defense attorneys chipped away at Babich's story. They pinned the blame on the two defendants of the original seven who had changed sides: Babich and his ad of sales, Burlakoff. They painted Babich as an arrogant frat-boy type who snuck around conspiring with Burlakoff and began cashing out his stock as soon as the feds started sniffing around, ultimately making $45 million. "He must have known something that somebody else didn't because John Kapoor didn't sell any stock," Wilkinson had said in her opening statement.

Wilkinson had some success undermining Babich by highlighting his slipperiness on the question of when he became aware that the speaker program was an illegal scheme. The prosecution sought to establish that it was corrupt from the get-go, that Burlakoff in particular had made it clear early on what the intentions were, but Babich didn't consistently pose it that way. His timeline was most dubious when it came to his wife, Natalie, whom he appeared to want to protect. He claimed that he didn't know she had been running sham programs with Heather Alfonso until the moment, years later, that she pled guilty to doing it.

Wilkinson suggested that Babich had gotten himself a great deal with the government by offering up the story they wanted and pointing the finger at Kapoor. Babich had not yet been sentenced when he testified (as is typical in such situations), and he was out of jail on bond. Wilkinson seemed to enjoy forcing him to acknowledge that while the defendants were facing the hardest moment of their lives, he had recently been playing golf at a private club in Arizona. (She didn't mention that the defendants were out on bail too.) Babich bristled at the suggestion that he was in an enviable position: "I've already pled guilty to two felonies, ruined my name, ruined my family's name. I don't think there's much upside to me from here."

Kapoor's attorney emphasized repeatedly that in pleading guilty, Babich had agreed to forfeit just $3.5 million. Wilkinson asked if Babich would lie in order to keep the other $40 million-plus that he made from a criminal scheme, leading to a rapid-fire exchange.

"This isn't about money for me," Babich said. "It's about the truth."

"But you lied to make that $45 million, didn't you?"

"I followed the direction of my boss."

Wilkinson managed to shake Babich's stoic facade and bring out some testy replies that suggested he had some feelings about Kapoor to get off his chest.

"You were paid a lot more money than anyone else in the company, weren't you?" Wilkinson asked.

"Yes I was," Babich said. "I took a lot more crap than everyone else, too."

"Forty-five million dollars of crap, you would say, right?"

"Compared to his wealth, it's a drop in the bucket."

Under government questioning, however, the picture Babich painted had a lasting effect. He recounted weighty private conversations with Kapoor that no other witness could have described, and those details dealt significant blows. If you believed Babich, Kapoor's reactions to the arrests of Madison and Awerbuch were only too telling: they didn't cause him to change course at all. With Insys under subpoena, Kapoor hired people to improve compliance and then gave them the stiff arm when they threatened to cut into sales. When the speaker program was audited by an outside firm, Kapoor decided that reps should be given notice when the auditors were going to show up at an event "to make sure we got a good report card," Babich said.

Prosecutors also used Babich's testimony to introduce a piece of evidence that had little to do with the defendants in particular but made for the most media-friendly moment of the trial. It was a rap video produced by two members of the sales force and presented at a national sales meeting in 2015, while Kapoor sat in the back row, according to Babich. At the time, Insys was already in deep legal trouble and the opioid crisis was in full swing. The creators put their own lyrics to a song by the artist A$AP Rocky, and the recurring refrain celebrated the idea of pushing for high-dose prescriptions of Subsys: "I love titration, and that's not a problem. I got new patients and I got a lot of 'em." Singing and dancing alongside the Insys reps was a person dressed in costume as a 1,600-microgram spray bottle of Subsys, the highest available dose. At the end, Alec Burlakoff removed the costume.

The video was a spoof, part of a contest, a bit of fun. When it was played in court in its entirety for the jury, it came off rather differently. It was a symbol of a group of people who had completely lost touch with the gravity of the business they were in.

Far more significant than the video was the insight that Babich gave both the jurors and the broader public. He provided an unprecedented vantage point, from inside the C-suite, onto the marketing of a prescription painkiller. An indictment or a lawsuit or a congressional report affords the view of a hostile outsider looking in. Rarely does an insider speak. When whistleblowers occasionally come forward, they usually come from the lower ranks, like Ray Furchak and Mia Guzman. They certainly aren't the CEO. One reason that drug companies pay enormous sums to settle investigations before trial is to avoid a moment like this one—a former chief executive, under oath, describing how the business operates.

Babich's perspective allowed the jury to see that the key players at Insys operated in a larger industry context in which their actions, however corrupt, made a great deal of sense. In Babich's account, Insys leadership simply made a series of business decisions in order to overcome various obstacles to the goal of dominating the TIRF market. Their thinking was governed by an undeniable logic flowing downstream from the profit motive: *If Cephalon already has relationships with the top customers, we need to offer them something better. If Subsys prescriptions aren't getting reimbursed by the insurers, we need to game the system better than the competitors do. If Couch and Ruan are having trouble getting enough Subsys because their pharmacy's distributor is trying to comply with the law, we need to find a way around the problem and make sure the doctors don't defect to Galena.* It was a thought process in which the patients barely figured at all.

When Alec Burlakoff testified a week later, he helped fill in the picture Babich had created, painting in brighter colors. Mindful that Burlakoff was a wild card with plenty of liabilities as a witness, prosecutors had scheduled him later in the trial, hoping to all but prove the case before he appeared. Burlakoff could supply more detail—provided the jury believed him—about the defendants in sales who reported to him, all of whom he had hired: Rich Simon, Joe Rowan, and Sunrise Lee. Burlakoff was the fulcrum of the company, positioned between the top bosses in corporate and the sales force and doctors spread around the country.

The jury had heard all about Burlakoff for weeks by the time he appeared in court. When Wilkinson was reading aloud from one of Burlakoff's emails in order to question Babich about it, she interrupted herself: "He was kind of a dramatic guy, wasn't he?"

"Extremely," Babich replied.

In person, Burlakoff did not disappoint. Always a talker, he came ready to unleash his story. Witnesses were routinely asked to identify defendants in court by pointing at them. Most of them raised a hand in a gingerly way, conditioned by society that pointing at someone is rude. Burlakoff raised a stiff right arm and index finger, pointing without compunction.

He moved and fidgeted on the stand like a movie wiseguy, thrusting his shoulders back, rolling his head from shoulder to shoulder to stretch his neck, jutting his chin away from his collar as he adjusted his tie. He unfurled his answers in articulate paragraphs and made few excuses for what he had done. Asked what Kapoor's role was at Insys, Burlakoff leaned into the microphone and spoke slowly: "To run every aspect of the company from *A* to *Z*." He appeared to be enjoying himself immensely.

The attorneys and judge were less pleased.

A trial is typically a choreographed event, adhering to rules and conventions that can seem arbitrary or even downright counterproductive to the project of arriving at the truth. Just when a witness is saying something revealing, she's often cut off by a volley of objections because she has unknowingly crossed some line or another.

In the ritualistic theater of trial testimony, it is really the questioner who runs the show, in the sense that the witness is supposed to be limited to answering what is asked. The attorney posing the questions, who knows in advance roughly what the witness has to say, carefully weaves through the material, swerving to avoid land mines, in order to create the picture most favorable to his position. That picture, of course, is utterly incomplete and badly skewed—a problem that is theoretically remedied when the other side gets its turn and engages in the same routine. This can be a highly frustrating exercise for the witness. It is a natural instinct, for example, that when you are asked a yes-or-no question and a simple "yes" would create a misleading impression, you want to elaborate: "Well, technically yes, but that leaves out something important . . ." Instead of saying that, you're supposed to suffer through being misrepresented and hope that the other side gives you a chance to explain, which may never come to pass.

Alec Burlakoff could not be controlled in this way. He was an unmanageable witness, constantly setting off the land mines as he strayed far outside the bounds of the question.

Sunrise Lee's attorney, Pete Horstmann, asked Burlakoff, "You don't always tell the truth, right?"

"Absolutely not," he replied. "I'm in sales. I worked for Dr. Kapoor."

Exasperated by one of Burlakoff's unsolicited shots at her client, Wilkinson raised her voice. "Is there a story you want to get out? Is that the idea?"

"That's what I'm here for and I'm doing it," Burlakoff shot back.

Judge Burroughs repeatedly turned to Burlakoff, sitting to her left and beneath her, and admonished him. "I'm going to tell you this one more time," Burroughs said. "Okay? You listen to her question, and you answer it. No speeches." Burroughs twice enlisted Burlakoff's lawyer, George Vien, to rein him in. Vien had no formal role in the proceedings because his client was not on trial; he had to be summoned from the hallway.

Burlakoff didn't stick to the prosecutors' script either, though he was their witness. The government sought to establish that during the investigation, when Joe Rowan was due to turn in his cell phone pursuant to a federal subpoena, he intentionally broke it at a ski resort to bury evidence. A fellow senior sales manager would testify that Rowan had bragged about doing it, in Burlakoff's earshot. But on the stand, Burlakoff said, "I do not believe Joe Rowan destroyed the phone, nor have I ever heard him say he destroyed the phone."

Burlakoff was highly combative toward Sunrise Lee's lawyer— "you're a jerk," he told Horstmann—but at one point Burlakoff suddenly handed him a gift. Out of nowhere, Burlakoff said he thought the sales rep Holly Brown was lying about Lee's giving a lap dance to Dr. Madison. Brown had already testified for the government and described the alleged lap dance under oath, drawing headlines. Horstmann blinked at Burlakoff in silence for a moment, looking stunned, then said, "I'll move on."

It was an extraordinarily charged moment for Sunrise Lee when Burlakoff took the stand. She had been, as she saw it, completely at his mercy at Insys. After he had walked into her life and taken a big chance on her, she viewed Burlakoff as her "savior" and sole supporter in power at the company. Their stormy affair only put her in a more vulnerable position. "You capitalized on her appreciation for your personal benefit, correct?" her attorney asked Burlakoff. ("Incorrect," he replied. "Not personal. Professional.")

At Insys, though Lee was promoted to upper management, she said she felt excluded from the in crowd of pharma veterans in senior roles, such as Karen Hill, who knew the rules and how to game them. Lee was aware of the talk internally that she had no real sales ability or smarts. Then she was fired. Now she was being prosecuted as if she had been one of the architects of the company's criminal strategy. She still clung to the fact that after her firing, Paul Baumrind of the FBI had told her in a message that she was "not a target" of the investigation. Somehow she became one. Now, while Hill pled to a lesser charge and was sentenced to home confinement, Lee was on trial for racketeering conspiracy, facing a twenty-year maximum sentence. And Burlakoff was testifying for the other side.

Burlakoff's tone was all over the map when the topic of his testimony turned to Sunrise Lee. In addition to jumping to defend her over the alleged lap dance (though he wasn't present), he said in response to a question about the timing of their romance, "I don't want to hurt Sunrise."

"You're here testifying against her," Horstmann said, over objections. "You realize that, right?"

It was unclear if he did, really, in the way that most people would. Blurting out his thoughts with abandon, at times he seemed not to grasp the gravity of what he was saying. Burlakoff described Rowan as his "best friend in the world" and their relationship as "phenomenal," appearing oblivious to the irony that he was implicating Rowan in court. Burlakoff kept giving Lee "credit" for raking in business from Awerbuch and Madison—thereby damaging her case tremendously. Her defense hinged on establishing her as a rookie in over her head, a mere tool. "She was the best salesperson I ever came across," Burlakoff said, then gratuitously added, "She took thousands of dollars from me in the first day I met her."

After all these remarks, Fred Wyshak, perhaps seeking to explain to the jury what was going on here, asked Burlakoff, "Do you, as you sit there today, still have feelings for Sunrise Lee?"

"I do," he replied. Lee recoiled and squinted at him, looking disgusted. Her mother, watching from the gallery, quietly hissed and shook her head.

When Wyshak questioned Burlakoff for the government, the two developed a rhythm, a theatrical patter. Wyshak tried to get out ahead of a problem by bringing up the fact that Burlakoff had lied to investigators on tape for hours back in 2016, before his arrest.

"I saw myself in a heap of trouble, panicked, and hoped I could talk my way out of it," Burlakoff said.

"That didn't work, did it?" Wyshak replied.

"No."

A veteran of organized-crime cases, Wyshak could work with a witness who broke things down to plain language and spoke bluntly about the dark arts of the trade. Whether or not jurors found Burlakoff credible, he and Wyshak cut through the medical jargon and told them a story that was colorful and direct.

Referring to the top prescribers that Insys targeted, Wyshak asked, "Were some of those doctors pill mill operators?"

"Yes," Burlakoff said.

"No secret about that, right?"

"None whatsoever."

Wyshak questioned whether it would make any sense, if the speaker program were legitimate, to enlist some of these doctors: "How realistic was it to expect a large number of attendees to hear, for example, Paul Madison speak?" Burlakoff replied,

One hundred percent unrealistic. Paul Madison was
known to be running a pill mill, which often brings a
negative connotation. I understand that. But being raised in
pharmaceuticals, in pain management at Cephalon and Insys,
especially from our coaching as far as targeting from Dr.
Kapoor and Mike Babich, pill mills for us meant dollar signs.
That's what we saw, dollar signs. It was not run the other way.
It was run *to* the pill mill.

Some of Burlakoff's testimony came off as a little too well crafted, shaped for maximum impact. When he recounted laying out the quid pro quo to specific doctors, the accounts were suspiciously similar and frank. Although it was believable, from seeing him in action, that Burlakoff had no shortage of nerve, jurors might have wondered whether anyone would pitch an illegal scheme to a doctor quite so baldly as he claimed. It also seemed implausible that Sunrise Lee had made that kind of outright pitch to Dr. Awerbuch in her first two weeks on the job, as Burlakoff claimed.

The defense had plenty of material to draw on to depict Burlakoff as untrustworthy. Wilkinson waved a whole binder of it at the government as the two sides bantered during a break. She hammered away at the blatant contradictions between his testimony and his recorded statements during that 2016 meeting. She also highlighted for the jury that Nat Yeager had accused Burlakoff on tape of lying—and now the government was posing him as a truth teller.

What exactly Burlakoff said about his intentions with the speaker program in his job interviews with Kapoor and Babich became a focal point of the trial. What did Kapoor know exactly when he hired his turnaround artist and gave him the go-ahead? After Beth Wilkinson undermined some of Burlakoff's claims and sowed some doubt on cross-examination, Wyshak came back and asked Burlakoff if, in his first interview, he actually used the word "bribe." Most people in the room likely expected him to say that of course it wasn't quite so explicit. But Burlakoff replied, "I did."

Wilkinson pounced. She pointed out later, in her closing argument, that Babich disputed there was any such discussion, and she ridiculed the idea that Burlakoff had suggested to a perfect stranger in a job interview that they embark on a criminal conspiracy together. She had a point. Perhaps Burlakoff never said the word "bribe." In fact, perhaps some jurors thought that he was a serial exaggerator, a greedy manipulator, and worse. The fact remained that Kapoor hired him and promoted him. After the company came under investigation, Burlakoff continued running sales at Insys for another year and a half.

"You saw him testify for a week," Nat Yeager said of Burlakoff in the government's closing statement. "Would you put him in charge of sales strategy for a Schedule II drug, the most potent opioid in the United States?"

Even if you doubted Burlakoff on the details, if you placed him in the overall context of the trial, a coherent story took shape. After the education the jury had received in the business of pharmaceutical sales, that story was not so hard to believe. It was a story in which everyone on the highway was driving at seventy-five miles per hour in a fifty-five zone, and Insys was going eighty-five.

Everybody does it is not a legal defense. Just as you won't be able to escape a speeding ticket by pointing out that all the cars around you were speeding too, defense counsel in the Insys trial could not rely on the argument that some of the conduct their clients were accused of was commonplace in the industry. They couldn't explain to the jury that in cases similar to this one, most companies just paid money to settle the matter and moved on. The prosecutors didn't have much cause to point out the industry big picture either; the government was trying to establish that these particular individuals were guilty of a very serious crime. But throughout the trial, *everybody does it* hovered just outside the frame and sometimes peeked through.

Elizabeth Gurrieri, for instance, testified that back when she worked at McKesson, one of the biggest corporations in America, processing prior authorizations for giants such as Pfizer and Glaxo-SmithKline, she would tell insurers, just as she did at Insys, that she was calling from the doctor's office. In other words, she would lie.

Mike Babich and several other witnesses conveyed that the most aggressive moves to court Dr. Ruan and Dr. Couch—culminating in Kapoor and Babich flying to Alabama to seal a suspect deal—were not made in a vacuum; they were made to counter Galena's own suspicious relationship with the doctors. Kapoor said he "won't be outbought by Galena," according to Napoletano. After their battle played out, in 2017, Galena paid millions to resolve Department of Justice allegations that it paid illegal kickbacks directed at Couch and Ruan, among other doctors. No one went to jail.

It was Alec Burlakoff, with his unmanageable speeches, who did the most to contextualize Insys's conduct within the norms of the industry. At times it was as if he were testifying against the drug business at large. Even if you discounted for his tendency to exaggerate, the facts made it hard to dismiss what he was saying. Cephalon paid speaker money to Xiulu Ruan, Heather Alfonso, and Gavin Awerbuch, all before Subsys existed. The main difference between the speaker program at Insys and at other companies, Burlakoff suggested, was that other drugmakers made more effort to disguise their true intentions.

Explaining why Insys hired Steven Chun's girlfriend, Burlakoff said that it was simply customer service, that you couldn't say no to a doctor like Chun. Why? He would have taken his business elsewhere. "She wanted to work in the industry," Burlakoff said. "She would get a job somewhere, sir."

Burlakoff said that when he and Joe Rowan discussed paying Dr. Ruan in exchange for prescriptions, "it was the same conversation we've had for probably a decade," dating back to their days at other companies.

So Rowan was already familiar with the concept? Wyshak asked. "Of course."

"Why do you say 'of course'?"

"It's considered the dirty little secret that everybody in pharma is aware of," Burlakoff said.

20   THE VERDICT

At 1:55 p.m. on May 2, 2019, a young woman shoved open the large door as she left Courtroom 17 and came skidding out into the near-empty hallway. It was Alexandra Gliga, a defense attorney for Joe Rowan. She broke into a run, her legs constricted by her skirt, her high heels sounding out a rapid *clack clack clack*. She was searching for her co-counsel, Mike Kendall, who needed to be pulled out of another hearing in the building, set to begin in five minutes. Gliga glanced at a reporter as she passed and said one word: "Verdict."

Inside the courtroom, approximately nothing had transpired for nearly four weeks. Each morning, the jurors arrived to deliberate and went directly to the jury room, which was situated in a private area past the rear door of the courtroom, behind the bench. Then, around six hours later, they left, day after day. For weeks, they didn't even have any notes or questions for the judge, so they left no hints about what was happening in their sanctum. Rumors circulated that one juror brought bacon for the others every morning, that another was seen working out at a gym across the street. It was as if they had moved in. Reporters and lawyers spotted the jurors only occasionally, as they entered or left the building, and tried to read their body language. Were there warring factions? No attorney involved in the case could recall ever waiting so long for a verdict.

Jury selection in late January had become a distant memory. By now, entering May, daffodils and fresh mulch and T-shirts could be seen outside the courthouse.

The atmosphere around the case had changed. After the government had rested, two months into trial, the defense had put on a case lasting less than three days. They called an expert and two off-label patients, grateful for Subsys, as witnesses, planting the idea that attempts to restrict the drug to cancer patients were arbitrary and unfair, a matter of insurers trying to save money. The witnesses underscored the idea that Subsys was a valuable drug, the best in its class, offering relief from debilitating pain. Was this case really in the same category as a conspiracy to illegally distribute, say, heroin or cocaine?

The defense's closing arguments hung the blame on those who had a motive to please the prosecution: Elizabeth Gurrieri, Michael Babich, and, most of all, Alec Burlakoff. Because the essence of a RICO conspiracy is an agreement, rather than the criminal acts themselves, the defense highlighted the points where Babich, Burlakoff, and Napoletano contradicted one another and suggested a climate of ongoing dispute at the company. The fact that bribes and fraud had occurred was irrelevant, defense counsel stressed, if these particular defendants hadn't agreed to be a part of it. Outside the jury's view, as the lawyers sparred in motion hearings, Judge Burroughs had continued to sharply question the way the government had approached the case, suggesting they overreached and overcharged it. The evidence supporting one of the RICO predicates—illegal drug distribution—was "pretty darn thin," she said.

Maybe the jury thought the same. With each passing day, hopes were rising for the defense. The passage of time implied doubts and disagreements, just what the defense was looking for.

The attorneys and defendants weren't required to come to court each day during deliberations—only to stay close by, within ten minutes' range. Most rarely entered the courtroom or even the building. The prosecutors and federal agents stayed on the ninth floor for the most part, in the U.S. Attorney's Office. All the parties were hanging on any word from the jury, but for the most part they were doing it invisibly.

When the word went out that the jury had reached a verdict, only three or four people were present in the courtroom. Then, with astonishing speed, people arrived in droves. Inside six minutes, the room was nearly at capacity. The courtroom clerk had alerted all counsel by text message, and the news had pulsed outward rapidly from there. Federal agents on the case began to fill the gallery on the government side of the room. Ten or fifteen journalists rushed into the media section one at a time, sliding into their pews and swinging open their laptops. The prosecutors entered—Fred Wyshak and Dave Lazarus, then Nat Yeager. At the rear of the courtroom, dozens of staffers from the U.S. Attorney's Office poured in and stood three or four deep along the back wall. Their boss, then U.S. Attorney Andrew Lelling, appeared in court for the first time and was given a seat. Newly arrived court security officers, also summoned on late notice, struggled to contain the flow.

Judge Burroughs entered from chambers and took the bench. The defendants and their attorneys hustled up the aisles, passing through the spectators, and found their places in the well. Rich Simon and Joe Rowan wore sneakers with their business suits—no time to change.

Kapoor was the second-to-last defendant to enter, flanked by his lead attorneys: Kosta Stojilkovic at his left side and Beth Wilkinson at his right. After they sat, Wilkinson ducked her head close to Kapoor and spoke softly, looking him in the eyes, gesturing with her right arm as if to explain the sequence of events that was about to unfold in court.

By the time Sunrise Lee entered, along with her mother and stepfather, she had to squeeze through a large, government-friendly crowd at the back of the room. The defense contingent in the gallery was vastly outnumbered. Family and friends had largely stayed away from court during the proceedings. Joe Rowan's wife, Denise, traveled back and forth from the Florida Panhandle to attend much of the trial and even the deliberations, but she happened not to be in Boston at that moment. She was home, with the couple's teenage children. No one of course knew, until minutes ago, that after four weeks of waiting, today would be the day.

With everyone in place, the courtroom clerk, Karen Folan, left through the far door, toward the jury room. After a brief interval, the door swung open again. Some of the crowd instinctively rose to their feet, anticipating by a second or two the loud call that soon came from Folan: "All rise for the jury."

The foreperson, Mikeljon Freitas, was a stout man with a heavy Boston accent who worked as a manager for a utility company. He had been randomly selected as foreperson by the judge at the end of trial, not chosen by his fellow jurors, but he had quickly established himself as an effective leader within the jury room. He would steer the discussion out of dead ends and call a break when debate threatened to become heated.

The group had worked meticulously. Over the weeks of deliberations, they had used one juror's particularly detailed notes as a guide and essentially run back through the trial from the beginning, reviewing the exhibits introduced into evidence, with a focus on key witnesses. There were more than twelve hundred exhibits in boxes spread about the room.

By the last day, the jurors were mentally drained. At the same time, they felt a rising anxiety about what they were preparing to do. They knew that they held the lives of these defendants in their hands, and the burden of that responsibility became a heavy presence in the room, jurors said. Some of them had become close to one another. In accordance with the rules, multiple jurors said, they never discussed the case until deliberations began. That left a conversational void that they filled by talking about their work, their families, their personal lives.

In the final hour before the verdict was announced, the foreman addressed every juror in turn, working his way around the table, asking for a verbal assurance that they were in agreement with the decision. One of them, Patricia Hazelton, had just lost a cousin, and the funeral was to be held the next morning. As the other jurors asked her if she was sure she was ready to handle the emotions of returning a verdict, she had tears in her eyes but said she was prepared to go ahead. Another juror, Michelle DaCosta, worried that as the verdict was read aloud in court, her legs would shake or she would begin to cry. The group decided to do a trial run. One juror read the verdict form aloud while the rest stood silent.

Now the group of twelve entered the courtroom, their faces betraying no expression, and stood in front of their assigned chairs. They did not look at the defendants. At the far right of the front row, the man in seat nine, a postal worker, put a steadying hand to the back of the woman to his right.

"Mr. Foreperson," the clerk said, after asking the rest of the courtroom to be seated, "has the jury reached a unanimous verdict?"

"Yes, ma'am," Freitas said.

He passed the verdict form—one page for each defendant—to the clerk, who turned and handed it up to Judge Burroughs. Standing at the bench and bending over, the judge reviewed the stapled papers silently, one by one, then turned again to the front page and flipped through them once more. The turning of the pages could be heard in the gallery. The courtroom had gone silent.

The judge passed the papers back to the clerk, who asked the defendants to rise to their feet. She began to read aloud.

The first defendants to receive the news were Mike Gurry and Rich Simon. They were both found guilty. Gurry's square jaw remained raised, and Simon's hands stayed in his pockets.

When Sunrise Lee heard "guilty" after her name, she looked quickly down and to her left, as if lightly slapped across the face.

By now, as the clerk moved on to Joe Rowan and called his name, he looked weakened, seeing the odds turn against him. His body and head leaned slightly to his right. Moments after the word "guilty" was spoken, he reached with his right hand toward his pants pocket. His hand trembled violently, as if in a spasm.

Finally it was on to John Kapoor. He was the last to be charged in the case, some twenty months before, and now the last to learn his fate. He was found guilty of racketeering conspiracy, in a resounding verdict. The jury found that he had conspired to commit all five of the alleged predicate offenses. Hearing the words, he tilted his head slightly forward.

And that was all. The government had reached the top of a cor-porate power and toppled the entire structure.

As the audience filed out of court, Joe Rowan, sitting where he had been for months, borrowed his attorney's phone and placed a call, relaying the news to his family. His face held composure, but his head stayed tipped forward as he spoke softly. He looked leaner than he had just weeks before. He had been fasting dawn to dusk and praying.

The prosecutors and other government officials poured out into the hallway, where hugs and congratulations were being exchanged. Paul Baumrind, the FBI agent, wept openly as he left the court-room. Reporters huddled around the victors. A light rain spattered the glass.

A few minutes later, back in the courtroom, the only people present were the defendants and their counsel. There was nothing to greet them outside the door but the ebullient mood in the hall and the TV cameras staked outside the building, waiting for them to emerge. Inside the courtroom, it was deathly quiet and still.

The Insys executives would not be sentenced until almost eight months later. Meanwhile, other ramifications of the Insys scandal were still playing themselves out across the country, in separate proceedings. For legal reasons, the Boston jurors were never told that many of the doctors and former Insys employees they heard about at great length had already been prosecuted. (After the verdict, some jurors went straight to Google to satisfy their curiosity—*did anything happen to Couch and Ruan?*—and talked to one another about what they learned.) The outcomes of the numerous ancillary Insys cases varied widely, illustrating the leeway and power that judges are afforded in determining sentences.

Xiulu Ruan and John Patrick Couch were convicted by an Alabama federal jury on more than a dozen felony counts, including RICO conspiracy, and sentenced to twenty-one and twenty years in prison, respectively. The judge agreed with the prosecutors' view that Ruan was the driving force. In written correspondence from prison, Couch defended his credentials and record as a physician and criticized the tactics of the prosecution, the professional judgment of the government's expert witnesses, and court rulings that limited the defense's ability to put forth evidence in his favor. Couch argued that his fate was emblematic of a system that is making it impossible for chronic-pain patients to get care because doctors "are not willing to help them and wind up in federal prison for decades." Natalie Perhacs, the Insys sales rep for Ruan and Couch, was sentenced to six months of home confinement, along with probation and community service. The nurse-practitioners Justin Palmer and Bridgette Parker, from the Mobile clinic, both pled guilty to drug conspiracy charges, testified against their former bosses, and have since served prison time themselves.

In Michigan, Gavin Awerbuch was given a sentence of thirty-two months, well below the guidelines, and received a further reduction for cooperation. He was released from federal custody in May 2020, after less than thirteen months. In New Hampshire, Christopher Clough was convicted of anti-kickback charges and sentenced to four years of incarceration. Credited with acceptance of responsibility and cooperation, Natalie Levine Babich received a sentence in the District of Connecticut of six months' home confinement, followed by probation, as well as community service.

Like Natalie Babich and Karen Hill, Heather Alfonso received no prison time, only three years of probation. Elizabeth Gurrieri was also sentenced to three years of supervised release.

Most of these defendants also face major financial penalties. Many of them are unlikely ever to get out from under their debts.

Paul Madison has not been accused of any crime related to Insys. His indictment in 2012 on health-care fraud and other charges, which sparked debate within Insys, finally led to a federal trial in Chicago in 2018. He was convicted on all eleven counts.

In September 2020, Dr. Steven Chun and Dan Tondre, the Insys rep who called on him after Tracy Krane left, were both arrested, accused in a sixteen-count indictment of conspiracy and kickbacks as well as identification fraud. Chun and Tondre have pled not guilty. Tondre declined to comment, through counsel. An attorney for Chun, Mark Rankin, said, "Dr. Chun is a well-educated and ethical physician who was a speaker for Insys because he believed in the product and was willing to educate other medical professionals, and he took the speaker role seriously. The Insys speaker program in no way influenced Dr. Chun's decisions regarding the care of his patients."

Insys Therapeutics somehow remained in operation into 2019. The company was still marketing Subsys when its former top executives were convicted. In June of that year, Insys agreed to pay

$225 million and admitted to illegal promotion of Subsys, to resolve criminal and civil investigations by the Justice Department. The settlement stemmed from five whistleblower lawsuits filed years before. Mia Guzman, the rookie rep coached by Alec Burlakoff days after he joined the company, was the first of that group to file. Guzman and the other whistleblowers stand to collect a share of the funds recovered by the government in the settlement, a share that theoretically should be in the millions. But the company, having hemorrhaged cash for years, quickly declared bankruptcy after the settlement was finalized and later ceased operations, raising serious doubt as to how much money the United States (and the whistleblowers) will ever recover. Two hundred twenty-five million dollars is a fantastical figure. The Department of Justice is part of a large crowd of creditors fighting for scraps. Many patients who have sued the company are in the same scrum.

Ray Furchak, the first Insys employee to come forward and sound the alarm, is excluded from the scrum altogether because he dropped his early lawsuit after the DOJ declined to take up the case. Nat Yeager and his team in Boston weren't involved in that decision, but Yeager later said that while it was Insys who truly did the damage, "it's appropriate to look at the government's behavior" as well, "and you look back at it and say, of course we could have done better and we wish we went forward at that time."

As Insys fell apart, a significant portion of its former wealth, ironically, went to high-powered law firms hired to defend not only the company but its former executives and sales staff. To varying degrees, Insys funded the defense of the seven defendants in Boston and other former employees, at least until they were convicted, because of indemnification clauses in their employment contracts. Very little money, meanwhile, has gone to the patients victimized in the scheme. Of the tens of millions in restitution that the defendants must relinquish, the vast majority is owed to health insurers who paid for Subsys. The most that patients will get from that pot is a refund of their co-pays.

With bankruptcy court approval, Insys sold off Subsys to another company. As of this writing, the product is still on the market.

———

In January 2020, the five trial defendants returned to the federal courthouse in Boston to be sentenced. Over the course of two weeks, they and the cooperators who turned, Mike Babich and Alec Burlakoff, each had a dedicated hearing and stood before Judge Burroughs. The hearings formed a crescendo of a kind, taking place roughly in order of seniority, climbing the hierarchy and ending with Kapoor.

Since the conclusion of the trial, the judge had delivered a significant blow to the government. Despite her evident respect for the jurors, Burroughs vacated part of their verdict—a ruling that the government would appeal. The conviction of all the defendants still stood, and it was unclear whether their sentences would even be affected, but Burroughs ruled that, contrary to the jury's findings, the government had not proven that the defendants involved in the kickback scheme specifically intended that Subsys be prescribed with no legitimate medical purpose—only that they "did not care" if that occurred as a result of their bribes. It was a fine distinction, and foes of Insys reacted with outrage. Judge Burroughs further alienated them with some remarks in court that downplayed the wrongdoing. The judge described the case at one point as "pretty garden-variety insurance fraud, with the bribery." Burroughs's decision negated, for the time being, the most symbolically potent predicate of the RICO conviction—that like a street gang the defendants had conspired to commit illegal drug distribution. It was a significant precedent that a pharmaceutical executive could be convicted of such an offense.

Nevertheless, all the defendants still faced the potential of significant jail time. The statutory maximum was twenty years, though no one expected the sentences to reach that high. Both sides had a chance to make recommendations to the judge, and the prosecutors initially asked for sentences ranging from five to fifteen years, depending on the defendant.

In the end, Mike Gurry and Rich Simon were both sentenced to thirty-three months in prison. Joe Rowan received twenty-seven months.

On the eve of Sunrise Lee's hearing, her counsel, Pete Horstmann, used the occasion of his sentencing memorandum to unleash a screed, posing Lee as a woman used, a mere instrument of the men who ran the show at Insys and directed her to do exactly what she did. Their treatment of her, he wrote, was emblematic of an opioid industry that should have been "boarded-up" long ago. Big Pharma had "weaponized" the exploitation of women as sexual lures for male doctors, Horstmann argued, and Insys's leaders had taken the next logical step. Rather than descending on college campuses to tap "cheerleaders and models" as sales representatives, Alec Burlakoff had turned to "gentlemen's clubs, not Clemson or Alabama."

For her part, Lee looked more saddened than defiant when she entered court the following day to be sentenced, accompanied by family. When she briefly addressed the judge, she stood unsteadily and could barely be heard. Her account of how she had ended up in her position was inadequate and confused. Judge Burroughs noted Lee's lack of pharmaceutical experience, her personal history, and the way in which Burlakoff recruited her into the company and the scheme. She was "in many ways extremely ill-equipped to deal with the situation at Insys," the judge said. Burroughs sentenced Sunrise Lee to one year and one day.

At Mike Babich's hearing, his wife, Natalie, appeared in the gallery in the second row, after having been absent throughout the trial. Addressing the court, the former CEO portrayed himself as a young man in over his head at Insys, caught between a boss who "berated" him and "was all controlling" and "a head of sales that could not be controlled." Babich tried to "play peacemaker," he said, with Kapoor and Burlakoff, as well as with Matt Napoletano, "who didn't get along with either of them." When Insys came under investigation and "we had lawyers all over the company," Babich thought he could be a tough guy from Chicago and "stick it out." Adding the pro forma words expected at sentencing, Babich said, "Your Honor, that's no excuse."

In the hearings for both Babich and Burlakoff, Fred Wyshak spoke for the government and made a forceful argument that the two deserved substantial credit for admitting their role and cooperating against the others. Although this is not an unusual phenomenon, it was nonetheless striking to hear the government go to bat for two men they had pursued for years and arrested at gunpoint.

When Burlakoff flew to Boston to talk to investigators without a lawyer back in 2016, Nat Yeager's voice had dripped with disgust. But at sentencing, his colleague Wyshak made a particularly impassioned case on Burlakoff's behalf. Having spent perhaps a hundred hours with Burlakoff, Wyshak said he found him to be "incredibly remorseful." The prosecutor said later that the relationship was professional, not personal, but it seemed apparent that a bond of a kind had developed between the two, across the fence between criminal and cop.

"Quite frankly," Wyshak said of Burlakoff, "I believe that he changed the entire complexion of this case" when he came forward. Wyshak implored Judge Burroughs to recognize the societal interest in rewarding people with leniency when they "assist the government in unraveling a case of this significance." Sometimes "you have to hold your nose," he said, and give a benefit to a criminal to serve a greater cause. Wyshak said "the primary objective of this prosecution, obviously, was to get to the top of the pyramid, with Mr. Kapoor," because "if you really want to deter this kind of conduct, you have to take out the top."

Judge Burroughs said she agreed about the importance of the case, citing "the shock waves that it sent through the pharmaceutical industry." But, she said, rewarding assistance can go only so far. She viewed Kapoor, Babich, and Burlakoff as "co-architects of this thing," she said. If someone at the bottom of the hierarchy flips, "that's an easy one," Burroughs said, but she worried about sending the message that you can be up at the top and "do the very worst thing and then erase it by cooperating."

Judge Burroughs came down a little bit harder than the government asked. She sentenced Alec Burlakoff to twenty-six months in prison, and Mike Babich to thirty months.

———

That afternoon, a capacity crowd came to court for the sentencing of the Insys founder. Since his conviction, authorities at the University at Buffalo had swiftly voted to remove the names John and Editha Kapoor from a building that had been named after the couple in recognition of their longtime philanthropic support. A large group of patients appeared for Kapoor's hearing, to tell their stories before a microphone and press for a severe punishment. "I don't want to read the rest of this," a man named Mark Gruenspecht said, slapping down his notes in the middle of his wrenching remarks. "I really don't." He had described in painful detail a life on the highest dose of Subsys, prescribed by a well-compensated doctor, a life that he sometimes "begged" would come to an end. "The fact is," he went on, "that the mastermind behind this whole scheme was John Kapoor."

Kapoor's lead attorney, Beth Wilkinson, spoke on his behalf. She made a plea for the judge to consider his age and to take into account the whole person. Wilkinson pointed to the undisputed reality, so incongruous with his behavior at Insys, that Kapoor has given enormous amounts to charitable causes—over $128 million, she said—with a focus on helping people with cancer, and has shown great generosity to those around him in his personal life. In every way, Wilkinson said, he has taken care of his brother, who suffers from "extreme limitations" in the wake of a coma.

When Kapoor himself addressed the judge, it was the first time, since his arrest, that he had spoken more than a few words in court, or in any other public forum. He and the other defendants might as well have watched their own trial from the gallery.

Leaning his hands on a table as he stood and consulted his notes, Kapoor appeared frail. He spoke once more of his late wife's suffering as the genesis of his ambitions for Subsys. "There are two things that cancer patients fear," he said. "One is death, and the other is pain."

Kapoor's grandfatherly tone was difficult to square with the many accounts of his screaming tirades at Insys subordinates. He turned to his right and looked at the patients and their families, telling them he was "heartbroken" by their words. He said that the doctors Insys called on were enrolled in the TIRF REMS program and "understood what Subsys was and what risks it carried." The attempt to shift blame onto the doctors seemed unlikely to move the judge, much less the patients in the room. The evidence showed that Kapoor was well aware, during the scheme, that Insys was paying doctors who were prescribing Subsys to patients who were nothing like his late wife, people who should never have been taking the drug. Kapoor acknowledged that he was "relentless and demanding" and said that he "wanted to believe in Subsys maybe, perhaps, too much."

Judge Burroughs responded with words of empathy, acknowledging Kapoor's good deeds and his apparent "genius," before saying that she could not ignore his conduct and the harm it caused to so many people. "And I don't know what motivated you," she said. For some Insys defendants it was clearly money or adrenaline, she said, but "I don't know what it was with you."

After a long windup, with the tension growing in the gallery, Burroughs said, "It is the judgment of the court that the defendant, John Kapoor, is hereby committed to custody of the Bureau of Prisons to be imprisoned for a term of sixty-six months." Five and a half years was far from the fifteen that the government had asked for, but for an older man accustomed to freedom and luxury, it was a sanction with teeth.

Judge Burroughs gave the defendants dates when they were due to report to prisons, rather than ordering them taken into custody immediately. Alec Burlakoff chose not to seek any further delays; he was held in a prison camp and later sent to a halfway house to serve the balance of his sentence. After a lengthy series of court-ordered postponements, occasioned by concerns about the spread of COVID-19 behind bars, the rest all reported to federal facilities around the country to begin serving their terms. An appeals court would later uphold the convictions and go a step further, reinstating the jury's findings of guilt with respect to illegal drug distribution and restoring the full force of the jury verdict. The Boston defendants were the first pharmaceutical executives sent to prison in connection with the opioid epidemic.

———

When Mike Babich's lawyer Wick Sollers was arguing at sentencing that Babich was a man out of his depth at Insys, he made a revealing remark, almost in passing. Sollers pointed out that Babich had no regulatory background when he was named CEO, "no compliance training, nor any meaningful legal or compliance infrastructure that would protect the company and him from what ultimately befell them." This was, of course, an inadequate defense for what Babich did—but it also carried the unmistakable ring of real insight. Sollers would never have stated the subtext of his comment directly, but it was nonetheless clear: *if only Kapoor and Babich had had a good lawyer on hand—if only they had protected themselves—they never would have gotten in trouble.*

If John Kapoor had been the type of person who took the precaution of hiring and empowering a couple of in-house legal and regulatory professionals from the start, the Insys story would have unfolded much differently. Anyone with regulatory experience would have looked around at the competitors and tried to dial back the most flagrant excesses so that Insys wouldn't stick out so much in the crowd.

A solid compliance department would have ensured better operational security. Reps might have used drop-down menus, not free-form messages, to report to headquarters about doctors so that the brass wouldn't be exposed to the unsavory details. The sales force would have been trained that you don't type "very shady pill mill" in an email. If anyone did that anyway, the company would have cut ties to the clinic, in case an investigator came calling. If Matt Napoletano could have summoned backup from a company lawyer, he might have convinced Kapoor that it was a terrible idea to track the ROI of a speaker program in a spreadsheet. (If Napoletano meant to bury that document so it was never found, as Mike Babich claimed, he didn't succeed. It became Government Exhibit 197, probably the most damning piece of evidence at trial.)

Major drug companies don't create spreadsheets like that. At the pharma giant Novartis, the chief compliance officer stated in presentations, "If you don't have to write it, don't. Consider using the phone."

With the normal precautions in place, the Insys speaker program would likely still function today as a way of rewarding and inducing prescribing, as such programs do throughout the business. Subsys would still be widely prescribed to patients without cancer because Insys would still be targeting pain specialists with few cancer patients—just like the rest of the TIRF manufacturers. A top prescriber might occasionally lose a license or even get arrested, but when the authorities sifted through the evidence during the investigation, Insys would come away clean; its relationship with the doctor would look just like everyone else's.

Of course, the company would never have climbed so high so quickly if it had stayed inside the lines. The approval rate at the IRC alone gave Insys a huge edge over Cephalon and Galena. But Kapoor had an excellent drug. Over time, it would have clawed at least some market share away from the competition—perhaps a lot of it. Some patients undoubtedly would have been prescribed Subsys unnecessarily, and some of them would have become addicted, even died. But no one at Insys would face any personal consequences for it. The seven defendants in Boston might still be working at the company, making great money. John Kapoor would be able to retire whenever he wanted, buildings still adorned with his family's name.

With a good general counsel and a real compliance department, the executives would still have put a lot of people at risk—but not themselves. At the Babich hearing, when Sollers expanded on the theme of his client's vulnerable position at Insys, he said that Babich lacked "guardrails" in a highly regulated industry, that he lacked a "regulatory safety net." A proper big-league pharma company has guardrails and safety nets. The beauty of a guardrail is that if you drive too fast, you might damage your car but you don't drive off the mountain. The beauty of a safety net is that you can be reckless and you'll never get hurt.

ACKNOWLEDGMENTS

It is a commonplace observation that writing a book can be a lonely endeavor. What isn't discussed often enough, however, is that all works of journalism are fundamentally collaborative enterprises. The more sensitive the story, the more the author relies on the bravery, time, and care of sources who place their trust in a person who started out as a stranger. For many of the sources who spoke to me, I was probing the worst chapter in their lives. The book owes a heavy debt to those who shared with me their perspective, their time, and sometimes the documents in their possession. Typically, they had little incentive to talk to me, and many reasons not to do it. Some were parties to active litigation. Others had appeared as witnesses before a grand jury, in secret, and expected that they might be called as witnesses in a trial. A number of them had not spoken to any other media before. These sources knew that speaking to a reporter could complicate their situation and that no one would compensate them for it. They also knew that they would have no control over the finished product. But they participated in the book nonetheless. These people are too numerous to name, and many have chosen not to be named, but I thank them. Their participation made the book possible.

Many of my sources made the book immeasurably better but go unnamed in the main text or appear only fleetingly, owing to my narrative approach. With the exception of a few of the attorneys and investigators in the Insys trial in Boston, authorities who uncovered pivotal information and shared their knowledge with me are barely visible to the reader because the book favors a tight focus on the central figures at Insys itself and at the clinics the company relied on.

Elizabeth McCarthy of the U.S. Attorney's Office in Boston was a major help, over a period she probably thought would never end. Christina Sterling also provided assistance. Special Agents Paul Baumrind, Vivian Barrios, Terrence Dupont, and spokespersons Kristen Setera and Laurel Sweet of FBI Boston deserve my thanks.

Defense counsel in the Boston trial treated me with professionalism and respect when they had reasons to be on guard. They included Pete Horstmann, Mike Kendall, Steven Tyrrell, and, on the team representing John Kapoor, Beth Wilkinson, Kosta Stojilkovic, Chan Sethi, and Sean McGrew.

Christopher Bodnar, an Assistant U.S. Attorney in the Southern District of Alabama, played a direct role in the events as one of two prosecutors on the *U.S. v. Couch* team, but he also walked me through the intricacies and folkways of federal criminal procedure on numerous occasions, helping me understand what was occurring in the many Insys-related court proceedings, not only his own case. His coworker Deborah Griffin as well as Michael Burt and Kevin Downey of the DEA provided insight about the Couch and Ruan story, as did several unnamed patients of the clinic.

For my reporting on the Awerbuch case, my thanks to Marc Heggemeyer and Katherine Harris of HHS–OIG and Travis Lloyd and Mara Schneider of the FBI.

Richard Franklin was very helpful on the subject of drug development. Caleb Alexander shared expertise about the TIRF REMS program. Andrew Kolodny and Adriane Fugh-Berman, foes of the prescription-painkiller industry, spoke to me about the history of pain management and the role of drug companies. The attorneys Richard Hollawell, Aaron Moore, and Michael Rainboth, all involved in civil cases against Insys, gave me a lot of time.

When reporting on a subject that is still enmeshed in extensive litigation, it can often seem as if the system is ranged against you. Many people have an interest in restricting access to information, on both sides. Publicity can muck up the works of an investigation, so government litigants often keep mum and favor filing court documents under seal when they can—despite that they are public servants, paid by the taxpayers who are being kept in the dark. Meanwhile, defendants such as Insys have no desire to be exposed and often go to great lengths to suppress evidence, such as gagging a plaintiff as a condition of settling a civil case. In theory, judges protect the public's right to know; in practice, they're busy and sometimes too readily agree to the secrecy that both parties to a case find convenient. Freedom of information laws are invaluable but carve out exceptions that can make little sense, at least to me. I was lucky in this instance that the most important legal matter went to trial, producing a wealth of new information that would never otherwise have come to light. But luck should not be required. It is not only the media but democracy itself that relies on transparency. I would like to thank those who fight for it.

This story began, for me, as a feature published in 2018 in *The New York Times Magazine*, after many months of work. At the magazine, I was lucky to work with Luke Mitchell and Bill Wasik. In addition to skillfully editing the text down to the line level, they gave invaluable guidance from a higher altitude, informing my thinking about how to give shape to a massive amount of material. Cynthia Cotts and Alex Carp worked incredibly hard as fact-checkers on the article. I am pretty sure I learned more about reporting from them than vice versa.

When this project became a book, Yaniv Soha, my editor at Doubleday, became a close and invaluable collaborator. He believed in it from a germinal stage and invested a lot of intelligence, time, and attention in improving it in so many respects. The book is the endpoint of a lengthy conversation between us that began years ago, before it was written, and I will always remember the value of that give and take. Thanks also to Cara Reilly, a keen reader from the beginning.

Daniel Novack at Doubleday is precisely the lawyer you want in your corner when you're reporting a story rife with legal implications.

My agent, David Halpern of the Robbins Office, has my profound appreciation. He and Kathy Robbins took a chance on me some years ago, and since then, David has spent an inordinate amount of time advocating on my behalf, cheerleading for me, and dealing with my anxieties. I owe him a ton. My thanks also to Michelle Kroes at CAA.

Most of all, I am grateful to my family and especially my wife. Adelle was a source of tremendous support, even when I whined about sources who wouldn't call me back and the aggravation and futility of writing. In addition to making sacrifices to give me time and space to work, she gave wise advice all along the way, and she was an important early reader. I love her and our daughter, Isabel, more than I can say.

AUTHOR'S NOTE

The reporting for this book began in December 2016, when the arrests of Michael Babich, Alec Burlakoff, and four other former executives at Insys Therapeutics caught my attention. I began months of work on the story for a lengthy feature article in *The New York Times Magazine*. In the middle of that period, investigators reached the pinnacle of the company when Insys's founder, John Kapoor, then a billionaire, was himself indicted. By the time the article was published in May 2018, it was apparent to me that the story deserved a book-length treatment, not only because of its scope and importance, but because it was far from over.

The Insys saga generated a mountain of litigation, and the book draws from court records in dozens of cases, not all of which are mentioned. But legal documents such as indictments or civil complaints can be given undue weight. They offer unproven allegations that have not been contextualized, challenged, or stress-tested. Many times, however, the public has to content itself with that incomplete picture, because defendants so often plead guilty in criminal cases or settle in civil actions, particularly in the pharmaceutical business. No one needs to answer hard questions. A crucial aspect of the Insys story, to me, is that the saga progressed all the way to trial, in several cases, and thus afforded an unprecedented view into the workings of the painkiller industry amid a national crisis. I attended four federal criminal trials in the course of my reporting—in Alabama, New Hampshire, New York City, and Boston. Of these, by far the most critical was the trial in Boston of the senior Insys executives, in *U.S. v. Babich*, which took place from January to May 2019. I was present for every hour of that trial, including jury selection and weeks of deliberations, along with related hearings that were held in the months before, during, and after, outside the presence of the jury.

The legal record was supplemented by my independent reporting. This book draws from hundreds of interviews with more than a hundred people, only some of whom are named. These included former Insys employees, patients, doctors, nurses and other staff at pain clinics, public health officials, prosecutors, federal agents, plaintiff's attorneys, and defense attorneys. Many of them spoke to me dozens of times, despite the potential for legal or other repercussions.

Portraits of the personalities and habits of key figures in the book are often informed by numerous sources who interacted with them, named and unnamed. No pseudonyms are used, and there are no composite characters. Direct quotation is almost always drawn from my firsthand participation or from a recording or transcript. In a few instances, if two sources remembered a remark in an identical way, or one person was certain of a verbatim wording that wasn't disputed by anyone else present, I used quotation marks. But there is no "reconstructed" dialogue; I did not learn the gist of a conversation and render it in quotation marks.

The book generally eschews the quotation of commentators at a remove from the narrative. I did, however, rely on experts who generously lent their knowledge and guidance about, for instance, drug development, pharmaceutical marketing and distribution, the regulation of controlled substances, the practice of pain management, the rules and customs of federal prosecution, and more.

Although the events described in this book are heavily documented and litigated and were subject to my own best reporting efforts, what happened at Insys remains disputed. No one can say with certainty, for example, what transpired in a 2012 meeting involving four people. Even if all four answered questions truthfully, they would recollect the events differently and with varying degrees of detail. Moreover, numerous participants in the narrative are known to have lied, and some have given no public accounts. In relating the story, I have made judgments about credibility and plausibility and sought to be transparent about my sourcing, to the extent possible. An attentive reader will be able to discern a great deal, through the main text and the endnotes, about what accounts I have drawn from and where to turn to learn more.

I made sustained efforts to contact those discussed in the text. It is important to note that some of the people whose conduct was closely scrutinized in court and who feature centrally in this book declined to participate in the reporting process. After I made numerous attempts to seek interviews or statements, John Kapoor, Michael Babich, Matthew Napoletano, Michael Gurry, Richard Simon, and Joseph Rowan declined to comment, usually through counsel, or didn't respond to requests. Some of their attorneys cited pending appeals and other unresolved litigation. Gavin Awerbuch, Natalie Babich, Judge Allison D. Burroughs, Christopher Clough, Franc Del Fosse, Karen Hill, Paul Madison, Kourtney Nagy, Natalie Perhacs, Xiulu Ruan, Shawn Simon, Wick Sollers, Judson Somerville, Leslie Zacks, and a spokesperson for Cephalon parent company Teva Pharmaceuticals also declined to comment, through counsel or directly, or did not respond to requests for comment.

NOTES

KEY TO ABBREVIATIONS FOR SELECTED COURT CASES AND DOCUMENTS

Alfonso:	*U.S. v. Alfonso,* No. 15 Cr. 111, D. Conn.
Awerbuch:	*U.S. v. Awerbuch,* No. 16 Cr. 20636, E.D. Mich.
Babich:	*U.S. v. Babich,* No. 16 Cr. 10343, D. Mass.
Babich deposition:	Deposition of Michael Babich, Jan. 27, 2020, in *Fuller v. Insys Therapeutics Inc. et al.,* No. 17 Cv. 07877, D. N.J.
Clough:	*U.S. v. Clough,* No. 17 Cr. 37, D. N.H.
Couch:	*U.S. v. Couch,* No. 15 Cr. 88, S.D. Ala.
Davis and Zacks motion:	Government's Motion to Admit Certain Testimony of Danielle Davis and Leslie Zacks to Avoid Jury Being Misled, in *Babich,* March 17, 2019
Furchak:	*U.S. ex rel. Ray Furchak v. Insys,* No. 12 Cv. 2930, S.D. Tex.
Gurrieri:	*U.S. v. Gurrieri,* No. 17 Cr. 10083, D. Mass.
Guzman:	*United States ex rel. Maria Guzman v. Insys,* No. 13 Cv. 5861, C.D. Calif.
Hill:	*U.S. v. Hill,* No. 17 Cr. 139, S.D. Ala.
Jefferies report:	"Company Note: Insys Therapeutics Inc. (INSY)," an equity research report by the firm Jefferies LLC, Dec. 8, 2014
Kapoor sentencing memo:	Sentencing Memorandum on Behalf of John Kapoor, in *Babich,* Dec. 18, 2019
Kottayil:	*Kottayil v. Insys,* No. CV2009-028831, Superior Court of the State of Arizona, Maricopa County
LaCorte:	*Frank LaCorte, Kelly Moore-Martin, and Alec Burlakoff v. Eli Lilly and Company et al.,* Broward County Circuit Court, No. CACE02023118
Lee sentencing memo:	Defendant Lee's Sentencing Memorandum, in *Babich,* Jan. 21, 2020

Levine:	*U.S. v. Levine,* No. 17 Cr. 147, D. Conn.
N.J. AG Complaint:	*Christopher S. Porrino, Attorney General of New Jersey v. Insys Therapeutics Inc.,* No. MID-C-162-17, Superior Court of New Jersey, Chancery Division, Middlesex Vicinage, First Amended Complaint
Perhacs:	*U.S. v. Perhacs,* No. 16 Cr. 24, S.D. Ala.
Porrino:	*Christopher S. Porrino, Attorney General of New Jersey v. Insys Therapeutics Inc.,* No. MID-C-162-17, Superior Court of New Jersey, Chancery Division, Middlesex Vicinage
Rowan sentencing memo:	Sentencing Memorandum on Behalf of Joseph Rowan, in *U.S. v. Babich,* Dec. 18, 2019

SELECTED FIGURES, IN ALPHABETICAL ORDER, WITH ABBREVIATIONS
References to job titles indicate titles at the time of the events described.

Alfonso:	Heather Alfonso, an advanced practice registered nurse, based in Connecticut
Babich:	Michael "Mike" Babich, Insys chief executive officer, 2011–2015
Baumrind:	Paul Baumrind, special agent, Federal Bureau of Investigation
Beisler:	Susan "Sue" Beisler, Insys sales representative
Bryant:	Tony Bryant, Insys regional sales manager, 2012
Burlakoff:	Alec Burlakoff, Insys regional sales manager, then vice president and finally senior vice president of sales, 2012–2015
Chun:	Dr. Steven Chun, a pain management specialist in Florida
Couch:	Dr. John Patrick Couch, pain specialist and co-owner with Dr. Xiulu Ruan of Physicians Pain Specialists of Alabama
Clough:	Christopher Clough, a physician's assistant at a pain clinic in New Hampshire
Furchak:	Raymond "Ray" Furchak, Insys sales representative, 2012
Gurrieri:	Elizabeth Gurrieri, a prior-authorization specialist and then manager at Insys, 2012–2016
Gurry:	Michael "Mike" Gurry, Insys vice president of managed markets, beginning in 2012
Guzman:	Maria "Mia" Guzman, Insys sales representative, 2012–2013
Heggemeyer:	Marc Heggemeyer, special agent, U.S. Department of Health and Human Services–Office of Inspector General
Hill:	Karen Hill, Insys sales representative and then manager, 2012–2017
Kapoor:	Dr. John Kapoor, founder, majority owner, and executive chairman of Insys, later also the chief executive officer
Krane:	Tracy Krane, Insys sales representative, 2012
Lazarus:	David Lazarus, Assistant U.S. Attorney, District of Massachusetts, one of three prosecutors on the trial team in *Babich*

Lee: Sunrise Lee, Insys regional sales manager and later regional
                    sales director
Levine: Natalie Levine, Insys sales representative, 2013–2014, later
                    named Natalie Babich
Lloyd: Travis Lloyd, special agent, Federal Bureau of Investigation
Madison: Dr. Paul Madison, an anesthesiologist practicing in Illinois
                    and other states
Napoletano: Matthew "Matt" Napoletano, Insys vice president of
                    marketing, 2012–2014
Palmer: Justin Palmer, nurse-practitioner at Physicians Pain
                    Specialists of Alabama, working primarily under Dr. John
                    Patrick Couch
Parker: Bridgette Parker, nurse-practitioner at Physicians Pain
                    Specialists of Alabama, working under Dr. Xiulu Ruan and
                    Dr. John Patrick Couch
Perhacs: Natalie Perhacs, sales representative and later a manager at
                    Insys, 2012–2015
Rowan: Joseph "Joe" Rowan, Insys sales representative and later
                    regional sales manager and regional sales director
Ruan: Dr. Xiulu Ruan, pain specialist and co-owner with Dr.
                    John Patrick Couch of Physicians Pain Specialists of
                    Alabama
Simon: Richard "Rich" Simon, Insys regional sales manager, then
                    national sales director
Skalnican: Kendra Skalnican, a patient of Dr. Gavin Awerbuch's
Szymanski: Brett Szymanski, Insys sales representative and later a
                    manager, 2012–2016
Wilkinson: Beth Wilkinson of Wilkinson Walsh (later called Wilkinson
                    Stekloff), defense counsel for Dr. John Kapoor, in *Babich*
Witherspoon: Tamisan Witherspoon, formerly known as Tamisan Blanks,
                    a patient at Couch and Ruan's clinic in Mobile, Alabama
Wyshak: Fred Wyshak, Assistant U.S. Attorney, District of
                    Massachusetts, one of three prosecutors on the trial team in
                    Babich
Yeager: K. Nathaniel "Nat" Yeager, Assistant U.S. Attorney, District
                    of Massachusetts, one of three prosecutors on the trial team
                    in *Babich*

PROLOGUE

1   He was educated: Awerbuch testimony.
2   Awerbuch had around five thousand: Ibid.
2   With the near collapse: The employer is Nexteer Automotive, formerly
     called Delphi Corp.
2   More than half: Exhibit 2221.
3   In January 2013: Affidavit in Support of Criminal Complaint, in *Awerbuch*; Heggemeyer, author interview.

4   "That was where": Heggemeyer, author interview.

4   fentanyl is up to: Centers for Disease Control and Prevention, cdc.gov.

4   By 2017, fentanyl: "Drug and Opioid-Involved Overdose Deaths—
         United States, 2017–2018," Morbidity and Mortality Weekly Report:
         MMWR, Centers for Disease Control and Prevention, March 20,
         2020.

5   They visited a young mother: The account of this interview draws on
         author interviews with Heggemeyer, Lloyd, and Skalnican.

5   When the agents went to see: This account draws from Affidavit in Sup-
         port of Criminal Complaint, in *Awerbuch;* Awerbuch testimony, in *Babich;*
         Heggemeyer, author interview; and statement of Donna Andrews, for-
         merly known as Donna Giessinger, at the sentencing hearing for Michael
         Gurry, Jan. 13, 2020, in *Babich.*

6   she later acknowledged: Statement of Donna Andrews at the sentencing
         hearing for Michael Gurry, Jan. 13, 2020, in *Babich.*

6   Awerbuch often prescribed: Heggemeyer, author interview.

6   A typical prescription: N.J. AG Complaint.

6   Medicare paid: Affidavit in Support of Criminal Complaint, in *Awerbuch.*

6   "how deadly that drug": Heggemeyer, author interview.

7   "As soon as he saw us": Ibid.

7   By this point, Awerbuch: This paragraph draws from photographs from
         the execution of search warrants, in *Awerbuch;* Heggemeyer, author inter-
         view; forfeiture proceedings related to *Awerbuch.*

7   Waiting for him in a conference room: Baumrind, author interview.

8   The CEO, Michael Babich, had held up: "Best IPO of 2013: Insys Thera-
         peutics," *Fast Money,* CNBC, Dec. 27, 2013.

CHAPTER 1: THE MENTOR AND THE PROTÉGÉ

11   It was a quiet day: Details about Babich's job at Northern Trust and his
         upbringing draw from his testimony, in *Babich* and from Sentencing
         Memorandum on Behalf of Michael Babich and the letters of relatives
         and associates attached as exhibits, in *Babich,* Dec. 18, 2019.

11   Babich became the first in his family: Sentencing Memorandum on
         Behalf of Michael Babich, letter of Babich's cousin Donald Busse.

12   As Babich would come: The description of Kapoor's upbringing draws
         from Kapoor sentencing memo and the letters of his relatives attached
         as exhibits, as well as from statements made by Kapoor's attorney Beth
         Wilkinson at his sentencing hearing.

13   In India, he said: Matthew Herper and Michela Tindera, "An Opioid
         Spray Showered Billionaire John Kapoor in Riches. Now He's Feeling the
         Pain," *Forbes,* Oct. 25, 2016.

13   Kapoor came to the United States: Jimmy Magahern, "Meet the Million-
         aires," *Phoenix Magazine,* Aug. 2008; Wilkinson's opening statement for
         Kapoor, in *Babich.*

13   By the time Babich met him: Babich deposition.

14   In his mid-thirties: The account of Kapoor's early career draws mainly
         from trial testimony of Kapoor in December 2014 in *Kottayil;* Steven

Morris, "Exec Finds Life After Lyphomed," *Chicago Tribune*, Oct. 12, 1990; Arsenio Olaroso Jr., "In Health Care, He's Everywhere," *Crain's Chicago Business*, Feb. 18, 1995.

14 "hoping to get your pennies back": Babich deposition.

14 "At midnight": Olaroso, "In Health Care, He's Everywhere."

14 Lyphomed had a de facto monopoly: The drug was pentamidine, marketed under different brand names. See "Making a Killing on AIDS: Home Health Care & Pentamidine," a report by the City of New York Department of Consumer Affairs, May 1991; "Firm's Sharp Price Increase for Drug Attacked," *Los Angeles Times*, Oct. 31, 1987.

14 Protesters lay down: "American Greed: The Fall of an Opioid Mogul," CNBC, Feb. 8, 2021.

15 Lyphomed grew: Kapoor sentencing memo; Olaroso, "In Health Care, He's Everywhere"; "Fujisawa to Buy Lyphomed, a Critical-Care Drug Maker," *New York Times*, Sept. 2, 1989.

15 Beginning in 1987: See "Troubled Maker of AIDS Drugs Promises Better Quality but Faces New Problems," Associated Press, March 15, 1988.

15 Investigators in 1988 seized: "FDA to Keep Eye on Lyphomed," *Orlando Sentinel*, July 8, 1988.

15 Shareholders sued the company: *Harman v. LyphoMed Inc.*, No. 88 Cv. 0476, N.D. Ill.

15 Later, the FDA found: *Fujisawa Pharmaceutical Co. v. Kapoor*, 936 F. Supp. 455 (N.D. Ill. 1996); "Fujisawa USA Files $805.6 Mil. Lawsuit Against Ex–Lyphomed Chief Kapoor," *Pink Sheet*, Aug. 24, 1992.

15 In pretrial litigation: *Fujisawa Pharmaceutical Co. v. Kapoor*, 936 F. Supp. 455 (N.D. Ill. 1996), ruling of Judge Elaine E. Bucklo, July 25, 1996; *Fujisawa Pharmaceutical Co. Ltd. v. Kapoor*, 115 F. 3d 1332, Court of Appeals, 7th Cir., June 16, 1997.

15 "somebody not keeping good records": "Ex–Lyphomed Owner Sued in Drug Recalls," *Chicago Tribune*, Aug. 20, 1992.

15 When a congressional panel: "Congressman Faults F.D.A. on Generics," *New York Times*, March 8, 1991.

16 He settled the Fujisawa matter: Herper and Tindera, "Opioid Spray."

16 Fujisawa was left: "Ex–Lyphomed Owner Sued in Drug Recalls."

16 With his newfound wealth: This paragraph draws from Sentencing Memorandum on Behalf of John Kapoor and attached exhibits.

16 When companies he played: Mike Colias, "Die Hard," *Crain's Chicago Business*, Aug. 18, 2007.

16 "If something happens": Herper and Tindera, "Opioid Spray."

17 While relatives and friends: Kapoor sentencing memo and attached exhibits.

17 the need to "survive" him: Colias, "Die Hard."

17 The meeting was not: The account of Babich's early period at EJ Financial are drawn from Babich testimony.

17 Akorn was in lien default: Kapoor sentencing memo, letter of Ramesh Acharya.

17 after its stock dropped: *In re First Horizon Pharmaceutical Corporation*

Securities Litigation, No. 02 Cv. 2332, N.D. Ga., Plaintiffs' Second Consolidated Amended Class Action Complaint, April 20, 2007.

17   "'DO NOTHING' style": Consent Statement filed with the Securities and Exchange Commission, Oct. 1, 2004.

17   Meanwhile, down the hall: Babich testimony.

17   his assistant Nellie Oquendo tried: Oquendo testimony.

18   His affable demeanor: Colias, "Die Hard."

18   But he could turn cold: Babich testimony; Burlakoff testimony.

18   In his primary role: The account of the HealthSouth episode draws from Babich testimony.

18   "That turned out": Babich testimony.

18   "You're not going to believe": Ibid.

CHAPTER 2: THE BIG BET

20   John Kapoor summoned: The account of the early plans for Insys draws from the testimony of Kottayil and Kapoor, in *Kottayil,* and Babich testimony, in *Babich.*

21   Editha Kapoor battled: Kapoor testimony, in *Kottayil;* Kapoor sentencing memo.

21   "I've never seen": Kapoor sentencing memo, Exhibit 5, letter of Linda Hillock.

21   "I can tell you": Matthew Herper and Michela Tindera, "An Opioid Spray Showered Billionaire John Kapoor in Riches. Now He's Feeling the Pain," *Forbes,* Oct. 25, 2016.

21   In her final days: Kapoor sentencing memo, letters of relatives.

21   Kapoor called out: Kapoor sentencing memo, letter of Jason DeLeo.

22   Developing a brand-name drug: The descriptions of various drug-development paths draw from author interviews with Richard Franklin; see also Theodore H. Stanley, "The Fentanyl Story," *Journal of Pain* 15, no. 12 (Dec. 2014).

22   It would cost tens of millions: Kapoor testimony, in *Kottayil;* Babich testimony, in *Babich;* Babich deposition.

22   Fentanyl, the active ingredient: For the history of fentanyl and TIRF products, see Stanley, "Fentanyl Story."

23   The first TIRF for out-of-hospital use: Prior to the launch of Actiq, a similar product called Oralet was approved for use as a premedication before surgery.

24   In 2006, Actiq generated: Cephalon SEC filings.

24   Babich's version: Babich testimony.

24   As Kapoor has said himself: Kapoor testimony, in *Kottayil.*

25   A Cephalon internal study: A Cephalon internal document, later produced by the company in civil litigation, including *In re National Prescription Opiate Litigation,* No. 17 MD 2804, N.D. Ohio.

25   Recent legal challenges: In the most significant example, *U.S. v. Caronia,* the U.S. Court of Appeals for the Second Circuit found that a drug representative's presentation of truthful, non-misleading information about

off-label use could not be construed as criminal, owing to First Amendment protections.

26   In the end, fully a quarter: FDA Center for Drug Evaluation and Research's Clinical Review for Subsys, completed Dec. 15, 2011.

26   "If you're waiting to die": "Doubts Raised About Off-Label Use of Subsys, a Strong Painkiller," *New York Times*, May 13, 2014.

26   Insys would have a "crowbar": Jim Coffman, a former Insys district sales trainer in the Southeast region in 2012.

28   "These drugs, which are": The Spanos remarks appeared in a Purdue video called "From One Pain Patient to Another," shot in July 1997 and distributed by company sales representatives beginning in 1998, according to company records produced in litigation.

28   no foreign country: The United States ranked first internationally in a 2019 report of the International Narcotics Control Board. A 2016 report by the same organization indicated that in 2015, the United States consumed 30.2 percent of the world's prescription opioids.

28   Fentanyl and its analogs: "Drug and Opioid-Involved Overdose Deaths— United States, 2017–2018," Morbidity and Mortality Weekly Report: MMWR, Centers for Disease Control and Prevention, March 20, 2020.

29   As many as four out of five: National Institute on Drug Abuse, "Prescription Opioid Use Is a Risk Factor for Heroin Use," Oct. 1, 2015.

29   "The bodies are stacking up": "Hillbilly heroin: the painkiller abuse wrecking lives in West Virginia," *The Guardian,* June 24, 2001.

30   The company ultimately pled guilty: *U.S. v. Cephalon,* No. 08 Cr. 598, E.D. Pa.

30   "We are only going to focus": Dr. Clair Callan. Comment made at a meeting of the FDA's Anesthetic and Life Support Drugs Advisory Committee, September 17, 1997.

30   Similar allegations: Federal whistleblower actions brought under the False Claims Act by the Cephalon employees Matthew Cestra, Bruce Boise, and others alleged off-label promotion of Fentora. The company never admitted to Fentora misconduct, nor did it pay to resolve these investigations.

31   "We all know [Actiq]": "Narcotic 'Lollipop' Becomes Big Seller Despite FDA Curbs," *Wall Street Journal,* Nov. 3, 2001.

31   At a 2008 FDA joint meeting: FDA joint meeting of Anesthetic and Life Support Drugs and Drug Safety and Risk Management Advisory Committees, May 5–6, 2008.

31   "aberrant drug use behavior": Presentation of Lori A. Love, MD, PhD, Medical Officer, Controlled Substance Staff, FDA joint meeting of Anesthetic and Life Support Drugs and Drug Safety and Risk Management Advisory Committees, May 5–6, 2008.

32   Babich was surprised to find: Babich testimony.

32   He had taken on more work: Babich deposition.

33   "John's theory was": Ibid.

33   Another option: This paragraph draws from Babich testimony; Kapoor

testimony, in *Kottayil*; Babich deposition. Insys's generic was called dronabinol SG, for soft gelatin capsule. For years, Insys had been trying to develop a hard gelatin capsule that would be stable at higher temperatures, an effort that was ultimately abandoned. Dronabinol SG was approved in 2011 and brought in less than $7 million in net revenue in 2012, according to regulatory filings. Later, Insys stopped marketing it.

33   "a desperate position": These quotations and the discussion of the dire state of affairs in 2009 draw from the testimony of Kapoor and others in *Kottayil*.

33   Much of his funding: Kapoor testimony, in *Kottayil*; Insys regulatory filings.

34   "We had one product": Babich quoted in a profile of him, in "Pharm Exec's 2013 Emerging Pharma Leaders," *Pharmaceutical Executive*, July 1, 2013.

34   The controversies: Kapoor attributed the TIRF market decline to Cephalon's off-label marketing and associated patient deaths in his testimony in *Kottayil*.

34   The market was still worth: See Exhibit 407 in *Babich*, a January 2012 internal Insys presentation to its board of directors (erroneously dated January 2011 on the cover page).

34   Still, Subsys continued: The account of the second attempt at an IPO, the appointment of Babich as CEO, and the delivery of the phase III results draws mainly from Babich testimony, in *Babich*.

CHAPTER 3: THE PLAYBOOK

36   "My opinions were those": The quotation and the agreement to interview Napoletano come from Babich testimony.

37   Napoletano grew up: Napoletano's career background draws from his testimony and Babich's.

37   Only five branded TIRF products: The five were Actiq, Fentora, Lazanda, Abstral, and Onsolis.

37   there was real "upside": The quotation and the discussion of the appeal and drawbacks, for Napoletano, of a job at Insys draw from Napoletano's testimony.

38   He liked to see: Babich testimony.

38   "He was a total goob": Author interview.

39   "I am not going to start": Babich deposition.

39   For a time, Napoletano led: Napoletano testimony.

39   The Drug Enforcement Administration: Drugs classified as Schedule I "have no currently accepted medical use." Examples include heroin, LSD, and Ecstasy.

40   "low-cost model": The quotation is from Babich testimony. It also appears in Insys regulatory filings in reference to the company's hiring policies for its sales force. Napoletano's reaction to the lack of compliance and legal infrastructure and the friction between him and Kapoor draws from Babich testimony, Napoletano testimony, and Babich deposition.

40   "Once he makes up his mind": Babich testimony.

40   "Matt's not very short-winded": Ibid.

41   "private interaction": "Supreme Court Hands Drug Companies Twin Wins," NPR, June 23, 2011.

42   Approximately 1,100 practitioners: Exhibit 407, a January 2012 presentation to the Insys board by the executive team.

43   Because most TIRF scripts: Exhibit 290.

43   the top 25 or so: An internal Insys "target list" derived from third-party data, obtained by the author.

43   "the gurus of fentanyl": Babich deposition.

43   "KOL is a very": Author interview.

43   Though it wasn't billed: Babich testimony.

44   to "touch" them: Burlakoff, author interview.

CHAPTER 4: THE ROOKIES

45   Tracy Krane was living: Krane's account of her home life and of the beginnings of her connection with Insys comes from author interviews with Krane.

46   He was hiring his team: The account of Bryant's plans and impressions draws from author interviews with Bryant and internal Insys documents obtained from former employees.

48   Guzman was a fellow pharma rookie: The account of Guzman's career path and personality draws from author interviews with Guzman and with fellow Insys employees.

48   The job listing: Internal Insys document obtained by the author.

49   The West region in particular: Author interviews with former employees.

49   At another point: Sworn certification of Frank R. Serra, April 24, 2018, attached as Exhibit 43 to Memorandum in Support of Plaintiffs' Motion for Partial Summary Judgment Against Defendant John N. Kapoor, in *Porrino,* Nov. 23, 2020.

50   "one-day relationship": Babich testimony.

50   At Insys, he became involved: Ibid.; author interviews with former employees.

50   He believed in the "low-cost model": Babich testimony.

50   the company publicly touted it: Insys regulatory filings; also, at the Needham Life Sciences Conference in April 2014, Babich said, "We also have a unique commercial model which I believe lends itself well to our success. The majority of our sales representatives have no prior pharmaceutical experience." The remark is quoted in the Amended Class Action Complaint in *Larson v. Insys,* No. 14 Cv. 1043, D. Ariz.

50   The same model had been used: Babich testimony.

50   "We were willing": Ibid.

50   "cost-efficient" sales force: See, for example, Insys's Amendment 12 to the prospectus for its 2013 initial public offering, introduced as Exhibit 575.

50   "poor, hungry, and driven": Burlakoff testimony, in *Babich;* author interviews with former Insys managers.

50   "folks who were": Babich testimony.

50   At Insys, sales commissions: See June 28, 2016, email of Daniel Bren-

nan, then Insys's chief operating officer, attached as Exhibit 45 to Memorandum in Support of Plaintiffs' Motion for Partial Summary Judgment Against Defendant John N. Kapoor, in *Porrino,* Nov. 23, 2020.

51   Bonuses would also be uncapped: Babich testimony; testimony of sales rep Brett Szymanski.

51   One rep in his mid-twenties: Brett Szymanski testified that he graduated from college in 2009 and earned between $1.5 million and $2 million during his employment at Insys from early 2012 to October 2016. He was promoted midway through, but his earnings came mainly from bonuses earned as a rep, from 2012 to mid-2014. Exhibits show that Awerbuch's prescribing was responsible for the vast majority of those bonus payments.

51   "That was John's philosophy": Babich testimony.

51   He went over his allotted time: Ibid.

51   Around dawn the next day: The account of this meeting is drawn mainly from ibid.

52   Kapoor would call: Ibid.

52   He wanted each rep: Ibid.; author interviews with Insys sales managers.

53   Kapoor took matters: Napoletano testimony.

53   "Subsys is good": Ibid.

53   "pain is pain": For example, Complaint, Sept. 27, 2004, in *United States ex rel. Michael Makalusky v. Cephalon Inc.,* No. 04 Cv. 12066, D. Mass.

53   Napoletano went home: Napoletano testimony, in *Babich.*

53   They were among the first: Krane and Guzman, author interviews.

CHAPTER 5: THE ECOSYSTEM

54   shoveling approximately $80 million: Babich deposition.

54   Each of them was given: Testimony of multiple sales reps, in *Babich;* author interviews with sales reps.

55   Clinics would allow reps: Author interviews with a former Insys manager and reps in the industry.

55   "take care of us": Exhibit 642.

55   "That Fentora representative": Email from Simon to Krane, May 31, 2012, obtained by the author.

55   But after a relatively strong: Krane testimony, in *Babich;* Krane, author interviews.

55   She had been told by then: Burlakoff, author interview. Chun has said that he was not in the Cephalon rep's territory.

55   And she suspected: Krane testimony, in *Babich;* Aqsa Nawaz testimony, in *Babich.*

56   Mia Guzman tried to call on: Guzman, author interview; public records.

56   When a young Insys rep: These two paragraphs, including the quotations, draw from Holly Brown's testimony.

57   several of the top early prescribers: Exhibit 533, in *Babich,* shows the top prescribers for the first quarter after launch. The top three names were all present at the December 2011 advisory board event.

57   During the period: FDA Opening Remarks of Sharon Hertz, MD, Joint Meeting of the Drug Safety and Risk Management Advisory Committee

and the Analgesic Drug Products Advisory Committee, Aug. 3, 2018. Before there was a class-wide program called TIRF REMS, which was instituted in 2012, there were REMS for individual TIRF products on the market. Subsys was marketed solely under the class-wide TIRF REMS Access Program.

58   Each one appeared: Exhibit 6039 provides one example.

58   The best time to make a sale: Burlakoff, author interview.

58   patient information was anonymized: Babich testimony.

58   Kapoor, Babich, Napoletano: Ibid., substantiated by numerous data reports disseminated by email from the Insys executive Xun Yu, who worked in sales operations.

58   A deeply worrying trend: Babich testimony; Burlakoff, author interview; Burlakoff testimony.

58   In the first few months: Babich testimony; Napoletano testimony; author interview with former Insys sales manager.

59   Managers grumbled: Author interviews with former Insys sales managers.

59   Kapoor directed Babich: Babich testimony.

59   The regional managers: Serra certification, in *Porrino;* Bryant, author interview.

59   Kapoor was angry: Serra certification, in *Porrino.*

59   Babich didn't know: Babich testimony.

60   the company was spending: Insys regulatory filings. The 2013 10-K indicates $24.4 million in net losses for 2012.

60   "the worst fucking launch": Babich testimony.

CHAPTER 6: THE SALESMAN

61   His father made a living selling: Burlakoff testimony; Burlakoff, author interviews.

61   Before entering the business: The account of Burlakoff's pre-pharma career and the application process at Eli Lilly draws from author interviews with him.

62   Lilly assigned him: Burlakoff, author interviews; also, author interviews with a former Lilly rep trained alongside Burlakoff.

62   "blew it out of the water": Author interview with fellow Lilly rep.

62   He was presented with: Burlakoff, author interview, substantiated by documents.

62   "money hours": Burlakoff, author interview.

62   He developed a close rapport: Ibid.

63   "Since the day I started": Burlakoff's Answer to Interrogatories, dated May 2, 2003, filed in July 2003 in *LaCorte.*

63   He would tell reps: Author interviews with former Insys reps.

63   A co-worker he was coaching: Furchak, author interview.

63   There was resentment: Author interviews with a former Lilly co-worker of Burlakoff's.

63   Word spread that he: Author interviews with a former Lilly co-worker of Burlakoff's.

64   "bullshit": Burlakoff, author interview.

64 When he was a kid: Burlakoff, author interviews.

64 Burlakoff would sometimes talk: Author interviews with former Insys employees.

64 Alec's older brother: Discussion of the Burlakoff family and the culture of Kings Park draws from author interviews with Burlakoff.

64 When he started thinking: Ibid.

65 Along with other reps: The account of the Prozac Weekly switch scheme draws from author interviews with Burlakoff; Burlakoff testimony, in *Babich;* "Free Prozac in the Junk Mail Draws a Lawsuit," *New York Times,* July 6, 2002; "Depositions Reveal Prozac Strategy," *South Florida Sun-Sentinel,* July 15, 2004.

65 "This is appalling": "Free Prozac in the Junk Mail Draws a Lawsuit."

65 Eli Lilly terminated: *LaCorte,* Fourth Amended Complaint.

65 Two security officers: Burlakoff, author interview.

66 He said in the suit: *LaCorte,* Fourth Amended Complaint.

66 Burlakoff took home: Burlakoff testimony, in *Babich.*

66 A co-worker told him later: Burlakoff, author interview.

66 In a 2003 court filing: Burlakoff's Answer to Interrogatories, dated May 2, 2003, and filed in July 2003, in *LaCorte.*

66 Years later, however: Burlakoff testimony, in *Babich.*

66 A manager there had had his eye: Burlakoff, author interview.

66 "I killed it": Ibid.

67 He also garnered a reputation: Author interviews with a former Cephalon co-worker of Burlakoff's.

67 In 2012, Burlakoff heard: Burlakoff, author interview.

67 "Alec was a very sales-y individual": Babich testimony.

67 He had invited Burlakoff: Burlakoff testimony.

67 Burlakoff knew: For discussion of his intentions and conduct at the dinner, Burlakoff, author interview.

67 At the corporate office: Babich testimony; Burlakoff testimony, in *Babich.*

67 Hearing that Kapoor: Burlakoff testimony; Burlakoff, author interviews. Krane recounted, to the author, that Burlakoff described his interview in the same way.

68 "Alec made it very clear": Babich testimony.

68 At the end of the interview: Ibid.; Burlakoff testimony; Burlakoff, author interviews. In Babich's testimony, he appears to recall that Burlakoff had left the room when Kapoor made this remark; Burlakoff insists that he was still present.

CHAPTER 7: THE PROGRAM

69 Babich announced Burlakoff's hiring: In author interviews, Bryant and several sales reps in the Southeast consistently recall the timing and their inference from it.

69 One week after Burlakoff arrived: Krane recounted the ride-along in testimony and in author interviews. The date was substantiated in exhibits introduced through her testimony.

70 Chun worked out of the third floor: Author visit to the site, Feb. 2018.

70      $6 Million Man: Exhibit 2126. Babich recalled in testimony that Chun was referred to as the $9 Million Man, but the document suggests that $6 million was the actual figure used.

70   In the lingo: Burlakoff, Napoletano, and Babich testimony. The term was not unique to Insys. It was used, for instance, at Purdue Pharma.

70   Krane brought Burlakoff: Recollections in this passage draw mainly from author interviews with Krane.

71   perhaps four to twelve attendees: A sales manager in the industry indicates that between four and eight attendees is usually considered acceptable, perhaps three in a rural area. Another pharma sales source said six to twelve was the norm.

72   he spelled it out: Krane testimony; Krane, author interviews; Burlakoff, author interviews.

72   "boiled it right down": Krane, author interviews. Without recalling the specifics, Burlakoff confirmed that a conversation along these lines occurred.

72   He brushed off the question: This paragraph draws from Krane's testimony, in *Babich*, and author interviews with her. The account was consistent.

72   Paying speakers had been part: Exhibit 407, a January 2012 presentation to the board of directors, shows plans for speaker development; author interviews with former Insys sales managers.

73   Napoletano had helped develop: Napoletano testimony, in *Babich*.

73   At Insys, it would cost: Exhibit 207, in *Babich*, is a proposed marketing budget for 2013. It indicates a speaker-program budget of more than $2 million, not including ad boards and speaker-training costs. The cost was around $500,000 in 2012, for a program that began in August of that year.

73   With that kind of expenditure: Napoletano testimony, in *Babich;* Burlakoff testimony, in *Babich;* Burlakoff, author interviews.

73   He didn't have experience: Wilkinson, Kapoor's attorney, made this representation in court, in her questioning of Burlakoff.

73   "Matt would whisper": Babich testimony, in *Babich*.

73   According to him: Burlakoff testimony, in *Babich;* Baumrind testimony, in *Babich*, regarding Burlakoff's statements in interviews with him and other federal investigators.

73   virtually all of it was entrusted: Babich testimony, in *Babich;* Burlakoff testimony, in *Babich;* author interviews.

73   "understand the important nature": Exhibit 166.

73   Some seventy-five doctors: Exhibit 443.

73   Kapoor told them the story of Subsys: Description of the speaker-training event draws from the account of an Insys manager who was present.

73   The attendees included some: Exhibit 5513 shows invitees to the event, though not all were present. Gavin Awerbuch testified that he was present. Exhibit 293 indicates, as of September 2012, which prescribers had attended speaker training, and many were top writers.

74   "He brought us those whales": Burlakoff, author interview. Babich also

testified that Napoletano made important early introductions to prescribers, winning him the approval of Kapoor.

74   When Burlakoff traveled again to Krane's: This dinner episode draws from Krane, author interviews; Krane testimony; Burlakoff testimony; Nawaz testimony.

74   "He wasn't one": Burlakoff, author interview.

74   Burlakoff knew that Dr. Chun: Burlakoff and Krane, author interviews; Nawaz testimony.

75   Burlakoff had previously struggled: Burlakoff, author interview.

75   Krane had scheduled: Krane testimony.

75   Burlakoff made it clear: The account of Burlakoff's pitch draws from ibid.; Krane, author interviews; and Burlakoff testimony.

75   Chun began speaking: Internal documentation obtained from an Insys employee.

75   But Burlakoff still believed: Burlakoff, author interview.

75   "You don't fire people": Ibid.

76   Alec had met Joe Rowan: Ibid.; Burlakoff testimony, in *Babich;* statements in court of Rowan's counsel Michael Kendall; letters of support for Rowan attached as exhibits to Rowan sentencing memo.

76   After Burlakoff became: Burlakoff testimony; Burlakoff, author interview.

76   The two went line dancing: Former Lilly co-worker to Burlakoff and Rowan.

76   They were Methodists: Letters of support attached as exhibits to Rowan sentencing memo.

76   Burlakoff proposed to Mike Babich: The description of Rowan's hiring draws from Burlakoff and Babich testimony; Exhibit 167.

77   Ruan was a decile 10: Internal Insys target list obtained by the author.

77   Everyone at Ruan's clinic: Bridgette Parker, author interview.

77   When he was eating lunch: Krane, author interview.

77   This road trip became: Author interviews with Insys reps; audio recording of a conference call led by Burlakoff.

77   That was part of the reason: Burlakoff, author interview.

77   one of the biggest players: Testimony from multiple witnesses, in *Couch.*

77   a region that did brisk business: CDC data shows that Alabama was one of the top states in the nation in opioid prescribing rates, cdc.gov.

77   But Ruan was writing: Exhibit 533.

78   But Ruan's Subsys numbers paled: Babich testimony.

78   Within three months: Exhibits 197, 2359, and 50. The payments and prescribing are discussed in Babich's testimony.

78   "I am pretty sure": Exhibits 127 and 128.

78   The weekly graph of sales: The graph is reproduced in Exhibit 172.

CHAPTER 8: THE STANDOFF

79   In August 2012: Exhibit 171, the cover email to Exhibit 172, the "Plan of Attack" memo.

79   a lengthy document: Exhibit 172.

79   "grave concern": Burlakoff testimony, in *Babich*.

79   Data analysis: Babich, Burlakoff, and Napoletano testimony; Babich deposition.

80   A doctor had remarked: Babich testimony.

80   "We need to move": Exhibit 1480.

80   "force conversations, force the titration": Babich deposition.

80   Getting into the particulars: Burlakoff testimony; Burlakoff, author interview.

80   "While all opioids": "Statement from FDA Commissioner Scott Gottlieb, M.D., on New Steps to Strengthen Agency's Safety Requirements Aimed at Mitigating Risks Associated with Transmucosal Immediate-Release Fentanyl Products," March 27, 2019.

80   The FDA label: Available at fda.gov. The label is also called the medication guide or the package insert, because it is supplied for the patient inside the medication packaging.

80   Napoletano told Kapoor: Napoletano testimony.

80   On top of that: Exhibit 1501.

80   "John had made up": Babich testimony.

80   Burlakoff's approach: Burlakoff, author interview.

81   "You can't leave anything": Ibid.

81   "He just said the majority": Babich testimony.

81   The fact that one: Burlakoff testimony; Burlakoff, author interview.

81   "Alec has brought a fire": Exhibit 1488.

81   meanwhile Burlakoff felt: Exhibit 5363.

82   Just before Burlakoff: Exhibit 174.

82   Even in its nascent stage: Babich and Napoletano testimony; Burlakoff, author interviews.

82   Kapoor was disturbed: Burlakoff testimony; Napoletano testimony.

82   Kapoor said in a meeting: Napoletano testimony.

82   The boss told his: Napoletano, Babich, and Burlakoff testimony.

82   "You don't do that": Napoletano testimony.

82   "favored child": Babich testimony.

82   Rolodex of top doctors: Babich deposition.

82   Burlakoff had never gotten: Burlakoff, author interview.

82   "Last thing we want": Napoletano testimony.

82   In one meeting, Burlakoff proposed: Babich testimony.

83   "I don't care": Burlakoff, author interviews; Napoletano's testimony corroborates that Burlakoff expressed this sentiment, without using the verbatim quotation.

83   "I knew I had lost": Napoletano testimony.

83   at times he took on the demeanor: Burlakoff, author interviews; author interviews with former Insys sales managers.

83   "out of control": Babich testimony.

83   "No! I told you before": Napoletano testimony.

83   Kapoor shouted back: Babich testimony.

83   Napoletano went back: Napoletano testimony; Babich testimony.

84   "Matt was almost in tears": Babich testimony.

84   Napoletano wanted Insys: Ibid.; Burlakoff testimony; Burlakoff, author interviews; author interviews with former Insys managers.

84   Even Alec opposed the idea: Burlakoff testimony and author interviews.

84   Top management was already tracking: Babich testimony; Burlakoff testimony.

84   perhaps two or three dozen: Exhibit 290 shows 511 monthly prescriptions in September 2012, and 849 in December.

84   Doctors who get paid: See, for example, Colleen Carey, Ethan M. J. Lieber, and Sarah Miller, "Drug Firms' Payments and Physicians' Prescribing Behavior in Medicare Part D," *Journal of Public Economics* 197 (May 2021).

84   An analysis of data: "The More Opioids Doctors Prescribe, the More Money They Make," CNN, March 12, 2018. The article reports on a joint study by CNN and researchers at Harvard University.

85   "didn't want to be responsible": Burlakoff testimony.

85   Napoletano sat in his office: Babich and Napoletano testimony.

85   "in a tough spot": Babich testimony.

85   "You've got to give him": Napoletano testimony.

85   He said he would run: Babich testimony.

85   The four men gathered: Ibid.; Burlakoff testimony; Burlakoff, author interview. The document is Exhibit 197.

85   The documents were gathered in a pile: Burlakoff testimony; Babich testimony; Burlakoff, author interviews. Burlakoff testified that it was Napoletano who collected the documents at the end; Burlakoff recalled that it was Babich.

CHAPTER 9: THE PERFORMER

86   he gave a triumphant speech: The account of this speech draws from author interviews with Krane and Burlakoff.

87   "windshield time": An industry term invoked by Burlakoff, author interviews.

87   "I could fire you": Burlakoff's recollection, author interviews.

88   "He was trying to motivate": Krane, author interview.

88   Burlakoff had met someone: The account of the origins of the relationship between Burlakoff and Lee draws from author interviews with both.

88   He was using cocaine: Burlakoff discussed using all these drugs in his testimony.

88   He had naked pictures: Author interviews with Burlakoff and a coworker, a sales manager.

88   And on occasion: Burlakoff, author interviews; a trip to a Scottsdale strip club with one doctor is alleged in the United States' Complaint in Intervention, in *Guzman*, April 13, 2018.

88   She appeared at upper-echelon clubs: Lee, author interviews.

88   She approached the two men: Burlakoff, author interview.

89   She made him feel: Burlakoff, author interview.

89   Her roots were unusual: Lee, author interview.

89   "quality clients": This and all other quotations from Lee, along with descriptions of her state of mind, are drawn from author interviews with her.

90   Her parents: The discussion of the parents' marriage, custody arrangement, the zoo incident, and the years with Lee's father draw from the letters of support by Lee's relatives, attached as exhibits to Lee sentencing memo, and from author interviews with Lee. Lee's account reflects partly her independent recollection and partly, by her own admission, what she was told by her mother. Lee's father could not be reached for comment.

90   "My sister is the reason": Letter of Lee's sister, Mariana, dated June 7, 2019, filed as an exhibit to Lee sentencing memo.

91   she hadn't in fact finished: Burlakoff claimed that Lee didn't tell him she hadn't gotten her degree until after he had nominated her for the job; Lee said that it was Burlakoff who suggested she alter her résumé to disguise it. On the witness stand, Lee's counsel presented Burlakoff with a copy of her résumé with handwritten notations on it. He denied writing the notations.

91   Babich had just hired a rep: Burlakoff testimony.

91   Babich's view: Burlakoff, author interview.

92   "This is someone": Exhibit 683.

92   The two had met: Burlakoff testimony.

92   Back at summer camp: Burlakoff, author interview.

92   Sunrise Lee was introduced: Lee, author interview.

92   Questions quickly began: Author interviews with Insys employees; Lee, author interview.

92   *If some people are criticizing:* Burlakoff, author interview; Lee, author interview.

92   He wrote a significant amount: Internal Insys target list; emails of Holly Brown.

92   Insys management had identified him: Babich testimony.

93   physically imposing man: Holly Brown testimony.

93   He had taken over: *Village of Melrose Park v. Purdue Pharma*, Circuit Court of Cook County, 2018-CH-06601, Complaint and Demand for Jury Trial, May 23, 2018.

93   Giacchino had been stripped: "Doctor Has Playmate Wife, and Drugs for Sex Trouble," *Chicago Tribune*, May 14, 2010; "Former Riverside Pain Doc Faces Prison Time," *Riverside/Brookfield Landmark*, Dec. 18, 2018; "Dr. Millionpills Becomes Mr. Unemployed," *Chicago Tribune*, June 16, 2011.

93   he was frequently present: Brown testimony.

93   A *Chicago Tribune* journalist: The journalist was John Kass. The columns ran in 2010 and 2011. In addition to the two cited above, there were "The Doctor, the Centerfold Wife, and 1 Million Pills," *Chicago Tribune*, May 20, 2010, and "A Million Questions but No Closure, Even After a Year," *Chicago Tribune*, Dec. 19, 2010.

93   "all kinds of unsavory information": Brown testimony.

93   Purdue Pharma call notes: Court documents in *Commonwealth of Ken-*

tucky ex rel. Jack Conway v. Purdue Pharma, Pike County Circuit Court, Civil Action No. 07-CI-01303.

93   a number of major drugmakers: Burlakoff, author interviews; his assertion is substantiated by, for example, "Report from February 23, 2012, Pharmaceutical Compliance Roundtable," U.S. Department of Health and Human Services Office of Inspector General; "Compliance Challenges Within Medical Affairs," *Policy and Medicine,* May 6, 2018; and "The Perfect Storm: Qui Tam Actions in the Pharmaceutical Industry," *In-House Defense Quarterly* (Spring 2011).

94   Before Burlakoff was promoted: Babich testimony.

94   "I almost had a heart attack!": Burlakoff, author interview.

94   Again and again: Exhibit 2 is one of the messages. As Babich testified, there were repeated messages using the same language. One of them appears in Exhibit 668, which shows the email being forwarded to Burlakoff. Brown was simply updating the same memo on roughly a weekly basis.

95   "was a guy in Chicago": Babich testimony.

95   Reps for at least two: Exhibits 2, 668, and 5176.

95   "ticket to stardom": Burlakoff, author interview.

95   Burlakoff asked Holly Brown: Brown testimony.

95   "'SMILE and CLOSE'": Exhibit 6918.

95   Burlakoff said Madison: Burlakoff testimony.

95   For her part, Lee wasn't put off: Lee, author interviews.

95   "shady" or "sketchy": Brown testimony. Jodi Havens, another rep who visited the clinic, called it "kind of a shady setup" in her testimony.

96   "kind of off the record": Brown testimony.

96   they met at a popular hotel bar: Original indictment in *Babich,* Dec. 6, 2016; Lee referred to it as a restaurant and noted that she was staying in the hotel with her children.

96   "She was a legend": Burlakoff, author interview.

96   He started telling other managers: Exhibit 670, for example.

96   A few days after: Brown testimony; original indictment in *Babich.*

96   "really under the eye": Exhibit 6919.

96   "I am very confident": Email obtained through a public records request.

96   "Subsys thought leader": Exhibit 669.

96   Burlakoff hated the meddling: Burlakoff, Babich, and Napoletano testimony.

96   Three top Insys executives: Descriptions of the dinner draw from the testimony of Brown and Havens and exhibits introduced through their testimony; and Burlakoff, author interviews.

97   "heavy groping": Havens testimony. Brown described essentially the same actions in her testimony.

97   Mike Babich received an email: The email, sent on November 24, 2012, was included in an exhibit marked as number 664. It was never introduced into evidence at trial, but the author obtained it.

97   Babich went to Burlakoff's office: This paragraph draws from Burlakoff and Babich testimony.

97   "He said, 'Well, if you're a stripper'": Babich deposition.

97   The pictures, however: Burlakoff testimony and author interviews; Lee, author interview.

97   a federal grand jury: *U.S. v. Madison*, No. 12 Cr. 1004, N.D. Ill.

98   Word filtered up: Babich and Napoletano testimony; Lee, author interview.

98   Matt Napoletano wanted: Napoletano testimony.

98   Babich wasn't sure: Babich testimony.

98   they continued paying him: Starting in August 2013, as required by law, these and all other Insys payments were reported to the federal government and are publicly available through the Open Payments Data website, managed by the Centers for Medicare and Medicaid Services.

98   58 percent of the Subsys sold in Illinois: *The People of the State of Illinois v. Insys*, Circuit Court of Cook County, 2016CH11216, Complaint, Aug. 25, 2016.

CHAPTER 10: THE SPIEL

99   Prescriptions were up: Exhibit 290.

99   But a different and urgent problem: The general description of the prior-authorization process and its challenges for Insys draws from Gurrieri testimony; testimony of Amy Moyer-Carey, a representative of CVS Caremark; testimony of Clayton Boquet, a representative of Optum RX; the indictments in *Babich;* author interviews with Lazarus and Yeager, who served as prosecutors in *Babich*.

100   But even with this intervention: Napoletano testimony.

100   Insurers would sometimes make exceptions: Substantiated in patient charts introduced into evidence in *Babich* and discussed in a June 27, 2014, email sent by Gurrieri, included in Exhibit 393.

100   With Medicare plans: Amy Moyer-Carey testimony; Clayton Boquet testimony. To approve coverage, Medicare broadly requires that a medication be prescribed for an approved indication or for an off-label use deemed to be "medically accepted." There were no such off-label indications for Subsys.

101   According to Burlakoff: Burlakoff, author interview.

101   At other companies: Author interview with a senior sales executive at a competing TIRF manufacturer; Yeager has estimated 35 to 40 percent as the norm.

101   Dr. Kapoor, however: Burlakoff, author interviews; Napoletano testimony.

101   Kapoor began turning: Burlakoff, author interviews and testimony.

101   Gurry was a U.S. Navy man: Letters attached as exhibits to Defendant Michael Gurry's Sentencing Memorandum, in *Babich*, Dec. 18, 2019.

101   People who worked: Beisler testimony.

101   With the air: Author interviews with former employees; statements of Gurry's attorney Tracy Miner in court.

102   Mike Gurry sought out: Exhibit 399.

102   Meanwhile, though, he moved to hire: Exhibit 415.

102   Elizabeth Gurrieri: Gurrieri testimony.

102 on the order of $1.7 million: Exhibit 399.

102 whereas Insys projected: Exhibit 290.

103 "Mike, that's not a good idea": Napoletano testimony.

103 Napoletano said that you really don't: Ibid.

103 he again started: Babich testimony; Gurrieri testimony.

103 "We need you now": Exhibit 316.

104 Gurrieri began learning: Gurrieri testimony; Gurrieri's email in Exhibit 421 reflects the lessons she had learned over time.

104 Most insurers: As explained above, technically Gurrieri and her future colleagues in her unit were not calling insurance companies directly; they were calling the insurers' pharmacy benefit managers. For the sake of simplicity, I will refer to the entities that the IRC routinely contacted as insurers, insurance plans, or insurance companies.

104 "third-partied out": Quotation is from the testimony of Lindsey Meyer, later a prior-authorization specialist under Gurrieri; Gurrieri describes the phenomenon in her testimony, specifically pertaining to the early days of the IRC; Kimberly Fordham, another PA specialist, describes it in her testimony.

104 This was typically a requirement: Amy Moyer-Carey testimony; Clayton Boquet testimony.

104 Gurrieri said that Mike Gurry told her: Gurrieri testimony.

105 she presented herself: Ibid.

105 At one point, Gurrieri: Ibid.

105 began to keep track: Ibid.; one such sheet of paper is reproduced as page 103 of Exhibit 116, which wasn't introduced into evidence but was attached as Exhibit 1 to the Davis and Zacks motion, in *Babich*.

105 They also discovered: Exhibit 393, for example; Gurrieri testimony; Burlakoff testimony.

105 "Shit, everybody has difficulty": Burlakoff testimony.

105 Gurrieri instructed her team: Gurrieri testimony.

105 made no sense: Multiple patients, including Kendra Skalnican, testified that the dysphagia diagnosis Insys claimed they had conflicted with the fact that they were taking pills.

105 Gurrieri's unit: In later years, the name changed more than once—at one point it was the Patient Services Center, at another the Patient Services Hub—but the function remained the same.

106 Newly hired sales reps: Danielle Davis testimony; Beth McKey testimony; author interview with a former Insys sales rep.

106 IRC workers had to contend: Gurrieri testimony.

106 When the IRC changed buildings: Babich testimony.

106 The outgoing number: Testimony of Maury Rice, the Insys IT director who set up this system.

106 A few insurers: Gurrieri testimony.

106 Tricare: Author interview with a Tricare spokesperson.

107 Even if they had suffered: Gurrieri testimony.

107 "the spiel": Ibid.; Lindsey Meyer testimony; interview with a former PA specialist; Gurrieri text messages obtained by the author.

107   The first version: Gurrieri testimony; the different versions of the spiel were documented in internal Insys records filed with the court or introduced into evidence.

107   It was also: Gurrieri testimony.

107   The IRC's approval rate: Exhibit 290; Exhibit 2090.

107   In an email: Exhibit 2090.

108   She had a habit: Author interviews with a former PA specialist.

108   In a presentation: Exhibit 357.

108   sometimes vulgar and cruel: Exhibit 6201, discussed in Gurrieri testimony, provides examples.

108   In early 2013, Gurry communicated: Exhibit 2091.

108   He and Babich viewed: Babich testimony.

108   The company instituted: Ibid.; Gurrieri testimony; Gurry's remarks at his sentencing hearing, in *Babich*, Jan. 13, 2020.

108     $17 to $20 an hour: Lindsey Meyer testimony; Kimberly Fordham testimony; interview with a former PA specialist.

CHAPTER 11: THE WHISTLEBLOWER

110   Every month or two: Napoletano testimony and associated exhibits.

110   Soon after Burlakoff joined: The account of the introductory ride-along draws from author interviews with Furchak and Burlakoff.

111   The following day, Ray had occasion: Furchak, author interviews; Bryant, author interviews.

111   Some of the talk: Author interviews with Furchak, Krane, Guzman, and Jim Coffman.

112   "planted the seed": Furchak, author interview.

112   "I'm thinking I'm going": Coffman, author interview.

112   When he heard several reps: Bryant, author interview.

113   "Ray was really adamant": Krane, author interview.

113   "I gotta tell you": Furchak, author interview.

113   "I'm a stick-it-to-you guy": Ibid.

113   Furchak had a less altruistic concern: Furchak, author interviews.

114   Furchak received an email: Exhibit 44. The email, dated September 13, 2012, proposes that a starting dose of 100 micrograms is to be avoided, though the FDA label indicates that the initial dose of Subsys "is always 100 mcg."

114   One day later, Babich announced: Exhibit 1488.

114   *Qui tam* suits are a major enforcement tool: For a discussion of their importance, see a report by Public Citizen called "Twenty-Seven Years of Pharmaceutical Industry Criminal and Civil Penalties: 1991 Through 2017," March 14, 2018.

116   According to Furchak, the lawyer replied: Furchak's attorney declined to discuss the case.

116   On some of the calls: Yeager, author interview.

116   "If something happens to me": Furchak, author interview.

116   "We work on loyalty": Text message exchange with Jeffrey Goldstein, obtained by the author.

116 Furchak's legal complaint: Relator Ray Furchak's Original Complaint, September 28, 2012, in *Furchak.*

117 she was used as a conduit: Burlakoff, author interview.

117 As Furchak prodded her: All Hill quotations come from the Factual Résumé attached to Hill's plea agreement in *Hill,* July 11, 2017. The Factual Résumé draws from her recorded remarks on phone calls with Furchak. By pleading guilty, Hill agreed to the facts in this document. (Hill declined to be interviewed, after numerous requests.)

118 "I do not doubt": "Purdue, Executives Handed Hefty Fine," *Roanoke Times,* July 20, 2007. The remark was quoted by Senator Patrick Leahy at a July 31, 2007, hearing of the Senate Judiciary Committee, "Evaluating the Propriety and Adequacy of the OxyContin Criminal Settlement."

118 "expensive licenses": Specter's remark came in the Judiciary Committee hearing cited in the previous note.

118 When Ray Furchak: Furchak, author interview.

119 An attorney familiar: Author interview with a longtime lawyer for *qui tam* relators who has worked closely with government counsel.

119 Furchak's attorneys told him: Furchak, author interview.

119 The theme of the meeting: Burlakoff testimony.

119 A Texas sales rep: Author interview.

120 that debt would be instantly converted: Insys prospectus filed with the SEC; Babich testimony.

120 Institutional investors: Babich testimony; Insys filings.

120 Alec Burlakoff didn't join them: Burlakoff, author interview.

CHAPTER 12: THE WHALES

121 "The below 5 names": March 19, 2013, email of Alec Burlakoff, Bates stamped INS-BOS-00589621. The email, with redactions, was included in "Fueling an Epidemic: Inside the Insys Strategy for Boosting Fentanyl Sales," a 2018 minority staff report of the U.S. Senate Committee on Homeland Security and Government Affairs. The identities of the top five doctors Burlakoff refers to are confirmed by the Complaint in *State of Arizona ex rel. Mark Brnovich v. Insys,* No. CV2017-012008, Superior Court of the State of Arizona, Maricopa County.

121 John Kapoor and Mike Babich: Babich testimony.

121 In spring 2013, when Rowan: The discussion of events resulting in this hiring draws from the trial testimony of Natalie Perhacs and associated exhibits, in *Couch.*

122 She would be calling on Ruan and Couch: Factual Résumé in *Perhacs,* Feb. 17, 2016.

122 Ruan's standing appointment: See Exhibit 2359.

122 which he claimed ordered special food: Author interview with a former senior pharmaceutical sales executive who visited Ruan several times.

122 For a while, one nurse: Parker, author interview.

122 When Ruan asked: Lori Carver, author interview; Palmer, author interview.

122   Perhacs helped out: Palmer, author interview.

122   She wrote at least one rave review: Factual Résumé in *Perhacs*, Feb. 17, 2016.

123   "Please hide me": Palmer, author interview.

123   *"Wolf of Wall Street"*: Lynette Lord, author interview.

123   He was skilled: Lori Carver, author interview; Parker, author interview.

123   "He was just done": Palmer, author interview.

123   Couch had struggled: Couch testimony; Stipulation for a Probationary Certificate, John Patrick Couch, Medical Board of California.

123   At least one staffer: Affidavit in Support of an Application for Search Warrants, in *Couch*, June 25, 2015; a memorandum summarizing federal agents' interview of Justin Palmer, obtained by the author.

123   Couch had gone through a contentious divorce: Statement of Jody Breland Donald at Couch's sentencing hearing, May 25, 2017.

123   twice pursued legal action: Couch testimony, in *Couch*.

123   Couch owned a Porsche: The vehicle and license plate were photographed by investigators executing a search warrant at his residence.

123   He frequently hit on: Author interviews with Lori Carver and other employees of the clinic.

123   Couch would bring a guitar: Parker, author interview.

123   He played and sang: Author interviews with employees of the clinic; CNBC's *American Greed* episode about Couch and Ruan, March 5, 2018.

123   People who worked: Lori Carver and Palmer, author interviews.

124   "All we do is write narcotics": Palmer, author interview.

124   Office visits at the clinic: Trial testimony from several witnesses, in *Couch*.

124   A former longtime patient: This was Tamisan Witherspoon, who could not identify him in court during her testimony.

124   Justin Palmer grew tired: Palmer, author interview.

124   Thousands of scripts: Established in trial testimony, in *Couch*.

124   Palmer had struggled: Palmer, author interview; memorandum summarizing agents' interview with Palmer.

124   "Pills couldn't touch me": Palmer, author interview.

124   Palmer would walk around: Palmer, author interview; Parker, trial testimony, in *Couch*.

124   One day, an employee: Palmer, author interview; trial testimony of Tamara Dabney, in *Couch*.

124   Palmer said it was obvious: Palmer, memorandum of interview; Palmer, author interview; Palmer testimony, in *Couch*.

124   she felt at sea: Parker, author interview.

125   she later had trouble: Parker, trial testimony, in *Couch*.

125   A staffer recalled: Trial testimony of Ken Cross, in *Couch*.

125   Co-workers would look after: Parker, trial testimony, in *Couch*.

125   With Couch often checked out: Trial testimony of, for example, Sharon Noland, a nurse; Palmer, author interview.

125   Few people could understand: Author interview with a sales rep who called on the clinic.

125   He would deny raises: Lori Carver, author interview.

125   He held a large "open house": Author interview with a sales rep who called on the clinic.

125   Ruan was amassing: The automobile collection was discussed in detail in court documents in *Couch*, including forfeiture papers and the Second Superseding Indictment.

126   He accumulated so many: Investigators' photographs show the way the warehouse was arranged.

126   he went to some lengths: Affidavit in Support of an Application for Search Warrants, in *Couch*, June 25, 2015.

126   one of the largest pain practices: Trial testimony of Ken Cross, in *Couch*; Couch testimony.

126   Ruan and Couch advertised: Ruan trial testimony; testimony of FBI special agent Steven Sorrells.

126   Alabama was number one: Centers for Disease Control statistics, cdc.gov.

126   "We were always looking": Author interview.

126   "It was a gold mine": Author interview.

127   Reps jockeyed to earn: Author interviews with Lynette Lord and another sales rep.

127   "a factory": Burlakoff, author interview.

127   They also used security guards: Trial testimony of Alice Dominguez Buckley and Gary Douthitt, in *Couch*.

127   People would sometimes buy: Author interviews with the patients Alice Byrd Jordan and Devitt Fountain; trial testimony of Ashley Dominguez Buckley, in *Couch*.

127   On Ruan's initiative: Ruan testimony, in *Couch*.

128   The pharmacy was technically: Trial testimony of Ken Cross, in *Couch*.

128   Patients were strongly encouraged: Trial testimony of the nurse Sharon Noland, in *Couch*; Palmer, author interview.

128   When the pharmacy first opened: Lori Carver, author interview.

128   Their pharmacy billed: Factual Résumé in *Perhacs*.

128   At Insys, she easily cleared: The $572,000 cited in the previous paragraph would have amounted to a bonus easily exceeding $30,000 that month, given that sales commissions were 10 percent or more. In her entire tenure, she averaged better than $30,000 per month in total compensation, by the total figure she gave in her testimony.

128   She made President's Club: Author interviews with Burlakoff and former sales reps at Insys.

129   Kathy Burns worked: Kathy Burns's story draws from author interviews with Dwight Timothy Burns; his trial testimony in *Couch* and associated exhibits; and the trial testimony of Michael Burt, a DEA special agent.

129   "In literature, physicians": Exhibit 9-5 (8), in *Couch*, discussed in the trial testimony of Michael Burt, a DEA special agent.

130   Dr. Ruan received a letter: Trial testimony of Michael Burt, and Government Exhibit 9-11.

130   She was still misusing: Dwight Timothy Burns, author interview.

CHAPTER 13: AN INTERLOPER

131   Mike Babich was romantically involved: Babich testimony.

131   Matt Napoletano at some point: Napoletano testimony.

131   For his part, John Kapoor: Beisler testimony.

131   Napoletano once saw them: Napoletano testimony.

132   "being *thrown*": Exhibit 252.

132   "getting $2500 a pop": Exhibit 249.

132   "900 pound gorilla": Babich deposition.

132   At launch in early 2012: Ibid.

132   "I never in my wildest dreams": Babich email, Oct. 4, 2013, obtained through a public records request.

132   Back in the spring: Babich testimony; Exhibit 5863.

132   Galena had recently acquired: David Corin testimony, in *Couch*.

132   "the peon products": Babich email, Oct. 4, 2013, obtained through a public records request.

133   less than 10 percent of the market: Exhibit 2351. These products were Abstral, Lazanda, and Onsolis (the last no longer being marketed by this time). The branded version of Actiq, still on the market despite the presence of generic versions, was also a minor player, with a 4 percent share of prescriptions in 2012.

133   "Galena is at the rems mtng": Exhibit 5863; Babich testimony.

133   Galena was smaller: Author interview with a former senior sales executive for Galena.

133   Many people at the company: United States' Consolidated Response in Opposition to Defendants' Motions in Limine 1–13, in *Babich*, Dec. 19, 2018; author interviews.

133   a vaccine to prevent: The product was NeuVax. It was not ultimately commercialized by Galena.

133   The company attracted: Author interview with a former senior sales executive for Galena.

133   "are not aiming": Babich email, Oct. 4, 2013, obtained through a public records request.

133   "I was told Dr. Ruan": Perhacs trial testimony, in *Couch*; Government Exhibit 32-4 (1), in *Couch*.

134   It was the kind of thing: Babich testimony; Burlakoff testimony; Burlakoff, author interview.

134   "Protect Your TIRF": This was a 2015 national sales meeting. The motto appears in photographs from the meeting obtained by the author.

134   "DOUBLED their script count": Exhibit 264.

134   "We need to refocus": Ibid.

134   Insys was getting word: Burlakoff testimony; author interview with senior Galena sales executive.

134   "Alec, you don't": Burlakoff testimony.

134   Natalie Perhacs saw the Galena rep: Perhacs trial testimony, in *Couch*.

134   "Dr Ruan and Dr Couch": Couch Exhibit 173, in *Couch*.

135   "I do not know": Factual Résumé in *Hill*.

135   The Mobile doctors were both still: Exhibit 2000.

135   better than $100,000: Exhibit 1999.

135   Couch and Ruan's nurses: This paragraph draws from the trial testimony, in *Couch*, of Sharon Noland and Bridgette Parker, both nurses in the practice. The "flavor of the day" remark is Noland's.

136   "I couldn't give them": Parker testimony, in *Couch*.

136   "big push": Sharon Noland testimony, in *Couch*.

136   Galena wasn't paying the doctors: Trial testimony of David Corin, a Galena sales executive, in *Couch*; author interview with a former senior Galena sales executive.

136   But a Galena manager: Trial testimony of Corin, in *Couch*.

136   If Insys questioned him: Author interview with a senior sales executive for Galena.

137   He had hoped: A Ruan email to Li Ma, included in Government Exhibit 11-5, in *Couch*.

137   An article: "Is Galena Following in the Footsteps of Insys with Abstral?," *Seeking Alpha*, March 7, 2014. A Ruan email distributing and recommending the article is Government Exhibit 11-5 (12), in *Couch*.

137   When Ruan told the Galena team: Corin testimony, in *Couch*.

137   "This is the product": Government Exhibit 11-5 (8), in *Couch*.

137   The nurse-practitioner Justin Palmer: Palmer testimony, in *Couch*; Palmer, author interview.

137   The two doctors and Palmer: Memorandum summarizing agents' interview with Palmer.

137   approximately 30 percent: Corin testimony and associated exhibits, in *Couch*.

137   Natalie Perhacs finally decided: This paragraph draws from Perhacs testimony, in *Couch*; Factual Résumé in *Hill*; Babich testimony.

138   C&R was having trouble: See, for example, Couch's testimony, in *Couch*.

138   Under mounting scrutiny: "Red Flags and Warning Signs Ignored: Opioid Distribution and Enforcement Concerns in West Virginia," a report prepared by majority staff of the House Energy and Commerce Committee, Dec. 19, 2018; also, "Prescription Drugs: More DEA Information About Registrants' Controlled Substances Roles Could Improve Their Understanding and Help Ensure Access," a report of the U.S. Government Accountability Office, June 2015.

138   "We have prescriptions": Email of Bryan Crawford, Government Exhibit 58-1, in *Couch*.

138   C&R would run out: Author interview.

138   "They literally have": Exhibit 140, in *Babich*.

138   Ruan and C&R did press: Corin testimony, in *Couch*.

139   "This will destroy us": Exhibit 140, in *Babich*; Burlakoff testimony.

139   "He didn't like the optics": Burlakoff testimony; Babich testimony corroborates that Reimer had repeatedly warned against direct shipment.

139   Burlakoff knew that Ruan and Couch: Burlakoff testimony; Burlakoff, author interview.

139   John Kapoor and Mike Babich flew: Babich testimony.

139   They had rooms: The hotel receipts are Government Exhibits 32-7 (1) and
       32-7 (2), in *Couch*.

139   Entrepreneurs were always trying: Babich testimony.

139   It was far out of the ordinary: Babich testimony; Burlakoff, author inter-
       views. No one at Insys could recall to the author another instance where
       Kapoor traveled to see particular doctors, other than at larger events orga-
       nized and hosted by Insys.

139   "the top people": Babich testimony.

139   "Hopefully with a little help": Perhacs testimony and Exhibit 32-4 (6), in
       Couch.

140   Insys had made reservations: Babich testimony; Exhibit 465.

140   Rowan had helped line up: Trial exhibits; Burlakoff, author interview.

140   Ruan had already communicated: Exhibit 133.

140   Through the pharmacy: Babich testimony. One man who accompanied
       the doctors was Bryan Crawford, according to representations of the par-
       ties in court, in *Babich*. Another C&R representative might also have
       been present.

140   The bosses went ahead: Burlakoff testimony; Burlakoff, author interview.

140   Kapoor and Babich expanded: Babich testimony.

140   Still, Couch and Ruan: Ibid.

140   By the time the deal: Ibid.; the contract for direct shipment is included in
       Exhibit 150.

CHAPTER 14: "LETS GET A FEW MORE"

141   the company received a subpoena: Exhibit 688; Exhibit 2324.

141   Unbeknownst to the higher-ups, two new whistleblowers: One of the suits
       was *Guzman;* the other was brought by a member of the sales force based
       in the Midwest, Torgny Andersson. It was filed in 2013 in the District
       of Massachusetts but transferred to the Central District of California as
       U.S. ex rel. Torgny Andersson v. Insys, No. 14 Cv. 9179.

141   By the time she filed suit: This account draws from author interviews with
       Burlakoff and Guzman.

142   "I'm telling you": Burlakoff, author interview.

142   Guzman was surreptitiously recording: Excerpts from the recording were
       played for the jury in *Babich,* and transcripts of them were admitted into
       evidence. See Exhibits 2279, 2280, and 2281.

142   "Talk about scary": Exhibit 2279-02.

142   A U.S. Attorney's Office: Technically, it was multiple U.S. Attorney's
       Offices, in different jurisdictions, that took an interest in this recording
       and others like it.

142   When the subpoena arrived: This paragraph draws from Babich testi-
       mony and the board meeting notes of Zacks, attached as Exhibit A to
       Defendants' Opposition to Motion to Admit Testimony of Danielle
       Davis and Leslie Zacks, in *Babich,* March 22, 2019.

143   Announcing it in an internal memo: Exhibit 2324.

143 "there was a lot of anxiety": Napoletano testimony.

143 According to Burlakoff: Burlakoff, author interview.

143 he wasn't feeling pressure: Ibid.

144 "under the auspices": Ibid.

144 That message propagated: Author interviews with Lee and a former senior sales manager.

145 Mike Babich was interviewed: "Best IPO of 2013: Insys Therapeutics," *Fast Money,* CNBC, Dec. 27, 2013.

145 Babich would exercise: Exhibit 5847-1; testimony of the FBI agent Bridget Horan.

145 Zacks told Kapoor: Statement of Yeager in court, in *Babich;* board meeting notes of Zacks, cited above.

145 In the weeks following: Napoletano testimony; Insys internal correspondence.

145 Szymanski was another pharma rookie: Szymanski testimony.

146 the number one rep: Exhibit 2001.

146 As he approached: Szymanski testimony.

146 "for no legitimate medical purpose": Affidavit in Support of Criminal Complaint and other court documents, in *Awerbuch.*

146 *The New York Times* published: The print headline differed slightly: "Doubts Raised About Off-Label Use of a Painkiller," *New York Times,* May 14, 2014.

146 He was far and away: Affidavit in Support of Criminal Complaint, in *Awerbuch.*

146 Insys had been courting: Testimony of Szymanski, Awerbuch, and Burlakoff. The word "experience" comes from Awerbuch's recounting.

147 "crystal clear": Burlakoff, author interview.

147 Awerbuch thought the suggestion: Awerbuch testimony.

147 "Expect a nice 'bump'": Exhibit 36.

147 The bump materialized: Exhibit 91.

147 Lee helped cultivate: Lee, author interview.

147 "lit up a room": Burlakoff testimony.

148 "I need him to be": Exhibit 41.

148 The programs started out legitimate: Testimony of Awerbuch and Szymanski.

148 It was becoming a full-time job: Awerbuch testimony.

148 They had recently created: Exhibit 243; Babich testimony.

148 "Mike Babich described this hire": Original indictment in *Babich.*

148 As the relationship: Awerbuch testimony.

148 One patient, a middle-aged woman: Ibid.; Exhibit 5242.

149 The patient's life: This paragraph draws from the patient's statement at Gurry's sentencing, Jan. 13, 2020.

149 "god given talent": All quotations here are drawn from Exhibit 665.

149 a small compliance team: A Danielle Davis sworn statement, attached as Exhibit E to Defendants' Opposition to Motion to Admit Testimony of Danielle Davis and Leslie Zacks, in *Babich,* March 22, 2019.

149 One IRC staffer, Patty Nixon: "Fentanyl Billionaire Comes Under Fire

as Death Toll Mounts from Prescription Opioids," *Wall Street Journal,* Nov. 22, 2016.

149   Almost none of his Subsys patients: Awerbuch testimony.

149   "Yup. Fucked": N.J. AG Complaint.

149   Awerbuch and his wife tried to contact: Lee, author interview.

150   When the Awerbuch news broke: Burlakoff testimony; Exhibit 2130.

150   so he ran it by: Burlakoff testimony. Del Fosse did not respond to requests for comment.

150   The three men: Burlakoff, author interview.

150   "We were friends": Burlakoff testimony.

150   They were also trying: Baumrind, author interview.

150   Within hours, Baumrind coordinated: Ibid.

150   "Listen, I'm in trouble": Burlakoff testimony.

151   Awerbuch continued to press: Testimony of Burlakoff and Szymanski.

151   Awerbuch pointed at Burlakoff: Burlakoff testimony.

151   Szymanski knew Awerbuch best: Szymanski testimony.

151   He'd had the same instinct: Burlakoff, author interview.

151   "We may have been recorded": Szymanski testimony.

151   Kapoor's primary concern: Testimony of Babich and Burlakoff; Burlakoff, author interview.

151   Babich said he and Kapoor reviewed: Babich testimony.

152   He wanted to know: Ibid.

152   "in the war zone": Burlakoff testimony.

152   Rather than fire Brett Szymanski: Babich testimony; Burlakoff, author interview.

152   Burlakoff pushed for the move: Burlakoff, author interview.

152   Kapoor approved the promotion: Babich testimony.

152   he was authorizing huge expenditures: Wilkinson stated in court, "I think the company paid them over $30 million."

152   However, when Davis: Davis and Zacks motion, along with the attached Exhibit 1; Davis testimony.

152   Davis was in her early thirties: Testimony of Davis and Burlakoff; Burlakoff, author interview.

152   she was essentially "powerless": Babich testimony.

152   In a text message: Exhibit 2181.

153   He complained loudly: Exhibit 1602; Burlakoff testimony.

153   Davis believed: The government stated this to the court, in *Babich,* and confirmed it in interviews. Davis was not given the opportunity to address the matter in her testimony, which was circumscribed by the court for legal reasons.

153   He even submitted: Exhibit 1648; Burlakoff testimony.

153   "He knew he couldn't do": Burlakoff, author interview.

153   it was quadrupled: The budget was roughly $2.5 million in 2013 and $10 million in 2014, as substantiated in internal records and testimony. Zacks's board meeting notes and Davis's sworn statement both show that the company discussed internally that the speaker budget was out of line with peer companies.

153 In fall 2014, the doctor was invited: Exhibit 6000.

153 Sales staff were being told: Lee, author interview.

154 To those around him: Babich testimony; Burlakoff, to the author; author interviews with a former senior Insys sales manager.

154 On the one hand: Babich and Burlakoff testimony; author interview with a former senior sales manager.

154 Napoletano was haunted: Babich and Napoletano testimony.

154 "out of control": Babich testimony.

154 "covering his tracks": Burlakoff, author interview.

154 "We're all going to go": Babich testimony.

154 According to Napoletano: Napoletano testimony.

154 He was asked: Ibid.

155 prescriptions for Subsys had recovered: Third-party data from IMS Health, cited in the Jefferies report. Napoletano left in August 2014.

155 Market share had never: Exhibit 482; IMS Health data from the Jefferies report.

155 Insys was increasing the price: N.J. AG Complaint.

155 But the shares: Kapoor testimony, in *Kottayil*.

155 Alec Burlakoff was exercising: Burlakoff testimony; forfeiture papers in *Babich*.

155 he walked into a dealership: Burlakoff, author interview.

155 A December 2014 report: The Jefferies report.

155 A front-page *New York Times* article: "Drug Company Enlists Doctors Under Scrutiny," *New York Times*, Nov. 28, 2014. (A version of the story appeared online under a different headline on the previous day.)

156 "What *New York Times* article?": A Burlakoff email that Danielle Davis was questioned about in an October 2017 deposition taken by Aaron Moore, attorney for a Subsys patient named Jeffrey Buchalter, in *Buchalter v. Tham*, No. C-02-CV-16-002718, Circuit Court for Anne Arundel County, Md.

CHAPTER 15: FALL GUY

157 On May 8, 2015: Affidavit in Support of an Application for Search Warrants, in *Couch*, June 25, 2015.

157 Couch did not have a prescription: Couch testimony, in *Couch*.

157 the street price of opioid pills: Gary Douthitt testimony, in *Couch*.

157 it emerged that Galena: Order Instituting Cease-and-Desist Proceedings, in the matter of Galena Biopharma Inc. and Mark J. Ahn, Respondents, April 10, 2017.

157 The sell-off and revelations: Government Exhibit 11-5; David Corin testimony.

158 The deal amounted: Galena paid $7.55 million to resolve a federal investigation in the District of New Jersey alleging that Galena had paid multiple types of kickbacks to Couch and Ruan, as well as other doctors. The settlement was announced, via justice.gov, on September 8, 2017.

158 One late night: Bodnar, author interviews; Government Exhibit 9-8 (1).

158 "ran away from that money": Bodnar closing statement, in *Couch*.

158 At the doctors' trial: Witherspoon's account draws from her testimony, in *Couch*, and an author interview with her.

160 Alec Burlakoff was on vacation: Burlakoff, author interview.

160 several based on a spray-delivery platform: Insys regulatory filings, such as the 2015 10-K.

160 Subsys sales reached a peak: Insys regulatory filings.

160 According to the market-intelligence firm: Cited in "Americans Consume Vast Majority of the World's Opioids," CNBC, April 27, 2016.

160 Kapoor's stake: He beneficially owned 66 percent of the stock at the end of 2015, down from 68 percent at the end of 2014, according to Insys regulatory filings. In mid-2015, the market capitalization exceeded $3 billion.

161 "Do you think I should": Exhibit 2015 and attachments.

161 In April 2015, he produced: "Insys Therapeutics and the New 'Killing It,'" Southern Investigative Reporting Foundation, April 24, 2015. Boyd's outlet later changed its name to the Foundation for Financial Journalism.

161 He also unearthed some details: "Insys Therapeutics, Part I," Southern Investigative Reporting Foundation, Dec. 3, 2015.

161 pled guilty in June 2015: Plea Agreement, June 23, 2015, in *Alfonso*.

161 Alfonso had only recently: Alfonso testimony.

162 She had five children: Sentencing Memorandum of Defendant Heather Alfonso, Nov. 11, 2019, in *Alfonso*; Alfonso testimony, in *Babich*.

162 Insys sometimes targeted: Burlakoff testimony.

162 According to Babich, Matt Napoletano: Babich testimony.

162 "had come to rely": Alfonso testimony, in *Babich*.

162 In a *New York Times* article: "Nurse Pleads Guilty to Taking Kickbacks from Drug Maker," *New York Times*, June 25, 2015.

162 She had a more impressive: Levine testimony, in *Clough;* letter of Lauren Dodge, attached as an exhibit to Sentencing Memorandum on Behalf of Defendant Natalie Levine, in *Levine*.

163 started dating "formally": Babich testimony.

163 "I really was terrible": Levine testimony, in *Clough*.

163 a rep for a territory next door: The rep was Abraham Rosenberg. His father was Dr. Jerrold Rosenberg, a top prescriber in Rhode Island who later pled guilty to health-care fraud and kickback conspiracy charges in connection with Insys.

163 At the national sales meeting: Levine testimony, in *Clough*.

163 In the summer, Levine finally: Levine testimony, in *Clough;* Exhibit 156, in *Clough*.

163 Levine asked Clough: Testimony of Levine and Clough, in *Clough*.

163 He was friendly but peculiar: Author interview with Clough's patient Mackenzie Colby; testimony of Melissa Perusse and John Perusse, in *Clough*. Kasey Talon, a nurse-practitioner in the clinic where Clough worked, also testified, in *Clough*, that he was "very outgoing, very boisterous," but that his sense of humor was "a little bit inappropriate."

163 "They all knew": Clough testimony, in *Clough*.

163   One woman, Melissa Perusse: Testimony of Melissa Perusse and John Perusse, in *Clough*.

164   Clough said he did not recall: Clough testimony, in *Clough*.

164   Clough was going through a divorce: This paragraph draws from the testimony of Clough and Levine, in *Clough*.

164   Many of Clough's speaker programs: Testimony of Levine and Clough, in *Clough*.

164   "I needed someone else": Levine testimony, in *Clough*.

164   "male threat": Levine testimony, in *Clough*. It was Clough's attorney who spoke the words "male threat" while questioning Levine, but Levine agreed with the characterization.

164   Clough wrote approximately 84 percent: Assurance of Discontinuance, State of New Hampshire, Merrimack Superior Court, in the matter of Insys Therapeutics Inc., Jan. 18, 2017. The assurance was the result of an enforcement action brought by the New Hampshire attorney general's office.

164   Of his roughly 400: Clough testimony, in *Clough;* testimony of the FBI analyst Stacey Schendler, in *Clough*.

164   Only a handful: Clough testimony, in *Clough*.

164   "with any pharmacological": State of New Hampshire Board of Medicine, Final Order, In the Matter of Christopher Clough, PA. Gilbert Fanciullo, MD, was the medical expert.

164   "Christopher Clough was infatuated": Testimony of Jessica Crane Bradley (known as Jessica Crane at the time of the events), in *Babich*.

164   In a photograph: Exhibit 18, in *Babich*.

165   Natalie Levine left Insys: Levine testimony, in *Clough;* Exhibit 137, in *Clough*.

165   She didn't tell Christopher Clough: Levine testimony, in *Clough;* Crane testimony, in *Babich*.

165   Clough texted her: Levine testimony, in *Clough*.

165   "I knew the speaker program": Levine testimony, in *Clough*.

165   "uncomfortable with what was going on": Questioning of Clough's attorney Patrick Richard during cross-examination and Levine's testimony in response, in *Clough*.

165   Mike Babich sensed a chill: Babich testimony.

165   after settling an investigation: The investigation by the Oregon Department of Justice resulted in an Assurance of Voluntary Compliance, announced August 5, 2015, and a $1.1 million settlement. Settlements with other states followed.

165   In the late summer of 2015: Babich testimony.

166   "I knew it was D-Day": Ibid.

CHAPTER 16: "IT'S GOING DOWN"

167   As scrutiny mounted: Burlakoff, author interviews; Burlakoff testimony.

167   "They made a decision": Burlakoff, author interview.

167   In February 2016, Perhacs pled: Plea Agreement, Feb. 17, 2016, in *Perhacs*.

168 Perhacs had been brought onstage: Author interview with a former sales rep.
168 He had been advised: Burlakoff, author interview.
168 he spoke darkly: Lee, author interview; author interview with a former sales manager.
168 Lee said that in 2015: Lee, author interview.
168 Burlakoff said later that he was threatened: Burlakoff testimony.
168 He sent threatening text messages: *Breitenbach v. Insys*, No. 18 Cv. 164, D. N.J.
168 "Fuck you bitch": Exhibit 2175.
168 Alec spent a month brooding: This account draws from author interviews with Burlakoff and the journal he kept at the time.
169 Burlakoff couldn't stand: Burlakoff testimony; Burlakoff, author interview.
169 To arrange the meeting: Baumrind, author interview; Yeager, author interview.
169 With news of Burlakoff's approach: Baumrind, author interview; Baumrind testimony; transcript, obtained by the author, of investigators' May 2016 interview with Burlakoff.
170 the FBI agent told him gently: Baumrind, author interview.
170 Burlakoff was near tears: Burlakoff, author interview.
170 It was late afternoon on the Friday: Baumrind, author interview; Yeager, author interview.
170 "a number of individuals": All quotations from and descriptions of statements made at this interview draw from recordings and a complete transcript obtained by the author. Additional detail comes from the recollections of Burlakoff, Yeager, and Baumrind.
170 "to the wolves": Burlakoff, author interview.
170 "I know it's unhealthy": Burlakoff journal, reviewed by the author.
171 Burlakoff spun a tale: Yeager, author interview; Burlakoff, author interview; interview transcript.
171 Burlakoff won a battle: Napoletano testimony.
171 "continuing threat to the public": Texas Medical License No. H-6622, in the matter of the license of Judson J. Somerville, MD, Order of Temporary Restriction, Dec. 11, 2013.
171 Three of his patients had died: Texas Medical Board, Final Order, in the matter of the complaint against Judson Jeffrey Somerville, MD, Aug. 25, 2017. The order revoked Somerville's license in Texas.
171 Somerville was paraplegic: Somerville's personal website.
172 "I think all you're doing": Excerpt from transcript of the recorded interview, attached as Exhibit 3 to Defendant John N. Kapoor's Opposition to Government's Motion to Compel and for Sanctions, Dec. 3, 2018, in *Babich*.
172 "I never lied": Exhibit 6513-23.
173 "It's fucking over": Burlakoff, author interview.
173 Seven months later: Babich testimony.
173 Paul Baumrind was there: Baumrind, author interview.

173   Mike Gurry, the executive: Ibid.

174   Joe Rowan lived at the water's edge: Ibid.

174   Several people came to the door: Burlakoff, author interview.

174   The Department of Justice had charged: Original indictment, in *Babich*, Dec. 6, 2016.

174   It was just what Alec Burlakoff: Burlakoff, author interview.

175   *Forbes* magazine had published: Matthew Herper and Michela Tindera, "An Opioid Spray Showered Billionaire John Kapoor in Riches. Now He's Feeling the Pain," *Forbes*, Oct. 25, 2016.

175   Her family's attorney: Hollawell and Aaron Moore, the attorney representing the Subsys patient Jeffrey Buchalter in a Maryland suit, formed an informal duo, unearthing numerous records and deposing key figures despite significant resistance. Hollawell eventually deposed Babich and Kapoor, though Kapoor invoked his right to remain silent.

176   Then, at dawn one day: Spokesperson for the U.S. Attorney's Office of the District of Massachusetts.

176   No one answered: The account of the arrest relies on an author interview with Baumrind.

CHAPTER 17: THE PYRAMID

177   it has become increasingly uncommon: For the landscape of enforcement actions in the drug industry, an important source is the report "Twenty-Seven Years of Pharmaceutical Industry Criminal and Civil Penalties: 1991 Through 2017," by the consumer advocacy group Public Citizen, March 14, 2018. With no central repository for this data, Public Citizen filled a significant hole.

178   the so-called Yates memo: The memorandum, dated September 9, 2015, and titled "Individual Accountability for Corporate Wrongdoing," is a publicly available document.

178   "Corporations can only commit crimes": "Justice Dept. Sets Its Sights on Executives," *New York Times*, Sept. 10, 2015.

178   "a criminal enterprise": Government opening statement in the *Babich* trial, by Lazarus.

179   As Burlakoff said, nothing: Burlakoff, author interview.

179   "sends a strong message": The remark, by the then assistant attorney general Jody Hunt, appeared in a Department of Justice press release, "Insys Therapeutics Agrees to Enter into $225 Million Global Resolution of Criminal and Civil Investigations," June 5, 2019, justice.gov.

180   if the DOJ sent a strong message: Barry Meier, "Opioid's Maker Hid Knowledge of Wide Abuse," *New York Times*, May 29, 2018. The statistic comes from DEA data obtained by Eric Eyre of the *Charleston Gazette-Mail*.

180   Why did Purdue itself: Information, Nov. 24, 2020, *U.S. v. Purdue Pharma L.P.*, No. 20 Cr. 1028, D. N.J.

180   why was the founder and CEO awarded $14.5 million: This was Frank Baldino Jr. The number is derived from Cephalon public filings.

180   "we were bribing doctors": Burlakoff testimony.

180   Back in 2011, when Kapoor and Babich: The entire account of this interview meeting draws from the Babich deposition. Napoletano and Kapoor declined, through their attorneys, to be interviewed by the author.

180   Baldino was a science type: "Cephalon CEO Frank Baldino Jr. Dies at 57," *Philadelphia Inquirer,* Dec. 17, 2010; "Obituary: Frank Baldino Jr., 1953–2010," *Inc.,* March 10, 2011; "Frank Baldino Jr., Founder of Pharmaceutical Company, Dies at 57," *New York Times,* Dec. 21, 2010.

181   "Well, what about the fine?": Babich deposition.

181   An FBI special agent on the case: Barrios, author interview.

181   "No one thought": Baumrind, author interview.

182   "a crazy way": Burroughs made the remark at a status conference and motion hearing held on July 17, 2018, and is quoted in Chris Villani, "RICO Indictment Against Ex–Insys Execs Perplexes Judge," *Law360,* July 17, 2018.

182   an off-label marketing case: *U.S. v. Stryker Biotech, LLC,* No. 09 Cr. 10330, D. Mass.

183   Reichel was accused of conspiring: *U.S. v. Reichel,* No. 15 Cr. 10324, D. Mass.

183   cannot be convicted of bribery: Under the indictment that went to trial in *Babich,* the defendants were not charged with violating the Anti-Kickback Statute, only with RICO conspiracy, as noted above. The Reichel precedent was nonetheless relevant to the Insys case, of course, and very similar words ultimately appeared in the *Babich* jury instructions.

184   Elizabeth Gurrieri, who had reported: A Cooperation Agreement in *Gurrieri* was filed under seal on April 27, 2017.

184   "he did everything in his power": Baumrind, author interview.

185   "because the defense bar": Fred Wyshak, the Assistant U.S. Attorney, addressing the court in Burlakoff's sentencing hearing, Jan. 23, 2020.

185   That summer, Burlakoff and Vien: Burlakoff, author interview.

185   Investigators he had lied to: Baumrind testimony; Yeager testimony.

186   "He's the cock of the walk": Janelle Lawrence, to the author.

186   He and a longtime partner: Wyshak, author interview.

186   "bread and butter": Ibid.

186   Kapoor's defense counsel publicly scoffed: The statement was issued widely to the media and appeared in several news reports.

187   "Standing by their side": Burlakoff, author interview.

187   "You're not a rat": Burlakoff, author interview.

187   Wyshak had put his faith: The witness was Stephen "the Rifleman" Flemmi, in the trial of Francis "Cadillac Frank" Salemme (also presided over by Judge Burroughs).

188   "to keep Chris paid": Levine testimony, in *Clough.*

188   She had already pled guilty: *U.S. v. Levine,* Information and Plea Agreement, both filed July 11, 2017.

189   In the period after Kapoor had ousted: This paragraph and the next draw from letters written by Catherine Danz Schildgen and her mother, Mary Gauwitz, attached as exhibits to Kapoor sentencing memo.

189 he reached out to a server: Letter of Abraham Suarez, attached as an exhibit to Kapoor sentencing memo.

CHAPTER 18: THE MARKS

191 lawyers on both sides: Judge Burroughs overlapped in the Boston office with Wyshak and with Michael Kendall, who represented Joe Rowan.

191 a landmark affirmative-action case: *Students for Fair Admissions Inc. v. President and Fellows of Harvard College,* No. 14 Cv. 14176, D. Mass.

192 Sunrise Lee had been advised: Lee, author interview. The author obtained a letter from an attorney advising her to plead guilty, before she made a change in her representation. Closer to trial, she engaged in a "reverse proffer," she said, in which the government presents evidence to the defendant, seeking a guilty plea.

192 Judge Merrick Garland: "Weddings; Beth Wilkinson, David Gregory," *New York Times,* June 11, 2000.

194 Paul Baumrind of the FBI: Author interview.

194 she was swiftly replaced: Indictment in *U.S. v. Chun,* No. 20 Cr. 120, M.D. Fla. The indictment gives Tondre's hiring as December 6. Krane was fired November 30, according to her testimony. Internal correspondence obtained through public records requests confirms Tondre's employment in the first half of December. Aqsa Nawaz testified that the two were close.

195 The doctor had done volunteer work: Statements at Awerbuch's sentencing, in *Awerbuch.*

196 Most doctors have no tolerance: Burlakoff, author interview.

197 She too had pled guilty: Information, filed April 4, 2017, and Cooperation Agreement, filed April 27, 2017, in *Gurrieri.*

198 "look the jury in the face": Kosta Stojilkovic made the remark in arguments before Judge Burroughs, outside the presence of the jury.

198 Late one afternoon: The section about Skalnican and her testimony draws from author interviews with Skalnican; her testimony; Awerbuch testimony; and medical records admitted into evidence in the case.

CHAPTER 19: DIRTY LITTLE SECRET

204 Mindful that Burlakoff was a wild card: Yeager, author interview.

206 It was an extraordinarily charged moment: Lee, author interview.

207 "not a target": Voice-mail message obtained by the author.

207 while Hill pled to a lesser charge: Plea Agreement, July 11, 2017, and Judgment, June 4, 2019, in *Hill.*

CHAPTER 20: THE VERDICT

212 "Verdict": The reporter in question was the author.

213 The prosecutors and federal agents stayed: Baumrind, author interview.

CHAPTER 21: NO SAFETY NET

218   some jurors went straight to Google: Author interview with the juror Patricia Hazelton.

220   "it's appropriate to look at": Yeager, author interview.

226   the chief compliance officer stated: Novartis acknowledged in court that this occurred, in *U.S. v. Novartis*, No. 11 Cv. 11, S.D. N.Y., Stipulation and Order of Settlement and Dismissal, June 29, 2020.